GRAPHIC ARTISTS GUILD HANDBOOK
PRICING & ETHICAL GUIDELINES
7TH EDITION

P9-DER-497

GRAPHIC ARTISTS GUILD HANDBOOK
PRICING & ETHICAL
GUIDELINES

7TH EDITION

Editorial

Director and project coordinator:
Paul Basista

Project manager:
Simms Taback

Editors:
Kathie Abrams
Joseph Azar
Paul Basista
Frederick H. Carlson
D.K. Holland
Jeff Seaver
Lee Stewart
Paul O. Zelinsky

Consultants:
Tad Crawford
Iris Morales

Survey committee:
Kathie Abrams
David Febland
Polly Law
Jeff Seaver
Lee Stewart
Simms Taback
Paul O. Zelinsky

Editorial production:
Yvonne Perano

Executive Director,
Graphic Artists Guild:
Paul Basista

National President,
Graphic Artists Guild:
Simms Taback

Design

Art Direction:
Simms Taback

Cover art:
Daniel Pelavin

Interior design:
Peter Ross

Layout, typesetting and camera ready:
Ross Culbert Lavery & Russman, Inc.

Printing:
Horowitz/Rae Book Manufacturing, Inc.

Publisher:
Graphic Artists Guild

Distributors to the trade in the
United States and Canada:
North Light Books
A Division of F & W Publications, Inc.
1507 Dana Avenue
Cincinnati, OH 45207
1-800-543-4644
(In Ohio) 1-800-551-0884

Direct mail distribution:
Graphic Artists Guild
11 West 20th Street
New York, NY 10011
(212) 463-7730

CONTENTS

Graphic Design Prices and Trade Customs

Illustration Prices and Trade Customs

Salaries and Trade Customs

Surface Design Prices and Trade Customs

Business Management

Standard Contracts

On the Guild

ACKNOWLEDGMENTS

The first edition of the *Graphic Artists Guild Handbook, Pricing & Ethical Guidelines* was first published eighteen years ago as a 20-page booklet beginning with the words: "This is an imperfect document."

Still a long way from perfection, the *7th Edition* of the *Guidelines* has grown to reflect the sophistication of our membership and the complex issues and practices of the industries in which they work. It is their commitment, participation and knowledge that is the foundation of the Guild and of the *Guidelines*. Perhaps the most widely accepted and respected industry reference of its kind, over 50,000 of each of the *Guideline's* last two editions have been distributed, not only to artists and designers, but also to their clients. Clearly, the *Guidelines* has gone a long way towards improving industry standards for all involved since the first booklet appeared in 1973. This has been heartening for all of us involved in producing the book; it strengthens our resolve to continue providing this important service to the industry.

The editors of the *7th Edition* and the Guild's National Board of Directors would like to express its deep appreciation and gratitude to the members and consultants who have participated in making this edition the best yet and whose contributions to the *Guidelines* have been invaluable:

Volker E.H. Antoni
Robert Altemus
Ilene Avery
Ray Alma
Don Ariev
Edmond Alexander
Daniel Abraham
Terrence Brown
Diana Bryan
Essie Borden
Sue Barnes
Wallace Colvard
Tom Carnase
Carol Carson
Tad Crawford
Emily Ruth Cohen
Margaret Cusack
Gigi Cooper
Frank Costantino
Eileen J. Canning
Fred Carlson
Bob Carlson
Stuart David
Michael Doret
Paula Differding Burton
Eva Doman Bruck
William Drenttel
Carol Donner

John A. Duncan
Leo and Diane Dillon
Mary Grace Eubank
Louise Fili
Janice Fudyma
Joseph Feigenbaum
Tom Geismar
Neil Hardy
Joel Hecker
Enid Hatton
Dolly Hertz
Andy Hughes
Killian Jordan
Brad Joyce
Diane Kadah
Larry Katzman
Iva Kravitz
Kitty Krupat
Terry Le Blanc
Mell Lazarus
Robin Lazarus
Caryn Leland
Tom Lupo
Sara Love
Michele Manning
Jeff Massie
Jill Mayo
Barbara Nessim
Maureen Nappi
Regina Ortenzi
Pat Porter
Judith Raices

Reynold Ruffins
Craig Russell
Katherine Radcliffe
Ellen Rixford
Jim Roginsky
Judson Rosebush
Peter Ross
Sharon Rothman
Glen Serbin
Rita Sue Siegel
Rael Slutsky
Paul Shaw
Yvonne Shultis
Hari Singh
Karna Singh
Kitty Stavros
Stephanie Stouffer
Eva Szela
Michael Toomey
Charles Talley
Mary Thelen
Wendy Wall
Bill Westwood
Bridey Whelan
Roger Whitehouse
Mick Wieland
Barry Zaid
Hy Zazula
Nat Zimmerman

American Institute of Graphic Arts

American Society of Architectural Perspectivists

Association of Medical Illustrators

National Cartoonists Society

Joint Ethics Committee

Motion Picture Screen Cartoonists, Local 839 I.A.T.S.E.

San Francisco Society of Illustrators

Society of Illustrators

Society of Publication Designers

Surface Design Association

P R E F A C E

Putting a price on a creative work is a complex process for artists and for those who purchase artwork. This seventh edition of the *Graphic Artists Guild Handbook: Pricing and Ethical Guidelines* is compiled to help both artists and art buyers determine how to arrive at fair prices; it is also a guide to acceptable and ethical business standards for our industry.

The first edition of the *Guidelines* began in 1973 as a 20-page booklet. Since then it has matured; and our two most recent editions have each circulated more than 50,000 copies.

Leading members of the graphic arts profession have contributed to the *Guidelines* over the years, providing what has become the most respected single source of information for people who buy and sell creative work. But the *Guidelines* is not just a consolidation of selective wisdom and experience; it represents a universal consensus painstakingly gathered from national surveys unique in the diverse field of visual communications.

The *Guidelines* does not suggest maximum or minimum prices for artwork. Instead, it offers a solid base upon which to negotiate fair compensation for creative work. Artwork, by definition, differs from project to project. New artists compete with experienced professionals whose reputations help sell their work. Similarly, large corporations and fledgling firms compete in the same markets for consumers' attention. And the markets that graphic artists work in vary tremendously both in size and specialization. The *Guidelines* is an aid to both artists and art buyers who must cope with the complex *business* of visual communications.

This seventh edition contains new and expanded sections on computer arts, illustration and cartooning, graphic design, map, chart and surface design. All sections, including one on mastering the art of negotiation, have been updated to keep pace with the rapidly changing industries that Guild members represent.

The Graphic Artists Guild is dedicated to raising and maintaining ethical standards throughout the communications industry. Sometimes, abuses of industry standards stem from ignorance of established criteria, but many stem from attempts to take advantage of the unwary, the inexperienced and the unorganized. It is the Guild's aim to change these conditions.

Simms Taback
National President
Graphic Artists Guild

Introduction

This book provides both graphic artists and their clients with a current compilation of pricing methods, ranges and professional business practices applied throughout the industry. The growing complexity of uses, fee arrangements and business and financial considerations makes information of this type essential for all participants in the field.

The book addresses the major components in the graphic arts industry: Professional Issues and Practices, Pricing and Trade Customs, Standard Contracts and Business Management.

The chapter on *Professional Issues* updates clients and artists on the laws, new legislative initiatives, court decisions and trade practices that affect the sale of artwork. This chapter includes the most recent information on relevant portions of the copyright law, moral rights and fair practices legislation, tax issues, art contests and competitions, work on speculation and cancellation fees.

The chapter on *Ethical Standards* includes the communications industry's Code of Fair Practice and an overview of the various organizations that monitor industry practices.

Business & Legal Practices for Commissioned Artwork highlights the practical details that must be considered when negotiating a commissioned work, including information on business forms, ownership of original art, credit lines, sales tax and liability for portfolios and original art. Also included is a guide for freelance creators to determine their legal status as an independent contractor or an employee, which has profound implications on benefits, taxes and ownership rights.

The Professional Relationship gives new art buyers and beginning artists a sense of the relationships between artist and client in the communications industry. This chapter includes descriptions of various art buyers responsible for commissioning artists' work, how independent contractors operate in the market and how artists' representatives, brokers and other sources of talent relate to both client and artist.

The Pricing and Trade Customs chapters provide an overview of the many factors that must be taken into account by all parties who are responsible for pricing works of design or illustration. Factors that affect pricing, including such diverse elements as usage and reuses, per diem fees, royalties on merchandise for sale, billable expenses, special time demands arising out of unique style or deadline requirements and overall size of project or print order are discussed. Various methods of pricing, including per diem, hourly rate and using advertising page rates as the basis for compensation, are also evaluated.

The Guild's national pricing surveys report ranges of rates in virtually all design and illustration specialties. Each trade area listed in this section includes an introduction that explains the type of work covered in the charts and factors that affect pricing in the individual areas. The pricing charts should not be read without referring to these introductions or other portions of the book that describe all factors to be taken into account when pricing a specific job.

Illustration pricing ranges cover all media in Advertising Illustration (including magazine, newspaper, brochure, catalog, mailer, point of purchase, packaging, transitcar, film, audiovisual and motion picture and theater posters); Pre-production art (comps, animatics and storyboards); Institutional and Corporate Illustration (including adult, juvenile, children's books and textbooks); Editorial Illustration (including national, regional and trade magazines and newspapers); Architectural Rendering; Fashion Illustration; Recording Covers (compact discs, records and audiocassettes); Medical Illustration; Technical Illustration; Novelty and Miscellaneous Products Illustration; Marbling; and Limited Edition Prints.

A highlight of most of the specialty sections above is that the work and trade practices unique to that field of illustration are spelled out in detail. In this manner both art buyers and graphic artists will better comprehend the demands on time and talent necessary in each area of specialization.

Design pricing ranges cover the following areas: General Graphic Design (including corporate reports and brochures, magazine and newspaper advertising, logos, album covers, posters and point of purchase); Book Design (including text, trade and juvenile books); Book Jacket Design (including hardcover, trade paperback and mass market); Lettering (including built-up letterforms and typeface design and calligraphy for the corporate, publishing and private markets).

Price ranges for Surface Design (including apparel, decorative and home furnishing, wovens and knits, rugs and special orders), Cartooning, Animation, Production, Retouching, and Staff Salaries in advertising, corporate, design firms, publishing, broadcast, textile and animation are also covered.

Business Management is a guide to negotiation, recordkeeping, invasions and infringements of rights, copyright registration and other details of running a business.

Standard Contracts provides the most complete set of forms ever assembled for all work specialties in the industry. The forms are designed to handle most of the basic contract issues that arise between graphic artists and clients, although special situations (such as when royalties are involved) may require amplification or modification. These forms include model contracts for both graphic artists and art buyers.

The *Reference* chapter contains a useful bibliography, glossary of terms, index and data on the population of artists in the U.S. from government and industry reports. This section also provides more information about the Guild, and includes an application for membership.

Professional Issues

In the development of the U.S. Constitution, our nation's founders recognized the need to stimulate the spread of learning and the dissemination of ideas by creating protections for creators of intellectual property. Article I, Section 8, empowers Congress to *"promote the progress of science and useful arts by securing for limited times to authors and inventors the exclusive right to their respective writings and discoveries."* This established the foundation for our copyright laws, which acknowledge artwork as intellectual property and a valuable economic resource that is traded in the marketplace.

In today's visual world, the works created by graphic artists are among the most powerful vehicles that communicate ideas in our society. A successful illustration can singlehandedly sell a product on the market. A successful logo can instantly evoke a company's good will in the public mind. A successful poster can move an entire population to action.

Like other creative professionals (actors, musicians, dancers, writers, photographers), graphic artists occupy a special place in our society and economy. Their unique vision, skills and style form the basis on which they attract clients, sell their work and earn their livelihood. Like other professionals, graphic artists provide their highly skilled service and creative input within a framework of professional standards and ethics. But the work of graphic artists is vulnerable and requires the maximum protection of our laws, not only to prevent unauthorized exploitation, but also to ensure that artists can continue to work without economic or competitive disadvantages.

One of the primary goals of the Graphic Artists Guild is to help create a healthy partnership between artists and clients by encouraging adherence to fair practices. The Guild upholds the standard of a value-for-value exchange, recognizing that both client and artist contribute to a successful working relationship.

The Guild is mandated by its constitution and by its members to *"promote and maintain high professional standards of ethics and practice, and to secure the conformance of all buyers, users, sellers and employers to established standards."* Further, the Guild seeks to *"establish, implement and enforce laws [and] policies...designed to accomplish these ends."* The organization's legislative agenda, therefore, is based on the needs and desires expressed by its members and its constitutionally mandated goals.

The Guild is active in creating and monitoring public policy developments, including legislative initiatives at the local, state and Federal levels. The issues addressed include local proposals to control escalating studio rents, state laws to encourage fair practices and to protect artists' authorship rights, and Federal legislation to close the work-for-hire loophole of the U.S. Copyright Act, strengthen infringement protections, create tax equity for artists and develop a national standard for artists' authorship rights (moral rights).

The Guild has drafted model legislation and has lobbied locally and nationally on these issues. Early successes in California, Oregon, New York and Massachusetts created a wave of interest in artists' rights legislation. Most recently Georgia has passed legislation, with Guild involvement, that strengthens artists' protections against copyright infringement.

The Guild has helped create a coalition of artists', photographers' and writers' organizations representing over one hundred thousand creators. The Copyright Justice Coalition continues to focus its attention on finding a Federal remedy to the work-for-hire problem. More recently, the Guild has also bridged the gap to the fine arts communities by co-founding Artists For

Tax Equity (AFTE), a coalition representing nearly one million creators which successfully lobbied Congress for exemption from an onerous tax provision.

Legislation

Like most unions, professional organizations and trade associations, the Graphic Artists Guild monitors legislation and lobbies on behalf of its members. Lobbying activities involve members at local, state and Federal levels through individual chapters and the national office. Since 1976 several legislative objectives have been targeted by Graphic Artists Guild members: reforming the work-for-hire provision of the Federal copyright law, abolishing the immunity of state governments and institutions from money damages in infringement suits, establishing mandatory awarding of attorneys' fee to individuals and small businesses by proven copyright infringers, moral rights, fair practices and equitable treatment for artists under the tax laws.

Work-for-hire reform

"Work for hire" is a provision of the U.S. Copyright Act intended as a narrow exception to the general rule that the artist or author who actually creates the work owns the copyright to it. The provision transfers authorship and ownership to the employer or other hiring party who commissions the work, leaving the artist with no rights whatsoever. While such a result *may* be justifiable in a traditional employment setting, the freelance artist, considered to be an independent contractor for all purposes except copyright, has no access to any employee benefits which may compensate for the loss of that copyright and the future earnings it may represent .

Under the law, a work for hire can come into existence in two ways: (1) an employee creating a copyrightable work within the scope of employment; or (2) an independent contractor creating a specially ordered or commissioned work in one of several categories, verified by a written contract signed by both parties and expressly stating that it is a work for hire.

Freelance artists who are independent contractors can lawfully be asked to sign work-for-hire contracts to cover work only in the following nine categories:

1. A contribution to a collective work (such as a magazine, newspaper, encyclopedia or anthology);

2. A contribution used as part of a motion picture or other audio-visual work;

3. A supplementary work, which includes pictorial illustrations, maps, charts, etc. done to supplement a work by another author;

4. A compilation (new arrangement of pre-existing works);

5. A translation;

6. An atlas;

7. A test;

8. Answer material for a test; and

9. An instructional text (defined as a literary, pictorial or graphic work prepared for publication and with the purpose of use in systematic instructional activities).

These criteria apply only to work done on special order or commission by an independent contractor. If there is no written agreement, or if the agreement does not specifically state that the work is made for hire, or if it is not signed, or if the work does not fall into one of the above categories, then there is no work for hire and the artist automatically retains authorship recognition and copyright ownership.

Even as an employee, however, an artist may negotiate with the employer a separate written contract, apart from the employment agreement, which transfers copyright ownership to the artist in some or all of the work created in the regular course of employment.

CCNV v. Reid

Until recently, independent contractors were found in many cases to be subject to the employee clause simply because the work was, or could have been, supervised and controlled by the hiring party. Despite the absence of a written contract, authorship and all rights in their work were awarded to their clients.

In 1989, however, the Supreme Court ruled unanimously that the employee clause could not be applied to independent contractors. However, if the relationship between the artist and the hiring party was determined to be one of conventional employment based on the application of a rigorous test of thirteen factors, then the created work would be considered made-for-hire.

The landmark case pitted freelance sculptor James Earl Reid against homeless advocate Mitch Snyder and the Community for Creative Non-Violence (CCNV) over a commissioned sculpture created by Reid but conceived and partly directed by Snyder. Even though there was no written contract between the parties and even though sculpture does not fall into any of the nine categories for specially ordered works, the lower court found Reid to be an employee because he was under Snyder's "supervision and control" and awarded the copyright to CCNV.

The factors the Supreme Court relied upon in deciding whether James Reid was an employee or not were: (1) the hiring party's right to control the manner and means by which the product is accomplished; (2) the skill required; (3) the source of the instrumentalities and tools; (4) the location of the work; (5) the duration of the relationship between the parties; (6) whether the hiring party has the right to assign additional projects to the hired party; (7) the hired party's discretion over when and how long to work; (8) the method of payment; (9) the hired party's role in hiring and paying assistants; (10) whether the work is part of the regular business of the hiring party; (11) whether the hiring party is in business; (12) the provision of employee benefits; and (13) the tax treatment of the hired party.

The Court made it clear that no one of these factors is determinative, but that all the factors must be examined. In applying them to the Reid case, the Court clearly found Reid to be an independent contractor, not an employee.

The practical consequences of this landmark decision are that some clients (like certain magazine publishers), are re-examining their policies for insisting on work for hire; they are determining that it is more desirable and economical to purchase the transfer of only specific rights. Those clients who insist on work for hire will comply strictly with the requirement for written agreements expressly stating that a work will be for hire.

But while the Supreme Court's decision narrowed one loophole, it may have widened others. Under the "joint authorship" provision of the Copyright Act, a work may be presumed to be a collaborative effort between the artist and client, granting each party the right to exploit the work independently of the other, without regard to the importance of their respective contributions, so long as profits are accounted for and divided equally. In the Reid case, for example, it was ultimately decided that the sculptor retained the right to make two- and three-dimensional copies; CCNV retained the right to make two-dimensional copies such as Christmas cards and posters.

Work-for-hire abuses

Clients who want to force a work-for-hire arrangement may resort to other means which, while unethical, are not prohibited under current copyright law. Some big businesses coerce freelancers into either accepting work for hire or losing the assignment. Works originally commissioned without discussion of copyright ownership may become works for hire after the fact, if the artist endorses a payment check or signs a purchase order after work has begun on which work-for-hire terms appear (usually in fine print). Or work-for-hire contracts understood by the artist to be for a single project may actually have work-for-hire language that covers all future work assigned to a freelancer.

Work-for-hire remedies

The Graphic Artists Guild is categorically opposed to the use of work-for-hire contracts. In addition to being a participant in arguing the *CCNV v. Reid* case successfully on appeal and later in filing a Supreme Court brief on behalf of artist James Earl Reid, it has helped introduce legislation at both the Federal and state levels to close this loophole in the Copyright Act and to prevent the variety of abuses proliferating in the marketplace. This position is supported by a prestigious coalition of national organizations representing a broad spectrum of creators.

One bill recently introduced in Congress by Senator Thad Cochran (R-MS), would modify the work-for-hire provisions to better enforce the intent of the Copyright Act. The bill, which attracted the support of the U.S. Copyright Office, would (1) narrowly define *employee* as a "formal, salaried" worker; (2) absolutely distinguish employee works from specially ordered or commissioned works, so that they are mutually exclusive; (3) require that an agreement for commissioned works for hire be signed *before* the work begins; and (4) prevent the use of blanket work-for-hire agreements by requiring a separate prior written agreement for each work.

Further, anticipating loopholes in the "joint work" provisions, the bill would require that each contribution intended to become part of a joint work be copyrightable on its own merits (merely suggesting the idea or the title is not enough) and, in the case of specially ordered or commissioned works, that each contributor sign a written agreement before the work begins, specifically stating that it will be considered a joint work.

Hearings were held on this bill in the fall of 1989 by the Senate Judiciary's Subcommittee on Patents, Copyrights and Trademarks and the Graphic Artists Guild presented extensive testimony in its support. At this writing, the Guild continues to lobby for its passage.

The legality of work for hire at the Federal level prevents any state from abolishing it, under the Federal pre-emption doctrine. But states are free to add stiff restrictions to the Federal criteria. California, for example, passed legislation in 1982 which makes any artist hired under a work-for-hire contract eligible for full employee benefits for the duration of the contract. This bill was supported by the Graphic Artists Guild and other creators' organizations active in the state.

Initiatives for similar legislation are being conducted by individual chapters in other states. Most recently, the Georgia legislature, responding to active lobbying by the Guild's Atlanta Chapter, held hearings to consider work-for-hire restrictions based on the California model.

State's immunity from copyright infringement

The U.S. Copyright Act, in establishing sanctions (monetary damages, fines, injunctions) against infringement, intended these sanctions to apply to *"anyone who violates any of the exclusive rights of the copyright owner."* According to the Copyright Office, "anyone" was meant to include states, state institutions and state employees. But in 1985, the Supreme Court ruled in a 5-4 decision that the Eleventh Amendment to the Constitution, which generally grants states immunity from lawsuits and money judgments in Federal courts, could not be negated by Congress except by explicit and unequivocal language. Subsequent courts decided that under this test the Copyright Act's language was not specific enough and so opened the door for many state-funded institutions to use copyrighted materials without permission, without paying or giving

credit and without fear of reprisal from the copyright owner.

In 1990, Congress corrected this court-induced injustice by passing the Copyright Remedy Clarification Act. Now states and their instrumentalities are once again subject to all the penalties and sanctions for copyright infringement. Grassroots lobbying by the Guild and its members helped in this new law's passage.

Mandatory attorneys' fees

One specific sanction provided for in the Copyright Act allows judges, in their discretion, to make copyright violators pay their victim's attorneys' fees in addition to the damage award. Except in extreme cases, however, judges tend to let each party pay its own legal costs, and for freelance artists, damages awarded are often less than the costs of litigating an infringement. This tends to inhibit those who cannot afford the high cost of litigation from seeking redress in the courts.

In 1989, a bill was introduced to make the award of reasonable attorneys' fees mandatory whenever individual creators or small businesses successfully sued for infringement of their copyright. The Graphic Artists Guild joined a coalition of writers, photographers, filmmakers and videotape producers, spearheaded by the Training Media Association, in raising grassroots support for the bill. Unfortunately, the bill was never voted out of committee.

Moral rights and the Berne Convention

Moral rights derive from the French doctrine of *droit moral*, which recognizes certain inherent personal rights of creators in their works, even after the works have been sold or the copyright transferred. These rights stand above and distinct from copyright.

The doctrine traditionally grants to artists and writers four specific rights:
(1) The right to protect the *integrity* of their work to prevent any modification, distortion or mutilation which would be prejudicial to their honor or reputation;
(2) The right of *attribution* (or *paternity)* to insist that their authorship be properly acknowledged and to prevent use of their names for works they did not create;
(3) The right of *disclosure* to decide if, when and how a work is presented to the

public; and

(4) The right of *recall* to withdraw, destroy or disavow a work if it is changed or no longer represents their views.

Moral rights have long been an integral part of copyright protection laws in most European nations, but were largely rejected and ignored in the United States. In 1886, the U.S. refused to join the Berne Convention, a world-wide multinational treaty for the protection of literary and artistic works which accepted moral rights as a matter of course. Member nations participating in Berne are required to conform their copyright laws to certain minimum standards and to guarantee reciprocity to citizens of any other member.

But after 100 years, economic realities and skyrocketing foreign piracy forced the U.S. to seek entry into the Berne Union. By this time, several states had enacted various forms of moral rights statutes (due to a great part to Guild involvement), and certain elements of the doctrine were recognized in state and Federal courts. The "totality" of the American legal system, therefore, persuaded Berne administrators that the U.S. qualified for membership.

The 1976 Copyright Act also brought the U.S. closer to other Berne standards. Duration of copyright was extended from a term of 28 years, renewable once, to life of the creator plus fifty years. Regulations were also drafted to eliminate the formalities of placing a notice on and registering a work as prerequisites to suits for infringement.

In 1988, the U.S. became the 80th country to sign the Berne Convention, in effect extending protection to American works in 24 nations with which the U.S. had no separate copyright agreements, and stemming the loss of billions of dollars in royalties. Although works are now protected at the moment they are created, it is still advisable to affix a copyright notice (e.g., © Jane Artist, 1991 or Copyright, Jane Artist, 1991) as it bars the defense of innocent infringement in court. And, while foreign works are exempt, American works still have to be registered with the U.S. Copyright Office before their creators can sue for infringement, statutory damages and attorneys fees.

The Visual Artists Rights Act

Most of the cases which brought moral rights problems to the public's

attention revolve around mutilation of works of fine art, such as Pablo Picasso's *Trois Femmes*, cut into one-inch squares and sold as original Picassos by two entrepreneurs in 1986; the destruction and removal of a Isamu Noguchi sculpture from a New York office lobby; or the alteration by the Marriott Corporation of an historical William Smith mural in a landmark Maryland building.

A much-publicized case in the graphic arts area involved Antonio Vargas' series, the *Vargas Girls,* which ran in *Esquire* magazine. After Vargas' contract with *Esquire* expired, the magazine continued to run the series under the name *The Esquire Girls* without giving Vargas credit. Vargas brought *Esquire* to court but lost the case, because he had no rights left under the contract, even the rights to his own name.

Moral rights legislation at both the state and Federal level has been proposed and vigorously supported by the Graphic Artists Guild since the late 1970's. Successes in California (1979), New York (1983), Maine and Massachusetts (1985) and other states helped sustain the momentum to advance a Federal version.

Like actors, artists are judged on the basis of their last public performance. Members of the Graphic Artists Guild have testified strongly that appearance of their artwork with unauthorized alterations or defacement can damage a otherwise vital career. By presenting testimony about the problems that illustrators and designers face, the Graphic Artists Guild was able to broaden proposed legislation. The bills the Guild helped to pass recognize artists' on-going relationships with the work they create.

The *Visual Artists Rights Act* was finally enacted by Congress in 1990. While it is a positive first step toward comprehensive moral rights legislation, the Act has limited application and, ironically, may invalidate many state statutes which may be far more protective.

The law covers only visual arts and only one-of-a-kind works (defined as paintings, drawings, prints, photographs made for exhibition only and sculptures existing in a single copy or in a limited edition of 200 copies or fewer, signed and consecutively numbered by the artist). Specifically excluded are any kind of commercial or applied art (advertising, promotional, packaging); posters, maps, charts, technical drawings; motion pictures and other audiovisual works; books, magazines, newspapers, periodicals; electronically produced work; any work for hire and any non-copyrightable work.

The moral rights protected are limited to those of *attribution* and *integrity*. Any distortion, mutilation or other modification of a work must be intentional; mere natural deterioration is not actionable (unless caused by gross negligence). In addition, the Act places two burdens on the artist: to prove that a threatened act would be "prejudicial to his or her honor or reputation" and, in order to prevent destruction of a work, to prove that it is "of recognized stature." Since no guidelines are provided for either standard, their meaning will have to be determined in the courts on a case-by-case basis.

These rights exist exclusively with the artist during his or her lifetime and may not be transferred. They may be waived, but only by an express written and signed agreement. In case of a joint work, each contributing artist may claim or waive the rights for all the others. The Act also contains special provisions for removal of works that are parts of buildings (murals, bas reliefs), including a procedure to register such works.

A potential problem of this new legislation is that it invokes the doctrine of Federal preemption and appears to nullify any existing state laws which protect equivalent rights. The question, which will probably have to answered in the courts, is whether these statutes, many of which apply to other visual works or extend greater protections are completely preempted or only partially so.

Resale royalties

Another time-honored French doctrine which, like moral rights, transcends rights of copyright and ownership of the original work is known as *droit de suite*. It allows creators to share in the appreciating value of their works by guaranteeing a certain percentage of the profits every time a work is resold.

Such rights, known as resale royalties, already exist in California. A provision for resale royalties had been part of the original version of the *Visual Artists Rights Act*, but was later dropped because of strong opposition from art dealers, auction houses and museums. The Act does however, authorize the Copyright Office to conduct an in-depth study on the feasibility of implementing resale royalties legislation.

Fair practices

The Fair Practices Act, signed into law in Oregon (1979), in California (1982) and in New York (1983), clarifies who owns the original work of art when reproduction rights are sold. This legislation was drafted by the Guild's attorneys on the basis of concerns raised by Guild members.

The Act provides that an original work of art can become the property of a client only if it is sold in *writing*. The passage of this act reinforces one of the premises of the copyright law, which is that works of art have value beyond their reproduction for a specific purpose, and that this value rightly belongs to the artist who creates them. The Fair Practices Act will prevent clients from holding on to originals unless they have written sales agreements with the creator. Where it applies, this act solves the problems that can arise when clients believe they have obtained ownership of the original art when in fact they have only purchased reproduction rights, or when they believe they have obtained an original through an ambiguous oral agreement.

In Oregon and California, the law provides that if there is any ambiguity as to who owns reproduction rights, the ambiguity shall be resolved in favor of the creator/artist.

For artists whose livelihoods depend on resale of reproduction rights and on sales of original works, this law is critical. It also sets a precedent for clearing up any ambiguity about ownership, since a written transfer is now required.

Another important precedent to prevent unauthorized reproduction of artwork was set by a Georgia statute enacted in 1990. The *Protection of Artists* law requires commercial printers to obtain written affidavits from their clients attesting that the artist has authorized the reproduction of the work, when the art (painting, drawing, photograph or work of graphic art), costs $1000 or more. The law emphasizes the distinction between ownership of artwork and the right to reproduce it. Any use or reuse of artwork without the written permission of the artist is now illegal. The Atlanta Chapter of the Guild was instrumental in getting the law passed.

Tax equity

There is a popular misconception that artists donating their art to a charitable organization may deduct the "fair market value" of the work. In fact, artists may deduct only the cost of producing the work, i.e., the price of the canvas, paint and other materials. If, however, an artist sells the original, the buyer may donate the work and deduct the amount paid for it. As a result, artists have either withheld their valuable originals or sold them to private collectors, thus limiting public access.

Historically, artists, writers and politicians were able to donate their original art and manuscripts and receive the full fair market value deduction. In 1969, the situation changed dramatically. Congress sought to prevent politicians from receiving windfalls based on the donations of their papers. Broad legislation was enacted which resulted in inhibiting artists and writers as well as politicians. Since 1969, museums, which depend on artists' donations of original art to supplement their paid acquisitions, have documented a sharp drop-off in donated works.

Artists and writers have spoken out about this obvious inequity and have received the support of their professional organizations. They have acted in cooperation with museums, universities and libraries whose representatives believe that wider access to original art is in the public interest. The *National Heritage Resources Act* has been introduced in the U.S. Congress to answer these concerns.

Uniform tax capitalization

Prior to the 1986 tax act musicians, photographers, writers and freelance artists were generally permitted to currently deduct expenses (including research costs, travel, supplies, etc.) incurred in creating the final work product. The *Tax Reform Act of 1986* contained a provision which threatened to drive many artists out of business: *uniform tax capitalization.*

For tax purposes, anyone who created property *"embodying words, ideas, concepts images, or sounds"* were to be considered manufacturers; all the direct and indirect expenses related to each and every project could only be deducted as the work produced income, and only in proportion to the portion income received from the work. In many cases, the productive period of investment for a creative work would have been the complete period of copyright (the creator's lifetime plus fifty years).

The first problem with the capitalization of expenses was the lack of guidance on how to allocate indirect costs to each project; the second was how to determine the write-off period for these capitalized amounts. Ultimately, with normal deductions of business expenses disallowed, an artists' tax liability would have risen dramatically.

Responding to this serious threat, in 1988 the Graphic Artists Guild, along with the Society of Illustrators, the Foundation for the Community of Artists (FCA) and the Association of Independent Video and Filmmakers (AIVF) spearheaded "Artists for Tax Equity," a coalition representing 75 organizations and nearly one million artists. This grassroots effort successfully lobbied Congress to exempt artists and designers from the uniform capitalization provision.

Sales tax

The question of whether graphic artists and designers are obligated to collect sales tax from their clients is problematic throughout the country. Many states which impose a sales tax on the retail purchase of goods consider the tax to apply to any transfer of artwork, regardless of whether the original art is sold (tangible personal property) or merely a right of reproduction (intangible personal property). Other state requirements are unclear or ambiguous as to whether the collection of sales tax is required when only rights of reproduction are sold. Some states even impose a sales tax on services.

Generally, the tax is charged by the artist, who must be registered to collect and remit it, to any non-exempt client who does business in the same state as the artist. Out-of-state clients may be subject to a "use" tax in their home states (the equivalent of a sales tax, but imposed on out-of-state purchases), which they are responsible for reporting and paying.

Exceptions to the tax do exist in certain circumstances, such as intermediate, non-retail sales, occasional sales, specific uses (printing, advertising), or when the buyer is tax-exempt. But regulations as well as rates vary tremendously from state to state. Many graphic artists who were unaware or confused about sales tax requirements have found themselves liable for large amounts of uncollected back taxes, interest and penalties. Some of the Guild's local chapters are working with state tax authorities to develop clear and coherent guidelines for graphic artists and the sale of their work.

New technology

In recent years, computers have become a part of professional artists' day-to-day lives. Artwork is composed and enhanced on computer, stored and altered, transmitted by satellite to disks. Artwork created on computer is used in virtually all markets and fields.

The U.S. Congress has become concerned with the effects of new technologies on society and the marketplace. The Graphic Artists Guild and some of its members were asked to provide testimony about the impact of the technology and the need for public policy development.

Artists expressed concern that their work can be stored in electronic "image banks" or electronic information networks and manipulated and used without their knowledge or permission. While unauthorized uses and alterations already occur, artists are concerned that these kinds of abuses will proliferate unless public policy is shaped to prevent them.

There is also some concern that a technological training gap may emerge between those who have the resources to gain access to new computer systems and those who do not.

While there is potential for great harm to creators, the new technologies offer the possibility of great creative advances. A public policy emphasis for research into technologies that will support the goal of protection of authorship rights is essential.

With access to training on new computer systems, artists can create a new "graphics vernacular" to transmit society's messages in a vital and immediate way. The Guild will continue to advocate the protection of authorship rights in the light of new technological developments.

Employment issues

Many graphic artists who are treated as, or believe themselves to be, freelancers (independent contractors), may actually be considered employees in the eyes of the law. A California comic book publisher, for example, was recently audited by the Internal Revenue Service (IRS) which determined that the artists, letterers, inkers, etc., hired out-of-house by the publisher were not independent contractors, but employees engaged in homework. The IRS focused on whether the individual artists performed services according to the company's specifications; using materials furnished by the company and on whether the services were not in the nature of a single transaction but were part of a continuing relationship with the company for which services were provided.

Similarly, some designers think they are "fulltime freelancers" because they are paid a flat daily or weekly fee. But they may work 9 to 5 for a single client, at the client's premises, using the client's materials and facilities, over a series of projects. If the relationship were examined by a government agency, they might be determined to be employees. Government is less interested in job titles than it is in the actual working relationship between the worker and the hiring party.

There are advantages and disadvantages to each situation for both the artist and hiring party. For every employee, an employer is legally obligated to pay 7.65 per cent of gross income up to $53,400 in social security tax (FICA) and additional premiums for unemployment, disability and workers compensation insurance. Employers may also be obligated to provide optional fringe benefits like paid vacations, comprehensive medical and hospitalization insurance, employer-funded pension plans and profit-sharing to every employee. But when an independent contractor is hired, only a flat fee is paid, simplifying the bookkeeping. Depending on the freelancer's fee structure, significant savings to the employer on taxes, insurance and other fringe benefits may also be realized.

Freelancers who are independent contractors must pay the full 15.3 per cent FICA tax on adjusted gross income (rather than the 7.65 per cent that employees pay). Independent contractors must purchase their own disability coverage and have no access to unemployment or workers compensation. Furthermore, independent contractors must provide their own vacations, medical coverage (if available) and retirement.

Employees enjoy the security of a regular paycheck while independent contractors do not. Employees have a legal right to organize for the purposes of collective bargaining, a right denied to independent contractors. Employees, however, do not enjoy the freedom of working for whom they want, when they want as a freelancer might. Independent contractors also have the ability to significantly reduce their taxable income by deducting legitimate business expenses.

Clients should be aware that the Internal Revenue Service (IRS) takes a dim view of independent contractor relationships. From the government's perspective, employers use so-called independent contractors to evade employment taxes. If independent contractors are hired, the employer should be sure there is a reasonable basis on which to rely in the event of an audit.

The IRS relies on usual common-law factors to determine whether an individual is an employee or an independent contractor, similar to those on which the Supreme Court relied in *CCNV v. Reid* (see "work for hire," above). In addition to those factors, the IRS may also examine the method of payment (independent contractors are usually paid by the job, not by the hour) and whether the hiring party has the right to fire at will.

There are risks to both artists and their clients by not treating their relationship correctly. In the case of the comic book artists, the IRS penalized the publisher with an amount equivalent to three years of income tax withholdings, penalties and interest, totaling $100,000. Freelance artists found to be an employees may have their business deductions disallowed, resulting in greater tax liabilities.

Speculation: Ethical and unethical practices

The Graphic Artists Guild is unalterably opposed to any artists being asked to work on speculation because of the inherent risks to the artist in such circumstances. Art buyers should not ask artists to work on a project unless a fee has been agreed upon in advance.

Artists must be equitably compensated at any time they are requested to create artwork. Working on speculation places all the risks on the artists without a commitment on the buyer's part.

For example, it is considered an unethical practice for a buyer to be in the position of deciding only upon completion of the art whether or not to compensate the artist. This situation occurs in agreements where payment becomes dependent on the "buyer's satisfaction" or "on publication."

In royalty arrangements for commissioned art, an advance should be provided. Payment of the advance allows the artist to

recoup expenses and to manage the financial demands of the project in a more timely and realistic fashion.

Similarly, if a buyer decides to cancel a job through no fault of the artist, cancellation fees must be paid at all times to compensate the artist for expended time, effort and expenses.

Art contests, except under special circumstances, are also opposed because of their speculative nature. For contest guidelines approved by the Guild, see the section following.

However, when artists create artwork on their own initiative and then seek to sell it to a buyer for speculative marketing, it is considered ethical speculation and not in violation of this rule.

For example, if an artist's proposal for a book is accepted by a publisher and a royalty arrangement is negotiated, the artist and publisher are taking a mutual risk in their investment. The compensation to both parties is speculative, meaning both are dependent on the market response to the product.

Contests and competitions

In 1980, the Graphic Artists Guild together with Designers Saturday (DS), a furniture manufacturers association, developed a competition to meet two goals: to produce high-quality art for the DS annual show and to provide a competition that was ethical and appropriate for professional artists. At the same time, the Guild was receiving complaints from artists around the country concerning the unethical nature of most contests that they were asked to enter.

The results of the experiment with DS were so successful that the Guild decided to see if other competitions and contests could be structured to accomplish the goals met by the DS model.

In an effort to gain a clearer picture of the competition scene nationwide, the Graphic Artists Guild Foundation, with a supporting grant from the National Endowment for the Arts, conducted a nationwide survey of art and design competition holders, as well as an informal poll of jurors and competition entrants.

This study resulted in the establishment of a list of guidelines for three types of art competitions: those held by art-related organizations/associations to award excellence in the field; those for which the winning entries are used for commercial purposes; and competitions held by non-profit organizations where the winning entries are used for non-profit purposes.

Among the findings of the surveys were that:

By far, the largest and most expensive competitions are those operated by associations ancillary to the advertising industry, such as art directors; clubs and industry trade magazines. The purpose of these competitions is to honor excellence within their own communities. While these competitions do not require that original art be submitted, the sponsoring organizations generally charge high entry fees for members and non-members alike. These competitions generally attract the highest volume of entrants.

The greatest barrier to attracting professional artists as entrants in competitions is work on speculation. Most professional artists reported that they did not want or could not afford to take time from income-producing projects to create original work for a competition on a speculative basis. The most popular type of competition for this group is based on work already produced or published.

In most cases, the process for selecting a jury for competitions appears to be quite good. However, jurors noted that often the criteria or process for judging the work is vague or poorly articulated.

Another abuse listed by professional artists concerning competitions is the requirement for all-rights transfers by all entrants to the competition holder.

In response to the data received from the competition study, the following guidelines were developed:

Competitions by art-related organizations/associations to award excellence

1. The call for entry shall define clearly all rules governing competition entries, specifications for work entered, any and all fees for entry and any and all rights to be transferred by any entrants to the competition holder.

2. Jurors for the competition shall be listed on the call for entry. No juror or employee of the organization holding the competition shall be eligible to enter the competition.

3. Criteria for jurying the entries and specifications for the artwork to be submitted in all rounds shall be defined clearly in the call for entry as a guide to both entrants and jurors.

4. Deadlines for notification and process for notification for acceptance or rejection of all entries shall be listed in the call for entry.

5. Any and all uses for any and all entries shall be listed clearly in the call for entries, with terms for any rights to be transferred.

6. For the first round, tearsheets, slides, photographs or other reproductions of existing work shall be requested in order to judge appropriateness of style, technique and proficiency of entrants. This round shall result in the choice of finalists. If samples from this round are not to be returned to the entrants, that fact shall be listed clearly in the call for entries.

7. If the competition ends in an exhibition, hanging or exhibition fees paid for by the entrants shall be listed in the call for entries.

8. After the first round, the jury may request original art for review. The competition holder shall insure all works against damage or loss until the work is returned to the artist. All original artwork shall be returned to the artist. Any fees charged to the artists for the return of artwork shall be listed in the call for entry.

9. Artwork shall not be altered in any way without the express permission of the artist.

10. All entries and rights to the artwork remain the property of the artist, unless a separate written transfer and payment for the original has been negotiated.

11. If work exhibited by the competition is for sale, any commission taken by the competition holder shall be listed in the call for entries.

Competitions where the winning entries are used for commercial purposes

1. The call for entry shall define clearly all rules governing competition entries, specifications for work entered, any and all fees for entry and any and all rights to be transferred by any entrants to the competition holder.

2. Jurors for the competition shall be

listed on the call for entry. No juror or employee of the organization holding the competition shall be eligible to enter the competition.

3. Criteria for jurying the entries and specifications for the artwork to be submitted in all rounds shall be defined clearly in the call for entry as a guide to both entrants and jurors.

4. Deadlines for notification and process for notification for acceptance or rejection of all entries shall be listed in the call for entry.

5. Any and all uses for any and all entries shall be listed clearly in the call for entries, with terms for any rights to be transferred.

6. For the first round, tearsheets, slides, photographs or other reproductions of existing work shall be requested in order to judge appropriateness of style, technique and proficiency of entrants. This round shall result in the choice of finalists. If samples from this round are not to be returned to the entrants, that fact shall be listed clearly in the call for entries.

7. The number of finalists chosen after the first round should be small. The finalists shall then be required to submit sketches or comprehensive drawings for final judging. All finalists shall receive some portion of the award. This eliminates the speculative nature of the competition.

8. Agreements shall be made with each artist working at the final stage, prior to the beginning of work (Graphic Artists Guild contracts or the equivalent can be used). The agreements shall include the nature of the artwork required, deadlines, credit line and copyright ownership for the artist, and the amount of the award.

9. Any work of finalists not received by the required deadline or not in the form required and agreed upon shall be disqualified. All rights to the artwork that has been disqualified shall remain with the artist.

10. The winners shall produce camera-ready or finished art according to the specifications listed in the call for entry. Artwork submitted shall not be altered in any way without the express permission of the artist.

11. The value of any award to the winners shall be at least commensurate with fair market value of the rights transferred. The first place winner shall receive an award that is significantly greater than that of other winners.,

12. The competition holder shall

insure original artwork in their possession against loss or damage until it is returned to the artist.

Competitions held by non-profit organizations or where the winning entry is used for non-profit purposes

1. The call for entry shall define clearly all rules governing competition entries, specifications for work entered, any and all fees for entry and any and all rights to be transferred by any entrants to the competition holder.

2. Jurors for the competition shall be listed on the call for entry. No juror or employee of the organization holding the competition shall be eligible to enter the competition.

3. Criteria for jurying the entries and specifications for the artwork to be submitted in all rounds shall be defined clearly in the call for entry as a guide to both entrants and jurors.

4. Deadlines for notification and process for notification for acceptance or rejection of all entries shall be listed in the call for entry.

5. Any and all uses for any and all entries shall be listed clearly in the call for entries, with terms for any rights to be transferred.

6. For the first round, tearsheets, slides, photographs or other reproductions of existing work shall be requested in order to judge appropriateness of style, technique and proficiency of entrants. This round shall result in the choice of finalists. If samples from this round are not to be returned to the entrants, that fact shall be listed clearly in the call for entries.

7. The number of finalists chosen after the first round should be small. The finalists shall then be required to submit sketches or comprehensive drawings for final judging. All finalists shall receive some portion of the award. This eliminates the speculative nature of the competition.

8. Agreements shall be made with each artist working at the final stage, prior to the beginning of work (Graphic Artists Guild contracts or the equivalent can be used). The agreements shall include the nature of the artwork required, deadlines, credit line and copyright ownership for the artist, and the amount of the award.

9. Any work of finalists not received

by the required deadline or not in the form required and agreed upon shall be disqualified. All rights to the artwork that has been disqualified shall remain with the artist.

10. The winners shall produce camera-ready or finished art according to the specifications listed in the call for entry. Artwork submitted shall not be altered in any way without the express permission of the artist.

11. The value of the award should, if possible, be commensurate with the fair market price for the job. For non-profit competition holders, exceptions may be made depending on the budget and use of the artwork for the competition.

12. The competition holder shall insure original artwork in their possession against loss or damage until it is returned to the artist.

Graphic Artists Guild Foundation Seal of Compliance

As a service to competition holders and entrants, the Graphic Artists Guild Foundation will review calls for entry to ascertain whether they meet the minimum standards listed in the guidelines above. If a competition holder meets these standards, they are eligible to carry the Graphic Artists Guild Foundation's Seal of Compliance for ethical competition calls for entry. A sliding fee scale for the reviewing calls for entry is available to accommodate the budgets of both non-profit and profit competitions. For further information, contact the Graphic Artists Guild Foundation, 11 West 20th Street, New York, NY 10011.

Cancellation and rejection fees

The Graphic Artists Guild strongly supports the *Code of Fair Practice* article that condemns the practice of work on speculation. All assignments should provide for a fee, even in the event of cancellation or rejection. Written agreements between artists and buyers should contain a "cancellation provision" or "rejection provision" based on the following principles.

Cancellation provision

The client agrees to pay the artist a cancellation fee if the assignment is cancelled for reasons beyond the artist's control.

1. If cancellation occurs prior to the completion of the finished art, the cancellation fee shall be no less than 50 per cent of the original fee.

2. If cancellation occurs after the completion of preliminary work and prior to the completion of finished art, the cancellation fee shall be from 50 to 100 per cent of the original fee, depending on the degree of completion of the finished art at the time of cancellation.

3. If cancellation occurs after the completion of finished art, the cancellation fee shall be 100 per cent of the original fee.

4. All necessary and related expenses shall be paid in full.

5. In the event of cancellation, the client obtains all of the originally agreed-upon rights to the use of the artwork (except in royalty arrangements).

6. If preliminary or incomplete work is cancelled and later used as finished art, the client will pay the unpaid balance of the original usage fee.

7. Both artist and client agree to submit any dispute regarding cancellation fees to the Joint Ethics Committee or other forum for binding arbitration.

Rejection provision

The client agrees to pay the artist a rejection fee if the preliminary or finished is not found to be reasonably satisfactory and the assignment is terminated.

1. If rejection occurs prior to the completion of finished art, the rejection fee shall be no less than one-third of the original fee.

2. If rejection occurs after the completion of preliminary work and prior to the completion of finished art, the rejection fee shall be from one-third to 100 per cent of the original fee.

3. If rejection occurs after the completion of finished art the rejection fee shall be from 50 to 100 per cent of the original fee. In no event shall a rejection fee on completed artwork be less than 50 per cent of the original fee.

4. All necessary and related expenses shall be paid in full.

5. In the event of rejection, the client does not obtain any rights to the use of the art-

work. Rejected work may not be used for reproduction by the client without a separate
fee.

6. Both artist and client agree to
submit any dispute regarding rejection fees
to the Joint Ethics Committee or other
forum for binding arbitration.

The cancellation and rejection fees
shown in these guidelines are commonly
accepted. These fees are flexible. If preliminary work is unusually complex or the
assignment was required to be done on a
very short deadline, the artist could reasonably expect higher cancellation or rejection
fees. However, the minimums for cancellation or rejection fees are necessary to
protect artists, since additional assignments
from other clients may be turned away to
provide time for completion of the cancelled
assignment.

The Guild monitors abuses that
occur with regard to cancellation fees. Even
if contracts are verbal (or written but lack a
cancellation provision), clients and artists
should follow the accepted trade practices
reflected in the Guild's cancellation guidelines. Any failure to follow these standards
should be reported immediately to the
Grievance Committee of the local Guild
chapter.

ETHICAL
STANDARDS

Ethical Standards

Code of Fair Practice

In 1945 a group of artists and art directors in the City of New York, concerned with the growing abuses, misunderstandings and disregard of uniform standards of conduct in their field, met to consider possibilities for improvement. They reached the conclusion that to be successful, any effort must start with the most widespread backing, and further, that it must be a continuing, not a temporary, activity. On their recommendation, three leading New York art organizations together established and financed a committee known as the Joint Ethics Committee

The Joint Ethics Committee Code of Fair Practice for the Graphic Communication Industry

Formulated in 1948, and revised in 1989, the Code was conceived to promote equity for those engaged in the various aspects of creating, selling, buying and using graphic arts.

Relations between artists and buyers

The word "artist" should be understood to include creative people in the field of visual communications such as illustration, graphic design, photography, film and television.

This code provides the graphic communications industry with an accepted standard of ethics and professional conduct. It presents guidelines for the voluntary conduct of persons in the industry which may be modified by written agreement between the parties.

ARTICLE 1.
Negotiations between an artist or the artist's representative and a client should be conducted only through an authorized buyer.

The Graphic Artists Guild is mandated by its constitution and its members' concern to monitor, support and foster ethical standards in all dealings between graphic artists and art buyers. This activity is accomplished through Guild programs for members, through cooperation with related organizations and legislative activity on local, state and Federal levels.

As part of its responsibility in this area, the Guild is a sponsor of the Joint Ethics Committee, which through mediation or arbitration resolves disputes between graphic artists and clients in the New York area.

Along with its support of the Joint Ethics Committee, the Guild has its own Professional Practices and Grievance Committees that work with members in addressing issues of professional relations between artists and buyers and assist members in resolving violations of agreements and commonly accepted trade standards. As with all other Guild programs, these committees draw from members' experiences in the field, track industry standards and publicize any changes in the field that affect contracts and trade practices.

ARTICLE 2.

Orders or agreements between an artist or artist's representative and buyer should be in writing and shall include the specific rights which are being transferred, the specific fee arrangement agreed to by the parties, delivery date and a summarized description of the work.

ARTICLE 3.

All changes or additions not due to the fault of the artist or artist's representative should be billed to the buyer as an additional and separate charge.

ARTICLE 4.

There should be no charges to the buyer for revisions or retakes made necessary by errors on the part of the artist or the artist's representative.

ARTICLE 5.

If work commissioned by a buyer is postponed or cancelled, a "kill-fee" should be negotiated based on time allotted, effort expended and expenses incurred.

ARTICLE 6.

Completed work shall be paid for in full and the artwork shall be returned promptly to the artist.

ARTICLE 7.

Alterations shall not be made without consulting the artist. Where alterations or retakes are necessary, the artist shall be given the opportunity of making such changes.

ARTICLE 8.

The artist shall notify the buyer of any anticipated delay in delivery. Should the artist fail to keep the contract through unreasonable delay or non-conformance with agreed specifications, it will be considered a breach of contract by the artist.

ARTICLE 9.

Asking an artist to work on speculation is not deemed professionally reasonable because of its potentially exploitative nature.

ARTICLE 10.

There shall be no undisclosed rebates, discounts, gifts, or bonuses requested by or given to buyers by the artist or representative.

ARTICLE 11.

Artwork and copyright ownership are vested in the hands of the artist.

ARTICLE 12.

Original artwork remains the property of the artist unless it is specifically purchased. It is distinct from the purchase of any reproduction rights.* All transactions shall be in writing.

ARTICLE 13.

In case of copyright transfers, only specified rights are transferred. All unspecified rights remain vested with the artist. All transactions shall be in writing.

ARTICLE 14.

Commissioned artwork is not to be considered as "work for hire."

ARTICLE 15.

When the price of work is based on limited use and later such work is used more extensively, the artist shall receive additional payment.

ARTICLE 16.

If exploratory work, comprehensives, or preliminary photographs from an assignment are subsequently used for reproduction, the artist's prior permission shall be secured and the artist shall receive fair additional payment.

ARTICLE 17.

If exploratory work, comprehensives, or photographs are bought from an artist with the intention or possibility that another artist will be assigned to do the finished work, this shall be in writing at the time of placing the order.

ARTICLE 18.

If no transfer of copyright ownership* has been executed, the publisher of any reproduction of artwork shall publish the artist's copyright notice if the artist so requests at the time of agreement.

ARTICLE 19.

The right to remove the artist's name on published artwork is subject to agreement between artist and buyer.

ARTICLE 20.

There shall be no plagiarism of any artwork.

ARTICLE 21.

If an artist is specifically requested to produce any artwork during unreasonable working hours, fair additional remuneration shall be paid.

ARTICLE 22.

All artwork or photography submitted as samples to a buyer should bear the name of the artist or artists responsible for the work. An artist shall not claim authorship of another's work.

ARTICLE 23.

All companies and their employees who receive artist portfolios, samples, etc. shall be responsible for the return of the portfolio to the artist in the same condition as received.

ARTICLE 24.

An artist entering into an agreement with a representative, studio, or production company for an exclusive representation shall not accept an order from nor permit work to be shown by any other representative or studio. Any agreement which is not intended to be exclusive should set forth the exact restrictions agreed upon between the parties.

ARTICLE 25.

No representative should continue to show an artist's samples after the termination of an association.

ARTICLE 26.

After termination of an association between artist and representative, the representative should be entitled to a commission for a period of six months on accounts which the representative has secured, unless otherwise specified by contract.

ARTICLE 27.

Examples of an artist's work furnished to a representative or submitted to a prospective buyer shall remain the property of the artist, should not be duplicated without the artist's consent and shall be returned promptly to the artist in good condition.

ARTICLE 28.

Contests for commercial purposes are not deemed professionally reasonable because of their potentially speculative and exploitative character.

ARTICLE 29.

Interpretation of the Code for the purposes of mediation and arbitration shall be in the hands of the Joint Ethics Committee and is subject to changes and additions at the discretion of the parent organizations through their appointed representatives on the Committee.

Submitting to mediation and arbitration under the auspices of the Joint Ethics Committee is voluntary and requires the consent of all parties to the dispute.

Artwork ownership, copyright ownership and ownership and rights transfered after January 1, 1978, are to be in compliance with the Federal Copyright Revision Act of 1976.

The Joint Ethics Committee

The Joint Ethics Committee is composed of four members with three votes from each of the following organizations: Advertising Photographers of America, American Institute of Graphic Arts, American Society of Magazine Photographers, Inc., The Art Buyers Club, The Art Directors Club, Inc., Society of Illustrators, Inc., Society of Photographers and Artist Representatives, Inc. and The Graphic Artists Guild, appointed by the directing bodies of each organization but serving jointly in furtherance of the purposes for which the Committee was founded.

Members of the Joint Ethics Committee are selected with great care by their respective organizations. Their selection is based upon their experience in the profession, their proven mature thinking and temperament and their reputation for impartiality.

The operating expenses of the Committee are defrayed by the sponsoring organizations. The time and services of the members are voluntarily contributed. The Committee zealously upholds the ethical standards set forth in the Code and invites any and all reports of violations.

The Committee offers no legal advice on contracts, copyrights, bill collecting or similar matters, but does act on matters that it defines as violations of the Code. It meets one or more times a month to read and act upon complaints, requests for guidance and reports of Code violation. The proceedings and records of the Committee are held in strict confidence. In the interest of the profession typical cases are published periodically without identification of the parties involved. All communications to the Committee must be made in writing. When the complaint justifies action, a copy of the complainant's letter may be sent, with the plaintiff's permission, to the alleged offender. In the exchange of correspondence which follows, matters are frequently settled by a mere clarification of the issues. Further action by the Committee becomes unnecessary, and in many instances both sides resume friendly and profitable relationships.

When, however, a continued exchange of correspondence indicates that a ready adjustment of differences is improbable, the Committee may suggest mediation or offer its facilities for arbitration.

In the case of flagrant violation, the Committee may, at its discretion, cite the alleged offender to the governing bodies of the parent organizations and recommend that they publicize the fact of these citations when (a) the Committee, after a reasonable length of time and adequate notice, receives no response from the alleged offender or (b) when the Committee receives a response which it deems unacceptable.

The Committee's facilities are not limited to members of its supporting groups. They are available to any individual, business, or professional organization in the field of communications. There is a nominal fee of $25 to bring a complaint to the Committee's attention.

Mediation

When the offer of mediation is accepted, both parties meet informally under the auspices of a panel of mediators composed of three members of the Committee. If the dispute requires guidance in a field not represented in the Committee's membership, a specially qualified mediator with the required experience may be included. The names of members of the panel are submitted to both parties for their acceptance.

The conduct of a panel of mediators is friendly and informal. The function of the panel members is to guide, not to render any verdict. The panel's purpose is to direct the discussion along such lines and in such a manner as to bring about a meeting of minds on the questions involved. If mediation fails or seems unlikely to bring about satisfactory settlement, arbitration may be suggested.

Arbitration

A panel of five arbitrators is appointed. One or more is selected from the Committee and the remainder are chosen by virtue of their particular experience and understanding of the problems presented by the dispute. Names of the panel members are submitted to both parties for their approval. Both parties involved sign an agreement and take an oath to abide by the decision of the panel. The panel itself is sworn in and the proceedings are held in compliance with the Arbitration Law of the State of New York. After both sides are heard, the panel deliberates in private and renders its decision, opinion and award. These are duly formulated by the Committee's counsel for service on the parties and, if the losing side should balk, for entry of judgment according to law.

So far, every award has been fully honored. The decisions and opinions of the Committee serve as precedent for guidance in similar situations. The Committee's Code has been cited as legal precedent.

The Guild's Grievance Committee

The Graphic Artists Guild is committed to raising and maintaining ethical professional standards between graphic artists and art buyers. Most Guild chapters have a Grievance Committee to assist local members in resolving violations of agreements and commonly accepted trade standards. These committees provide Guild members with assistance in resolving individual disputes and preventing the occurrence of grievances in general.

Monitoring industry practices

Guild Grievance Committees encourage artists and art buyers of all disciplines to communicate instances of unprofessional practices encountered in the field. These reports enable the Committee to monitor business practices within the graphic communications industry. When such reports are not forwarded, vital information for the industry is missing and there is no opportunity to change unethical practices.

Graphic Artists Beware column

Buyers reported for flagrant, repeated or unresolved unprofessional practices are selected by the committees for citation in the "Graphic Artists Beware" column of the Guild's chapter and national newsletters. The intention of citing these companies and individuals is to keep the community of graphic artists aware of unethical or unfair practices. At the same time, the Guild puts buyers who use unethical or unprofessional practices on notice that they can no longer exploit artists with impunity.

Committee assistance

The Grievance Committees also provide guidance and assistance to Guild members in their personal efforts to seek resolution of grievances. The Guild is committed to seeing that its members are treated justly and fairly as professionals.

When a member's grievance is judged justified, the Committee contacts the member to discuss the case and plan an appropriate strategy for resolution. The Committee directs the member in the use of accepted business and legal procedures. Depending on the unique factors of each case, the Committee's assistance generally involves: (1) guiding the member's personal efforts to resolve the grievance, (2) directing communication with the buyer on the member's behalf, and (3) mediating, if requested by both parties, to achieve a private settlement.

If further action becomes necessary, other relevant alternatives are proposed by the Committee. These may include: (1) arbitration, (2) small claims court, (3) collection methods, (4) lawyer referral, or (5) litigation.

Members who wish to report unprofessional practices should forward them directly to the Grievance Committee at their local Guild chapter. Members requesting Grievance Committee assistance should also contact their Guild chapter. Please refer to the chapter on *Business Management*.

The Guild's Professional Practices Committee

The Professional Practices Committee of the Guild seeks to address the issue of professional relations between artists and buyers by fostering an ongoing dialogue with all commissioning parties.

The graphic communications industry, much as any other industry, has its instances of misunderstandings and disputes. At times these are inevitable due to the nature of interaction between people. However, a sizeable degree of contention in artist-buyer relations results from unawareness or disregard of common standards of professional practices.

It is the Guild's position that such problems can be reduced and that mutually beneficial and productive business practices can be advanced through discussion and negotiation. Both formal and informal communication between the Guild and major buyers has existed since the Guild's inception. The Guild has always acknowledged the legitimate concerns of both sides of professional issues. Through the activities of its Grievance Committees, the Guild seeks to contribute to a broader and fuller understanding and commitment to professional standards of practice.

Media articles

A principal means through which the Committee focuses attention on professional practices is to initiate research into specific issues and produce articles for industry and Guild publications. The selection of topics results both from monitoring industry practices and from correspondence received by the Committee.

Graphic Artists Aware column

The Guild periodically publishes a "Graphic Artists Aware" column as a means of acknowledging and informing its membership of advancements made in artist-buyer practices.

The column, which appears in national and local Guild newsletters, cites individual buyers and companies that have established improved terms for art commissions as a matter of policy. Such advances may have resulted through negotiations with the Guild, from communication with the Professional Practices Committee, or have been determined independently.

Business and Legal Practices for Commissioned Artwork

This section is designed to give both artist and buyer an overview of the business and legal issues that constantly arise in the graphic arts field. Since copyright is the basis of transactions between artists and clients, information on copyright is essential to a full understanding of professional practices. (Please refer also to the chapter on *Professional Issues*.)

Negotiation

Negotiation is an art in which each party seeks to accommodate its needs as well as those of the other party. Both artist and art buyer must have goals by which to judge a negotiation. A buyer, for example, must stay within the budget and obtain satisfactory art. An artist, like any business person, must earn enough to cover overhead and make a reasonable profit.

The more information each party has about the other, the more effective the negotiation. Artists who know the budget for a given job and know what other artists have been paid for similar work will have a good idea of what they can obtain. Similarly, buy-

ers who know standard ranges and contract terms will have a good idea of how to budget and what rights to buy. Of course, if either artist or buyer finds that the other party will not permit them to achieve their essential goals, then the negotiation will break down and the parties will seek to fulfill their needs elsewhere.

In all negotiations, the Guild encourages artists and buyers to adhere to the standards of the Joint Ethics Committee's Code of Fair Practice. (For detailed information on negotiation, please refer to "Negotiation" in the chapter on *Business Management*.)

Business Forms

It is in the interest of artists and art buyers alike to put any agreement authorizing the use of an artist's work into writing. These agreements should be specific in naming the rights that are being transferred and in describing the disposition of the original art, cancellation fees and other terms. Written agreements should also reflect the concerns of artist and art buyer in a way that will specifically address the issues raised in negotiations.

While it is possible to enforce an oral agreement, it is strongly recommended that artist and client confirm any agreement in writing. This is the best protection against faulty memories and future conflicts. A written agreement can also be a valuable tool in helping both parties clarify their needs. Getting it in writing is also evidence that both parties are professionals who treat the investment of their resources with care.

Agreements can be realized in many forms, including purchase orders, letters of agreement, memos, invoices and so on. A written understanding may be sent by mail, messenger or facsimile.

Terms

Contracts and purchase orders must contain provisions covering at least the following points:

1. The names of the artist and client, including the name of the client's authorized art buyer (the commissioning party).

2. A complete description of the assignment.

3. The fee arrangements, including fees for usage, consultations, alterations, travel time, cancellation fees and reimbursement for billable expenses. Payment terms should be described, including a schedule for advances, monthly service charges for late payment and royalty percentages and terms, where applicable.

4. Specifications regarding when and how the original will be returned.

5. Any agreement regarding copyright notice requirements and placement of the credit line.

6. The assignment of rights described in specific terms, normally naming a specific market category, medium, time period and geographic region. For example, *national* (region) *consumer magazine* (medium) *advertising* (market category) *rights for a period of one year* (time). A common formula for editorial assignments is *one-time North American magazine* (or newspaper) *rights.*

7. Responsibility for obtaining releases for the use of people's names and/or images for advertising or trade purposes should be defined.

For further information on contracts, please refer to the contracts section of this book and to the index for related topics. *The Legal Guide for the Visual Artist* by Tad Crawford (see Bibliography) is another excellent reference for contract information.

Copyright

The copyright law is the fundamental system of protections for artists that flows from the U.S. Constitution, Article 1, Section 8. Congress created the copyright law to foster the dissemination of ideas by providing economic rewards and protections to creators. The current copyright law became effective January 1, 1978.

Freelance artists' livelihoods depend on their ability to claim authorship for the pieces they produce. They build their reputations, and therefore their ability to attract clients and build a career, on the basis of past performance. Indeed, artists' careers succeed or fail by their skill and style in communicating the ideas and messages society needs to disseminate.

Copyright law defines artists' rights to control the usage of their original creative art and is the basis of pricing and fair trade practices.

A bundle of rights

Since an artist's copyright is a bundle of rights, each different usage, or right of reproduction, can be transferred separately. Fees are assigned based on the value agreed upon for the rights of reproduction being transferred. Any rights not specifically transferred remain the property of the creator.

The concept of selling limited usage, or limited rights, to a work of art for an initial fee is one of basic fairness. Since no one can be certain what a copyrightable work will ultimately be worth, estimating a fair price for a sale of *all* rights is difficult. Negotiations regarding the price for a commissioned work, therefore, are normally based on the usage the buyer indicates will be made of the work.

Transferring rights

Transfer of any rights except nonexclusive rights must be written and signed by the artist or the artist's agent and must specify what rights are being transferred. Nonexclusive rights, which can be transferred to more than one client at a time, may be transferred verbally.

For contributions to collective works (such as magazines, anthologies, encyclopedias, etc.) where there is no signed agreement, the law presumes the transfer of only nonexclusive rights for use in that particular collective work. All other rights remain vested with the artist.

Copyright must be transferred in writing for the transfer to be valid. Because ownership of the physical art may be transferred legally without a written contract, artists in California and New York lobbied successfully to create state laws that require ownership of original art to be transferred in writing.

Fair use and compulsory licensing

Copyright owners have the exclusive right to reproduce or sell their work, prepare derivative works (such as a poster copied from a painting), and perform or display their work. (The owner of a copy of the work may also display it). Anyone who violates these rights is infringing on the artist's copyright and can be penalized and prevented from continuing the infringement.

There are some limitations on artists' exclusive control of their work. Fair use is one such limitation. Fair use is a copyright law provision that permits someone to use a work without the artist's permission for a purpose that does not compete with or injure the market for the work, such as using an illustration in an article about the artist's career. Fair use also describes the use of a client assignment in an artist's portfolio.

Another limitation relates to the compulsory licensing provision of the law, which permits a noncommercial, educational broadcasting station to use published work without the artist's consent. Rates of payment for such use are established by the Copyright Royalty Tribunal and each station is required to publish a list of artists entitled to receive payment.

Work for hire

"Work for hire" is a provision of the U.S. Copyright law under which the employer or other commissioning party is deemed to have created the artwork for the purposes of the copyright law, leaving the artist with no rights whatsoever. And, since the artist is an independent contractor, he or she has no access to traditional employee benefits to compensate for the loss of copyright.

A work for hire can come into existence in two ways. First, work done by an artist who is an employee within the scope of his or her employment can be work for hire. An employed artist is usually defined as one who works at the employer's office during regular business hours on a scheduled basis, is directed by the employer and works with tools supplied by the employer. An artist in this relationship with an employer is an employee who is entitled to employment benefits and should be having taxes withheld from his or her paycheck.

Second, work created by a freelance artist can be work for hire if the artist and client sign an agreement stating that the work is to be for hire *and* the work falls under one of nine categories specifically enumerated in the law as eligible to be for hire. (See page 15 for more information on these categories.)

By signing a work-for-hire contract, a freelance artist becomes an employee for the purposes of the copyright law, but not for the purposes of labor law. In addition to losing the copyright, the artist receives no salary; unemployment, workers compensation or disability insurance; nor would they receive health insurance, sick pay, vacation, pension and profit-sharing that the company may provide to its formal, salaried employees.

When a freelance artist signs a work-for-hire contract, the employer becomes the creator for copyright purposes and owns all authorship rights. The artist has no further relationship to the work, cannot display it, copy it or use it for other purposes. The client may change the art and use it again without limitation.

Until recently, many unscrupulous clients attempted to gain the windfall benefits of work for hire without a signed agreement by claiming that extensive supervision, control and direction made the artist an employee and therefore the work was a work for hire. The Supreme Court resolved this issue in CCNV vs. Reid (refer to page 15), affirming that in virtually all cases, commissioned works executed by independent contractors cannot be work for hire unless the work falls under the nine specified categories *and* a written agreement is signed by both parties stated that the work is to be for hire.

In the *Reid* case, there was no written agreement between artist and client. In addition, the work in question was a sculpture, and was ineligible to be work for hire since it did not fall under one of the nine specified categories. One may conclude that advertising illustration, textile design, comic book illustration and other artworks which are not enumerated in the nine categories are similarly ineligible to be work for hire.

The Graphic Artist Guild is emphatically opposed to the use of work-for-hire contracts by commissioning parties. Work for hire is an unfair practice that gives art buyers economic benefit and recognition that belong to the creative artist. These contracts devalue the integrity of artists and their work by empowering buyers to alter the work in any way without consulting the artist and by preventing artists from obtaining any payment for the future use of their work.

Original art

Well-known illustrators can command high prices for the sale of their original art. In fact, many artists in graphic arts fields also sell their work through galleries, to collectors and to corporations. Original art may be exhibited, used as portfolio pieces, given as gifts or willed as part of an estate.

Concern for the protection of ownership of an original work stems not only from artists' interests in obtaining additional income based on the sale of the original, but also from their recognition that protecting the original is an essential part of protecting their reputations and careers.

Ownership of the physical art is separate from the copyright ownership. Like ownership of copyright and the rights that come with it, ownership of the original is vested with the artist from the moment that the artwork is created. Selling the physical artwork does not transfer any rights of copyright. Nor does selling a right of reproduction to a client give the client any claim to the physical artwork.

The artwork can be given to the client temporarily in order to make reproductions, but the client must take reasonable care of it and return it undamaged to the artist. For a separate fee, of course, an artist can sell the physical artwork to a client or to another party who wishes to buy it.

Registering copyright

Copyrights created after January 1, 1978, as well as those existing for work not published or registered, will last for the artist's life plus 50 years. Works copyrighted before 1978 will now run 75 years, but must be renewed on Form RE if renewal would have been necessary under the pre-1978 law. There is legislation pending to make these renewals automatic.

The work does not have to be published with a copyright notice or registered with the Copyright Office in order to be copyrighted. The artist has copyright as soon as the work is created. All artworks can be registered, whether they are published or not.

In 1989, the United States became a signatory to the Berne Convention, the most extensive international copyright agreement among nations. Under the Berne Convention, artists have no legal obligation to place copyright notice on their work or to register it. However, the Guild recommends strongly that artists continue both practices.

Failing to place copyright notice on artworks makes them vulnerable to so-called "innocent" infringers, who may claim they did not know the work was protected. Registration, though no longer necessary for artists to bring a lawsuit for infringement, is still required to collect statutory damages and attorneys' fees from infringers. That is a strong economic motive. Registration also limits the ability of a defendant to claim

innocent infringement. (Please refer also to "Moral Rights" in the chapter on *Professional Issues* and "Copyright Registration" in the chapter on *Business Management*).

Copyright notice

The copyright notice is Copyright or Copr. or ©; plus the artist's name, an abbreviation of the name or an alternate designation by which the artist is known; and the year date of first publication. For example, notice would take the form of: © Jane Artist 1991. (For more information, please refer to the chapter on *Business Management*.)

The copyright notice can be placed on the back of an artwork or, when it is published, adjacent to the artwork. Other reasonable placements of the copyright notice for published works are specified by the regulations of the Copyright Office. Pieces in an artist's portfolio should have copyright notice on them, including published pieces, when the artist has retained the copyright. It is best for artists to have their copyright notice appear with the contribution when it is published. This helps avoid certain risks of infringement.

Group registration

To cut the cost of registration, the Copyright Office provides that unpublished artworks can be registered in groups. For example, five numbered drawings could be collected in a binder and registered as "Drawings By Artist, Series 1." Only one fee would have to be paid and the art would not have to be registered again when published. A good reason to request copyright notice in the artist's name for contributions to periodicals is that it makes possible an inexpensive group registration of all contributions published in a one-year period with the copyright notice in the artist's name. Form GP/CP is used in addition to form VA for such a registration.

Original art does not have to be sent to the Copyright Office in order to register a work. While the copyrightable content of an artwork must be shown, this can be done with transparencies or photocopies.

Termination of rights transfers

Transfers of copyright may be terminated by the artist during a five-year period starting 35 years after the date of execution of the transfer. This right of reversion is an important feature of the 1978 copyright law when transfers or licenses are of exceptionally long duration.

The formalities of termination are detailed. Artists or their heirs whose grants of rights are approaching 35 years should contact the Copyright Office for forms and procedures. The exact form of notice is specified by, and must be filed with, the Copyright Office. Failure to comply with the proper procedures will lose artists their opportunity to reclaim rights to their creations until the grants otherwise terminate.

The right of termination does not apply to work for hire or transfers made by a will.

Further information on copyright

For further information on copyright, artists can send for a free copy of the Copyright Information Kit from the Copyright Office, Library of Congress, Washington, D.C. 20559. The kit includes a substantial packet of information on copyright and registration. Free copies of copyright registration applications can be obtained by calling the Copyright Office Hotline at (202) 479-0700 or (202) 707-9100.

Another source of information on copyright and related issues is the *Legal Guide for the Visual Artist* by Tad Crawford (see Other Resources).

Cancellation fees

When a commissioned assignment that has been completed is cancelled through no fault of the artist, the full fee must be paid. If the assignment is unfinished at the time of cancellation, artists customarily charge part of the original fee in proportion to the degree of completion. Such a cancellation fee should not be less than one-half of the original fee. Buyers usually, but not always, obtain all the originally agreed upon rights to the use of the work upon full payment of the original fee.

When royalty arrangements have been entered into, all rights to the artwork as well as possession of the original art must revert to the artist upon cancellation. Since payment to the artist was to be based on a percentage of anticipated product sales rather than a fixed dollar amount, an equitable cancellation fee must be negotiated. Such arrangements often include an artist's retention of any advance.

In the event of cancellation, all expenses incurred by the artist to date must be reimbursed in full.

Cancellation terms should be stipulated in writing in confirmation forms and purchase orders or these fees must be negotiated at the time cancellation occurs. Full payment of fees should be made contingent upon receipt of the artwork, not upon publication, to cover the possibility of cancellation after acceptance (as well as to receive timely payment). For a further discussion of Guild policy regarding cancellation fees, please refer to page 25.

Rejection fees

When a buyer rejects commissioned artwork as not reasonably satisfactory, the artist is customarily paid a rejection fee in compensation for time and effort expended. The fee for completed work is normally at least one-half of the original usage fee. If the assignment is unfinished at the time of rejection, the artist may charge part of the original fee in proportion to the degree of completion. Such a rejection fee should not be less than one-third of the original fee. In this situation a buyer forgoes any rights to the use of the artwork. All work and material must be returned to the artist.

Expenses

Graphic designers traditionally bill their clients for all the expenses of executing an assignment. Textile designers and illustrators have usually absorbed such expenses as art supplies because, for them, the amounts tend to be quite modest. Expenses such as shipping, photostats, film, costumes, model's fees, unusual travel costs, production expenses and consultation time should be billed to the client. These expenses shoud be agreed upon and set down in the original written agreement. Often a maximum amount for expenses will be indicated beyond which artists may not incur expenses without additional authorization by the client.

Credit lines

Illustrators usually incorporate their signatures on their artwork and those are typically reproduced as part of the piece. For important pieces, especially when a letter of agreement is needed to spell out the terms of usage and payment, artists may make making credit line requirements part of the deal.

For some this may mean a printed credit line with copyright notice, for others merely the reproduction of the signature in the artwork. In some cases, as is traditional with magazines, both credits may be agreed upon.

A copyright notice can be made part of the credit line simply by adding © before the artist's name and the year date of publication after the name (©Jane Artist1991). Such a copyright notice benefits the artist without harming the client.

Some magazine photographers require by contract that their fees will be doubled if an adjacent credit line is omitted. Given the modest rates for editorial work, the value of the credit line is as important as the fee. This activity does not constitute a trade practice, but it is becoming more common and is being adopted by some designers and illustrators as well.

Samples of work

I t is a courtesy for clients to provide artists with examples of the finished piece as it was reproduced. This piece, often called a tear sheet, can be used in an artist's portfolio and provides a view of the project in its completed form. Regardless of who owns a copyright in the artwork, artists' use of their own original art in a portfolio is permissible as fair use (one that is not competitive with those the copyright owner might make), except in cases of work for hire, when the client's permission needs to be obtained.

Sales tax

V arious states have different policies in regard to sales tax. In states that have sales tax, the rate usually ranges from 3 to 9 per cent. The tax is levied on the sale or use of physical property within the state. A number of exemptions exist, including special rules for the sale of reproduction rights. The applicable state regulations should be consulted.

Generally, services, including the services of transferring reproduction rights, are not subject to sales tax. Transferrals of physical property to a client (i.e., original art,

designers' mechanicals) shouldn't be taxed if they are part of a project which will be billed to a client later by a design firm or other agent, although a resale certificate may have to be obtained. Sales tax is applicable for end sales or retail costs only, not for intermediate subcontracting. An artist may have to file forms showing that materials were intermediate and thus not taxable.

Many tax laws are unclear in relation to the graphic communications industry. In any case in which artists are doubtful whether to collect the tax, it is safest to collect and remit it to the state sales tax bureau. If artists should collect the tax but don't, they, as well as their clients, will remain liable for the tax. (But, of course, it can be difficult to try to collect the tax from clients on assignments that have been performed in the past.)

Liability for portfolios and original art

I f an artist's portfolio is lost by an art buyer, the law of "bailments" (the holding of another's property) makes the buyer liable for the reasonable value of that portfolio if the loss arose from the buyer's carelessness. If the portfolio contained original art such as drawings, paintings or original transparencies, the amount in question could be quite substantial. The same potential liability exists with respect to commissioned artwork a client has agreed to return to the artist. A model "Holding Form" for use by textile designers appears in the contracts section of this book and can be modified for use by other disciplines.

The value or appraisal of originals, transparencies and other lost items can be verified in court by obtaining simple written assessments by an artist's client, art director, or vendor and presenting those figures to the party who lost the work or the claims court. The *full* value of the work, however, may be nearly impossible to calculate, since no one can be certain what a work will be worth over the life of the copyright. Artists who encounter this problem may need to demonstrate that their works have generated additional income through transfers of rights.

There are two ways to minimize the risks in the loss of original work. The first is with "valuable paper" insurance. That, however, is not sufficient, since as with any insurance, continued claims will lead to either prohibitive premiums or a complete loss of coverage.

Buyers also need effective systems for tracking and storing all original art in their offices. They should make sure that the receipt of every portfolio is recorded and a notation is made of its destination within the organization. If possible, buyers should avoid keeping portfolios overnight and on weekends. All original art should be logged out when it goes to any supplier, such as color separators or printers, and logged in when it returns. Finally, suppliers should understand that they may be held liable for any losses they cause as a result of the damage or disappearance of any original art.

Since the likelihood of guaranteeing protection in the handling of original art is remote, buyers should minimize legal risks through the purchase of suitable insurance and, more importantly, the installation of proper recordkeeping procedures.

Speculation

The Guild is unalterably opposed to work on speculation because of the risks to artists inherent in such requests. Artists who create their own work and seek to sell it are not in violation of this rule, but art buyers should not ask artists to work on a project unless a fee has been agreed upon. Art contests, except under special circumstances, are also opposed because of their speculative nature. For contest guidelines approved by the Guild, see the chapter on *Professional Issues*.

THE PROFESSIONAL RELATIONSHIP

The Professional Relationship

Our society and our economy rely on an extensive communications system, and graphic artists serve an increasingly visually sophisticated public. Economic projections for the next decade suggest that, on the whole, the graphic arts profession will continue to grow as fast as or faster than other professions, based on the importance of the communications industry. The field is competitive and clients can select among a wide range of graphic artists producing diverse, original, high-quality images.

Graphic artists are professionals dedicated to solving communications problems. Many run their own studios and are responsible for the day-to-day business matters that concern any entrepreneur. Those with their own studios must pay overhead, including insurance, taxes, studio rent, marketing costs, assistants, utilities, office equipment and other costs of doing business. Their rates are based on these costs, on their professional judgment, training, experience and on market forces; however, the fees that artists charge are based primarily on usage. Payment based on use is the foundation of the U.S. copyright law.

How artwork is commissioned

A client may commission artwork directly from an artist or indirectly, through an artist's representative or other agent. The Guild recommends that a written agreement be signed by both parties prior to the beginning of work. For more information about contracts, please refer to the chapters *Business and Legal Practices for Commissioned Artwork* and *Standard Contracts*.

Among those who commission artwork are the following art buyers:

The client

Graphic artists often specialize, focusing their talents on markets within the communications industry such as magazine or book publishing, corporate markets, manufacturing, retailing, advertising or broadcasting. Their clients may be individuals, small companies or conglomerates. Some clients purchase art on a regular basis and some are first-time or infrequent buyers.

Clients who buy art regularly usually have staff: corporate art buyers, art directors and other representatives with expertise in commissioning art assignments. In a large corporation, for example, the art director, art buyer or stylist in charge of hiring artists to work on projects probably has some knowledge of professional practices and pricing issues.

Clients who buy art occasionally may rely on art directors, design firms, studios or agencies with whom they have contracted for a particular project and who will, in turn, hire artists.

In both cases clients, as the experts in their own fields, must communicate their needs to the graphic artist in terms of the product and the market. The artists then bring their own style and expertise to bear in helping the client solve the visual communications problem posed.

The practical basis of a successful partnership between clients and artists is respect for ethical professional practices as well as the ability to describe problems effectively and/or envision solutions.

During initial meetings, artists and clients discuss possible solutions to the design problem, fees, usage and contract terms. These discussions create a relationship that addresses the concerns of both parties.

The art director

In many organizations, art directors are assigned simultaneously to a number of projects or accounts. They are responsible for finding the artists, negotiating the terms of the job and supervising the assignment.

Art directors bring together the talent for a project on the basis of knowledge of the client's concerns and the diverse styles of the professionals available. An art director may rely on advertising directories, call in artists to review their portfolios, place ads in the papers or contact employment services.

When speaking with artists, art directors need to be familiar with the time schedule for the project, the budget, how the artwork will be used and a variety of other factors.

Freelance artists negotiate rights, terms and fees with the art director or client. The factors described in this book are the basis of business dealings for graphic artists.

Advertising agencies

Artwork for advertising agencies is usually purchased by an art buyer or art director. The art buyer works with the art director to select the freelance artist to be used on a job and is responsible for negotiating purchase of usage rights and other terms. Art buyers often handle budgets, schedules, traffic and invoicing on each freelance assignment.

Often an art buyer will oversee assembling a selection of portfolios for review by the creative group to select a freelance artist for an assignment. Artists are selected based on the style of art needed and the portfolio submitted.

At the time of assignment, most agencies provide artists with a purchase order that details rights purchased, ownership of art, delivery dates for sketch and finish, prices for the completed assignment, cancellation fee at sketch and finish stages and any additional expenses such as delivery charges or shipping. All terms on a purchase order may be negotiated until terms agreeable to both parties are reached. When both parties have signed the purchase order, it signifies that a contract between them has been reached.

Rights purchased may be in any or all of a number of categories, which should be spelled out in the purchase order. Roughly in order of increasing value, some of these categories are:

Presentation and research use: Generally purchased at the lowest rates in the advertising market since the material will only be used in-house or in front of small groups. The agreement should cover an additional fee if the art is used extensively.

Test market use: Generally purchased at low rates for use in a limited number of test markets. As in *presentation and research use,* an artist's agreement should cover additional fees if use is expanded.

Point of purchase: Includes all point of sale materials such as signs, leaflets, shopping cart posters, catalogs, brochures, direct mail, etc.

Outdoor use: All posters that are not point of sale, such as billboards, painted bulletins, 30-sheet posters, transit posters, bus shelters, etc.

Publication use: Includes use in newspapers, magazines, Sunday supplements, internal publications and any material included as part of a publication, such as freestanding inserts.

TV use: Television rights only.

The above categories are examples of purchases of *limited rights.* Grants of limited rights may range from one-time to extensive use, but all rights being granted are clearly established in the purchase order, normally naming a specific market category, medium, time period and geographic region. For example, *national* (region) *consumer magazine* (medium) *advertising* (market area) *rights for a period of one year* (time). Exclusivity within the markets purchased ("noncompetition") is usually guaranteed. Sale of the original artwork is a separate transaction. Noncompeting rights may be sold.

Unlimited rights: The purchase of all rights connected with the product for all media in all markets for an unlimited time. In this sale, *the artist retains the copyright.* Rights that do not compete with the purchaser's product may be sold.

Exclusive unlimited rights means that the artist may not sell any use to anyone else. Sale of the original art is a separate transaction. The artist may display the work and retains authorship rights. Under copyright law, the artist may reclaim the rights granted after 35 years.

The vague term *"buyout,"* though widely used, means different things to different people. It is an imprecise term that can lead to misunderstandings. The Guild recommends that specific usage rights sold and status of ownership of the original art be stated in the agreement.

Representatives

Artists' representatives, or artists' agents, have the legal right to act on behalf of the artists they represent. They can legally obligate the artist, but only in matters agreed to in the artist-representative contract.

Artist-representative arrangements are best put in writing. Artists should have a lawyer read any contract and make certain the terms are clearly understood before signing. The Guild's standard Artist/Agent Agreement and Textile Designer/Agent Agreement can be found in the contracts section of this book. If a more casual relationship is undertaken, the Guild recommends that both parties sign a memo that spells out the responsibilities of each.

Some topics that should be considered when negotiating an artist-agent agreement are:

Exclusivity or nonexclusivity : In one kind of nonexclusive relationship, artists are free to promote their work in all markets, even those handled by the representative. Some representatives handle only certain markets, such as advertising or publishing, and artists retain the right to promote their work in other areas; this is also sometimes called nonexclusive. Other representatives handle all markets for which their artists produce and request that the artist work through them exclusively.

Exclusivity or nonexclusivity is a crucial issue in any contract, since artists must feel that all of their work will be marketed in the best manner. Representatives who ask for exclusive contracts should be willing to identify the other artists whom they represent.

Mounting of portfolio pieces, presentations, laminations, etc: The agreement should cover who pays for preparation of portfolio and promotion pieces. It should state for the record that these pieces remain the property of the artist and that they will be returned to the artist upon termination of the relationship.

Directory advertising, direct mail promotion, shipping of artwork, insurance, etc: Many representatives will split these costs with the artist or absorb them. The arrangement should be understood by both parties.

Billing: Whether it is wiser for agent or artist to handle billing will depend on the circumstances. A reputable party handling billing will supply copies of all purchase orders and invoices to the other party. If a purchase order does not exist, a copy of the check should be supplied to the other party. One practical benefit of this procedure is that if the person handling the billing dies, goes into bankruptcy or reorganizes, the other party has proof of what is owed. If the representative is handling billing, the Guild recommends that artists maintain complete records of all paperwork and any decisions made orally.

Commissions: The conventional artist-representative arrangement calls for a 25 per cent commission to the representative. In the textile design field, commissions range from 25 to 50 per cent.

Commissions should be based only on the fee paid to the artist, not on expenses normally billed to the client. Expenses should be subtracted from a flat fee before the commission is computed. If the agent is given accounts that artists had prior to retaining a representative (sometimes called house accounts), they are usually serviced by the agent at a lower commission rate.

Termination: This is a sensitive area for both agent and artist. Each party should be able to terminate on 30 days' written notice, but an agent may demand a continuing right to receive commissions after the termination date. This right should not apply to house accounts.

An agent might reasonably request the right to a commission on any assignments received by the artist for a period of three months after the termination date if the accounts were obtained by the agent. If an agent has represented an artist for more than six months, the right to receive commissions after termination might be increased by one month for each additional six months of representation (so that after two years of representation, the agent would receive commissions for six months after termination).

The circumstances in each case will differ, but artists should rarely agree to give agents commissions on assignments obtained more than six months after the effective date of termination. Of course, if an agent is entitled to receive a commission on an assignment obtained within the agreed time, it is due even if the client's payment arrives later than that time.

Subcontracting

Art directors, design firms or other art buyers who assume creative control of a project for a client often subcontract freelance artists for work they cannot create themselves. Payment is due from these contractors in a timely manner no matter when they receive payment from their client.

Brokers

Most brokers do not represent talent on an exclusive basis, relying instead on their contacts among clients and their knowledge of various talents to put together a deal. As with studios, some projects can be quite complex. Most of the points raised in the sections on representatives and studios would apply. It cannot be emphasized too strongly that price, relative responsibilities and working conditions should be established before accepting the assignment. *In the absence of a formalized artist-agent agreement, artists should establish a price that they consider adequate for the work*, leaving the broker free to negotiate above that price and keep the excess as a commission.

Sources of talent

There are several resources available to clients and artists to find and/or promote talent. Among the most widely known and used are the advertising directories. These directories generally showcase a specific type of work, such as illustration or graphic design. Artists purchase space in a directory that displays representative work chosen by the artist and gives a contact address for either the artist or the artist's representative. Other directories are compilations of juried shows. Directories also serve the industry as references for the types and styles of work being done in each field.

Among the best-known directories nationally are, for illustration, *American Showcase, Creative Black Book, Graphic Artists Guild Directory, Creative Illustration, New York Gold, Chicago Talent, The Workbook* and *RSVP*. Directories of juried shows include the *Society of Illustrators Annual, American Illustration* and *Art Directors Annual*. For design, *AIGA Annual, Creative Black Book, The Workbook,* and *Art Directors Annual*. There are many publications from juried shows in areas of special interest such as dimensional illustration, humorous illustration and international design and illustration. Directories can be requested from their publishers or found at most art supply stores.

Employment agencies and referral agencies in various cities around the country refer artists to clients for a fee. They operate in the same way that most employment agencies do, but specialize in the graphic arts markets. Often these agencies are listed in trade magazines and the telephone book. Some Graphic Artist Guild chapters offer referral services.

If none of the above established services for locating talent is available in a particular region, a client or artist can contact the local Guild chapter or other professional graphic arts organization and request referrals.

How Artwork is Priced

Graphic art is commissioned in highly competitive and specialized markets—there are *no* standard prices. Prices depend upon several factors: the use that the buyer intends to make of the art, the size and stature of the client, the graphic artist's reputation, the urgency of the deadline, the complexity of the art and so on. Actual prices are the result of negotiations between artist and buyer that take into consideration all relevant factors. Guidelines for pricing vary from discipline to discipline, so the information in this chapter should be supplemented by reading the appropriate sections on pricing for each discipline.

The prices listed in the *Guidelines* are based on nationwide surveys. They are not meant to be taken literally as specific prices; the nature of the art market makes this impossible. Our figures are benchmarks to help artists and buyers determine the value of a job according to its particular factors.

The pricing ranges that appear in this book reflect market conditions and do not necessarily represent what the Guild considers proper compensation for artists. Markets which are depressed or in which the supply of graphic artists exceeds the demand may offer inadequate compensation and substandard employment conditions.

Price determined by use

In order to encourage the free flow of ideas to the public, copyright law vests with the creator of every artistic or literary work a bundle of rights that can be divided and sold in any number of ways. Therefore, the price of graphic art is determined primarily by the extent of its use and the value derived thereby.

Graphic artists, like photographers, writers and other creators, customarily sell only specific rights to the use of their creative work. The intended use, or "usage," is indicated by specifying which rights of reproduction are being granted.

Some inexperienced art buyers assume that they are buying a product at a flat fee, with the right to reuse or manipulate the art however they wish. But sales, or grants, of reproduction rights are more like rental or licensing agreements in that only the right to use the art in a specific way for a limited time period is implied.

The basic standard of sale for a commissioned work of art is "first reproduction rights" or "one-time reproduction rights." Reuses, more extensive uses, uses in additional markets, foreign uses, etc., should receive additional compensation. Artists should consider the full potential value of the artwork when estimating the value of "exclusive," "unlimited," or "all-rights" agreements. Sale of the original, physical art is, under copyright law, not included in the sale of reproduction rights and, if desired, is normally a separate transaction.

In some cases (e.g., corporate logos, advertising, product identity), the buyer may genuinely need to acquire most or all rights. Buyers are generally aware that purchasing such extensive grants of rights will be more expensive than purchase of single or more limited uses. In other cases the buyer has no need for extensive rights. One of the responsibilities of both parties negotiating transfers of rights is to identify the buyer's needs and negotiate the transfer of only those rights.

Selling extensive rights or all rights at prices usually paid for limited rights provides the buyer with an unearned inventory of stock art and deprives the artist (and other artists) of income from additional uses and future assignments. For the client, paying higher prices for more rights than will be used is expensive and unnecessary. Additionally, purchasing more rights than are needed deprives the public of access to the work, since in most cases only those specific rights are ever exercised.

If buyers are asking for an "all-rights" or "work for hire" agreement to protect themselves from competitive or embarrassing use of the work, a limited rights contract can easily be drafted that prohibits such use by the artist.

All grants of rights should specify the category and medium of intended use and the title of the publication or product. Grants of rights may also specify edition, number of appearances and geographic or time limitations where appropriate. For example, *national* (region) *consumer magazine* (medium) *advertising* (market category) *rights for a period of one year* (time). A

common formula for editorial assignments is *one-time North American magazine* (or newspaper) *rights*.

The following chart gives examples of market categories and some of the media for which they buy art. Within each category there may be more media than space allows to be listed here.

Markets and media

Advertising
Animation
Collateral and direct mail
    (brochures, direct mailers,
    flyers, handouts, catalogs)
Consumer magazine
Display and exhibit
Newspaper
Newspaper supplement
Outdoor
    (billboards, bus and car
    cards, station posters)
Packaging
    (products, albums,
    CDs, cassettes, videos,
    software)
Point of purchase
    (counter cards,
    shelf signs, posters)
Poster
    (film, theater, concert,
    event)
Preproduction
    (storyboards, animatics,
    comprehensives)
Television
Trade magazine
Other

Book
Anthology
Mass market
Text
Trade
Other
    (Also specify hardcover or
    softcover edition, cover, jacket
    or interior, etc.)

Editorial
Consumer magazine
Educational audio-
    visual/filmstrip
Encyclopedia
Newspaper
Television
Trade magazine
Other

Institutional
Annual report
Audiovisual/filmstrip
Brochure
Corporate/employee publication
Presentation
Other

Manufacturing
Apparel
Domestics
Home furnishings
Jewelry
Novelty and retail goods
    (paper products, greeting
    cards, posters for sale,
    calendars, giftware, other)
Toys and games
Other

Promotion
Booklet
Brochure
Calendar
Card
Direct mail
Poster
Press kit
Sales literature
Other

Royalties

A good way of establishing price in relation to use is through a royalty arrangement. This is the accepted method of payment in the book publishing industry. A royalty is actually a percentage of the list or wholesale price paid to the artist based on the product's sales. Royalty arrangements also include a nonrefundable advance payment to the artist in anticipation of royalties before the product is sold. Royalties are not appropriate in cases where the use of the art does not involve any resale

or where a resale is difficult to monitor. See also "Licensing," below.

Licensing

When a design or illustration is developed to be marketed and sold as a product, it is usually done under a licensing agreement. Markets that customarily use licensing agreements include textiles, apparel, domestics, china, wall coverings, greeting card, paper products, giftware, novelty items, toys, posters, and other manufacturing. *Product licensing* applies to the marketing of any visual image for use in such markets. *Character licensing* refers to the sale of an existing or specially created character. Peanuts, the Muppets, Ninja Turtles, and the Simpsons are examples of characters who have been licensed successfully.

Peanuts and the Muppets were already famous characters and were licensed very easily. Other characters, such as the Care Bears, are carefully developed and marketed with a strategic and well-financed advertising campaign specifically for the purposes of licensing a variety of products. Many graphic artists base their business on creating images for licensing to one or more markets. Recently new companies have formed that specialize in representing licensed properties. They may even plan marketing support for these products through animated movies, TV series, publishing ventures, recordings and other forms of promotion.

Terms of licensing agreements

A license is an agreement whereby an artist, designer or developer who owns the rights to the art permits another party, usually the client, to use the art for a limited specific purpose, for a specified time, in return for a fee or royalty. At the expiration of the license, the right to use the property reverts to the owner.

Payment under licensing agreements normally takes the form of royalties. Royalties are usually a percentage of the retail or wholesale price or a fixed amount per item sold.

Licensing agreements should include a nonrefundable advance, and a nonrefundable minimum guaranteed royalty is advisable. The agreements should be also subject to requirements regarding sales, production or scheduling that provide for the best commercial exploitation of the design. If these requirements are not met, the license should terminate. In the event that this happens, the artist or owner is free to license the work to others for the same or similar uses.

Artists and owners should insist upon proper quality control of the product to prevent inferior goods and to maximize sales potential. It is up to the artist, in consideration of client needs, to set those standards. In the event that the client or manufacturer fails to meet these standards, the license should terminate.

The duration of a license must be spelled out clearly. Many licenses are for relatively short, fixed terms with renewal clauses based upon successful performance. This type of agreement is fair to both parties since it provides for continued license of the art only when the artist is assured of obtaining payment and the client is satisfied with the product.

It is important to differentiate between rights granted and those retained, since there are multiple markets available and more than one license agreement possible for a particular property. In an *exclusive* licensing arrangement, one licensee holds complete rights to market the property. A *nonexclusive* arrangement allows the artist or owner to license the same design to multiple or overlapping markets. An arrangement may specify noncompetition within one market, a form of limited exclusivity. The degree of exclusivity is an important factor when negotiating licensing agreements and compensation.

The artist or owner is entitled to periodic accounting statements with details of sales made and royalties due. And the artist should have the right to audit the appropriate books and records to verify the statements and to insure that payment is forthcoming.

Proper copyright notice must accompany the distributed art and, where possible, name credit should be given to the artist. This can be written into the licensing agreement.

An excellent book on the subject of licensing is *Licensing Art and Design* by Caryn Leland, published by Allworth Press (see Other Resources for ordering information). A Model Short Form Licensing Agreement appears in the chapter on *Standard Contracts*, reprinted from *Licensing Art and Design* by permission of the author.

Per diem rates

In some cases artists are hired on a per diem or day-rate basis. This is a perfectly acceptable method of pricing provided that the day rate reflects just compensation for the work and is agreed to by both artist and buyer beforehand.

Artists should establish a basic day rate for their work. This, together with an estimate of the number of days needed to complete the work, art direction, consultation, travel, etc., is the basis for a rough price estimate. *A word of caution:* Some jobs look deceptively simple, and even the most experienced artists sometimes encounter greater expenditures of time than antici- pated. Questions concerning delivery time, degree of finish, complexity, expenses and general responsibilities ought to be included in the estimate and it should be made clear than an estimate is merely that and is not binding.

A formula for calculating a per diem rate is to first total all business costs. Add a reasonable profit margin. Divide this total by 240 working business days annually. See also "Hourly rate formula," below.

Both artists and clients should be aware that certain working relationships may be considered traditional employment regardless of a "freelance" title. So-called "full-time freelance" positions, relationships which are steady and ongoing or relation- ships which extend over a series of projects may actually be considered employment under tax or labor law. In these cases, the artist may be entitled to basic employment benefits including unemployment, workers compensation and disability insurance. Other benefits like medical coverage, vacation, pension and profit-sharing may be due. Clients who do not withhold payroll taxes in these cases may be at risk with Federal and state agencies and may face penalties equivalent to the tax that should have been withheld. Please see the chapter on *Professional Issues* for further information.

Hourly rate formula

Whether pricing on a fee-for-use basis or by the hour, graphic ar- tists must know what it costs to conduct business in order to know whether the client's fee for each project will mean profit, break-even or loss. Establishing an hourly rate is a businesslike way of doing this.

One simple way to establish an hourly rate is to first total all annual business "overhead" expenses such as rent, utilities, insurance, employees' salaries and benefits, promotion, outside professional services, equipment, transportation, office and art supplies, business taxes and entertainment. Using the figures in Schedule C of IRS Form 1040 makes this task easier. Add in a reasonable salary for yourself that reflects current market conditions (see the chapter

on *Salaried Prices and Trade Customs*). Divide the total by 1680, which is the number of hours worked in an average year (52 weeks less four weeks' vacation, holiday and sick time). Add to this figure a reason- able profit margin of 10 to 15 per cent. The resulting figure is an hourly rate based on a 35-hour week that can be expected to cover all costs of doing business including the artist's own salary.

However, most artists, especially those who are self-employed, should divide the annual overhead figure by a much smaller number of working hours to allow for time spent on non-billable work such as writing proposals, billing and self-promotion. A figure from 20 to 45 per cent less, or roughly 900 to 1350 hours, is probably more practical and accurate. A profit margin should still be added.

When a project is being considered, it is important to closely estimate the required hours of work. This estimate multiplied by the hourly rate will demon- strate whether the client's fee for the project will cover costs. If it will not, the artist may negotiate with the client for more money, propose a solution to the project that will take less time or search with the client for another mutually agreeable alternative.

Many large jobs, such as corporate design projects, require that the hours involved be used as a gauge to see if the project is on budget.

Design firms usually have two hourly rates: one for principals and one for employ- ees. The difference is the salary level. For example, in the graphic design field, the hourly rate for a principal is, on average, $125 and for studio staff, $50 to $100.

Page-rate pricing

Page-rate pricing is primarily an illustrator's tool to gauge fees in the advertising and editorial markets for print media, although design firms who specialize in advertising may also rely on this method. It is a method of pricing determined by multiplying a given percent- age by the advertising page rate of a publication. Pricing for artists' fees, there- fore, is directly indexed to the same pricing system used by the publication and its advertisers. The page-rate calculation will reflect inflationary increases due to the spiraling costs of paper, printing and mailing (i.e., as the page rate rises, so will the fee).

Advertising page rates vary according to the type and circulation of a magazine and therefore provide a basic standard for measuring the extent of usage. These rates, therefore, provide a good barometer of a magazine's resources. As of January, 1991, for example, national consumer magazine *TV Guide*, with a circulation base of 15,800,000, receives $103,650 for a one-page black-and-white advertisement. Obviously, the *Guide* delivers a potential market to the advertisers that makes this cost worthwhile. *Business Week*, with a circulation base of 875,000, receives $39,720 for a black-and-white page. *Popular Mechanics*, circulation 1,600,000, costs $38,095. A page in the regional consumer magazine *New York*, circulation 437,412, costs $17,980. A page in specialty consumer magazine *Working Woman*, circulation 900,000, costs $25,005. Page-rate pricing reflects these different costs in the fees paid for artwork.

This method of pricing is best suited to so-called *higher-priced markets*, where a higher fee is more appropriate than otherwise recommended in the *Guidelines*.

Magazine advertising page rates and circulation information can be found in trade journals such as *Advertising Age* and *Adweek* and in the Standard Rate & Data publications *Business Publications* and *Consumer Magazines*, available in most business libraries.

The accompanying Page-rate Pricing Formula chart illustrates suggested percentages of page rates for different markets.

Page-rate pricing formula

Suggested percentages for pricing

Editorial

B&W page	B&W spread	Color cover	Color page	Color spread
PR* x 10%	PR x 12.5%	PR x 15%	PR x 13%	PR x 14%

Advertising

PR x 12.5%	PR x 13.5%	———	PR x 16.75%	PR x 17.5%

*Page Rate

Examples

	TV Guide	Business Week	New York
Circulation	15,800,000	875,000	437,400
Non-bleed B&W page rate	$103,650	$39,720	$17,980
Full-color page rate	$122,000	$60,380	$28,300
Advertising			
B&W page x 12.5%	$13,000	$5,000	$2,200
B&W spread x 13.5%	$14,000	$5,400	$2,400
Color page x 16.75%	$20,400	$10,100	$4,700
Color spread x 17.5%	$21,400	$10,600	$5,000

Examples (continued)

Editorial	TV Guide	Business Week	New York
B&W page x 10%	$10,400	$4,000	$1,800
B&W spread x 12.5%	$13,000	$5,000	$2,200
Color cover x 15%	$18,300	$9,100	$4,200
Color page x 13%	$15,900	$7,800	$3,700
Color spread x 17.5%	$17,100	$8500	$4,000

Page-rate pricing formula applied to 1991 advertising rates. Figures for black-and-white page and spread are based on advertising page rates for one page, single insertion, black and white, non bleed. Figures for color cover, color page and color spread are based on rates for one page, single insertion, full color.

Other pricing factors

Inflation

During periods of inflation, the Guild recommends that the government price index on cost of living increases for the date of publication of this edition be added to the figures contained in the price survey charts. The 1990 Consumer Price Index was 4.7 per cent. The cost of printing, paper, distribution, advertising page and TV rates and other elements of the communications industry rise as time passes. Prices paid for commissioned art should be reviewed yearly, and any increases in the inflation rate should be taken into consideration.

Size of print orders or ads

The reproduced size of the ad and the quantity (number) of the print order should be reflected accordingly as a factor in pricing.

Consultation

If a job requires extensive consultation, artists may estimate their hourly or day rate and add a consultation fee to the basic project fee. It is not uncommon, especially for a brief consultation to solve a particular problem, for the consultation fee to be substantially higher than a normal hourly rate.

The nature of the project, proposed usage, unusual time demands, and travel requirements are factors in estimating a consultation fee.

Large projects

In some markets, large orders may carry lower per-unit prices than single or smaller orders. In such cases, lower prices may be in keeping with standard business practices.

Billable expenses

Necessary costs of producing a job, such as model fees, prop rental, research time, typography, photostats, production, shipping and travel expenses should be billed to the client separately. Estimates should be included in the written agreement. Three-dimensional illustration, for example, may require substantial outlays for rental or purchase of materials and photography to achieve desired results. When artists are required to advance sums on behalf of the client, it is customary to charge a markup in the range of 15 to 25 per cent to cover overhead and provide adequate cash flow. 17.65 per cent is the standard markup used by advertising agencies.

Billable expenses for computer-assisted graphics and illustration

Artists who own computer equipment will consider their capital investment in their fees, but those artists who rent equipment or use out-of-house service bureaus should maintain strict records of expenses in order to bill the client. Billable expenses include rental fees, transportation to and from the equipment and any costs incurred in recording work on hardcopy, film or videotape. Fees paid for technical assistants, research and reference costs and expenses for preparing raw art (photos, stats, line art, etc.) for digitizing camera input are also billable.

Other expenses should be negotiated, for example, equipment or technology purchases to meet specific demands of the job (e.g., purchase of a new font or telecommunications program).

Artists should also follow basic markup considerations in equipment rental, particularly when time is spent negotiating for rental time or purchasing supplies and services. A customary markup is in the range of 15 to 25 per cent to cover overhead and provide adequate cash flow.

The going billable rate for computer animation/paint systems is $400 to $600 per hour. Rental fees range from $350 to $550 per hour.

Any artist working in this area should be aware that the newness of this technology and the speed with which the technology changes requires a continual review of expenses and charges.

Animation

Animation artists create the illusion of movement. Knowledge of movement and technical film details are essential for the animation artist. In the process of animation, the animation artist begins with a layout, which gives the "path" for movement. Following the model sheets of characters, which are based on the designer's concepts and are often supplied by an advertising agency (when doing a television commercial), the animation artist creates specific movement based on the written directions and camera instructions. These directions and instructions, along with any dialogue, music, or sound effects, are broken down frame by frame for 35-mm film. Often, the artist physically stages the action.

Generally, animation artists work for a studio but there are those in the Motion Picture Screen Cartoonists (MPSC) union who freelance. There are nonunion animation artists, but most artists employed by animation studios are covered by collective bargaining agreements negotiated by the artists' union.

Animation is used extensively in television commercials, medical and educational films, television specials, titles, feature films, special effects and the familiar Saturday morning cartoons. There are also independent animated films which are an entirely different art form with a broad spectrum of styles. Usually these are shown in film festivals or competitions that serve as showcases for the artist's work. A factor affecting pricing is whether one is a freelance or on staff. If the animation artist is freelancing, pricing is also affected by what category the animation falls under (e.g., the intricacy of the movement, how much movement there is and how intricate the drawings must be). This is decided upon before work is begun.

Animation is a highly specialized field, but advancement is possible according to one's skills. There are animation artists who also work in other areas; some are illustrators, designers for film and cartoonists. It does not follow that cartoonists or illustrators have the skill or patience to be animation artists. Most are satisfied with seeing their drawings animated by someone else's hand. Occasionally, artists who supply a design may want to try animating it.

In showing work, portfolios of storyboards, backgrounds, model sheets and similar items are useful to animation artists who have expertise and seek work in these areas. The animation artist's samples, however, are usually condensed onto a film reel or a video casette in order to show the true nature of one's ability in animating movement.

Most animation in this country is done with drawings that are then inked and painted onto cels. Other techniques of commercial value are computer animation, which can be hard edged, geometric, abstract or figurative; and three-dimensional animation (claymation), which has clay figures or puppets or any other three-dimensional object used to narrate a story; and highly realistic miniatures used in special effects.

Pay scales of temporary animation artists by classification*

Animation	Hourly	4-hour minimum call
Director	$34.29	$137.14
Assistant director	27.95	111.80
Production boards	34.29	137.14
Layout	32.14	128.58
Animation artist	32.14	128.58
Staff comic strip artist	29.81	119.25
Assistant staff comic strip artist	25.34	101.37
Sheet timer	27.95	111.80
Story sketch	26.68	106.72
Scene planner	26.38	105.53
Animation checker	25.35	101.42
Breakdown	22.14	88.56
Blue sketch	21.70	86.78
Inbetweener	21.27	85.07

Ink and paint
(inking, special effects, painters)

	Hourly	4-hour minimum call
Assistant supervisor	$22.94	$91.75
Head special effects	22.44	89.75
Special effects	21.80	87.18
Color modelist	21.91	87.64
Ink checker	21.80	87.18
Key xerox processor	21.16	84.63
Xerox processor	20.88	83.52
Inker	21.04	84.16
Painter	20.88	83.52

*Temporary work scale is 117.719% of the minimum basic hourly rate for each employee's classification. See *Salaried Prices and Trade Customs* staff salaries. All figures were suppled by the Motion Picture Screen Cartoonists, Local 839 I.A.T.S.E., and represent the union-negotiated pay scales for journeymen for the contract effective August 1, 1992 through July 31, 1993.

Minimum unit rates for television or theatrical storyboards*

	Unit rate	Health, welfare and pension hours
Short subjects *(4 to 7 minutes)*	$754.21	25
Short subjects *(7 to 11 minutes)*	913.33	30
Half-hour subjects	1,638.19	62
One hour or more	2,443.46	93

*Two re-works may be required after presentation without additional compensation. If additional re-work is required, an additional 20% of the original unit maximum shall be paid for each re-work. Any amount negotiated in excess of the above minimums may be applied against any additional compensation for re-work when due. All figures were suppled by the Motion Picture Screen Cartoonists, Local 839 I.A.T.S.E., and represent the union-negotiated pay scales for journeymen for the contract effective August 1, 1992 through July 31, 1993.

Cartooning

Cartoonists are humorous illustrators who create single-panel or multi-panel cartoons, comic strips, editorial cartoons or comic books. Many cartoonists also work in advertising, publishing, television, promotional and other general illustration markets.

Cartoons look deceptively easy to create because they are common and because of their relatively simple style. However, cartooning is a highly demanding specialization, with a long "apprenticeship" period usually needed before the cartoonist masters the skills to consistently bring together the various elements involved in a successful cartoon.

Magazine cartoons

The magazine cartoon is probably the most popular of the graphic arts. Media surveys invariably place cartoons among readers' first preferences.

Magazine cartoons (or gag cartoons) are created by freelance cartoonists who usually conceive the idea, draw the cartoon and then offer it for sale to appropriate magazines. Most cartoonists market their work first to higher-paying publications.

Cartoonists bring a unique blend of writing and drawing skills to every piece. They know how to stage a cartoon as graphic theater that instantly communicates the situation and characters. A good cartoon "says it" faster and with more impact than a paragraph of descriptive words and, most importantly, makes you laugh.

The pricing of freestanding magazine cartoons is different from that of other forms of illustration, because they are purchased at fixed rates as a complete editorial element, similar to a freelance feature article. Generally, all black-and-white or color cartoons published at a particular size are paid at the same rate. The exception is a handful of magazines (e.g., *The New Yorker*) that additionally compensates those cartoonist-contributors closely identified with their magazine. In these instances, the cartoonist may have a contract providing an annual "signature" fee, bonuses and, in a few cases, fringe benefits in return for first look at the cartoons.

A number of factors affect prices for magazine cartoons. Among them are: whether the cartoon is black-and-white or color, size of reproduction, the magazine's geographical distribution, circulation, impact and influence, importance of cartoons as a regular editorial element, the extent of rights being purchased, and the national reputation of the cartoonist. Since the list is composed of objective and subjective factors and the mix in each case is different, rates vary considerably.

Trade practices

The following trade practices are accepted as standard:

1. Payment should always be made on acceptance of the work, not on publication.

2. Artists normally sell only first reproduction rights unless otherwise stated.

3. Under copyright law, cartoonists retain copyright ownership of all work they create. Copyright can only be transferred in writing.

4. Cartoonists should never send the same original drawing to more than one U.S. publisher at a time. Multiple photocopy submissions are acceptable to many European and other overseas publishers.

5. Purchasers should make selections promptly (within two to four weeks) and return cartoons not purchased.

6. Return of original artwork to the artist is automatic unless otherwise negotiated.

7. The Graphic Artists Guild is unalterably opposed to the use of work-for-hire contracts, in which authorship and all rights that go with it are transferred to the commissioning party and the independent artist is treated as an employee for copyright purposes only. The independent artist receives no employee benefits and loses the right to claim authorship or profit from future use of the work forever. Additional information on work for hire can be found on page 15.

8. Terms of sale should be specified in writing in a contract or on the invoice. For example, if work is to be reprinted in a textbook, the following should be included:

"For one-time, nonexclusive, English language, North American print rights only, in one hardcover edition, to be published by *(name of publisher)*, entitled ____ . All additional requests for usage by your organization or any other publication, except as specified above, are to be referred to *(name of artist)* to determine the appropriate reprint fee."

Syndication

Many freelance cartoonists develop comic strips or panels for distribution to newspapers by national and international syndicates. Since the number of newspapers using syndicated material are limited, the field is highly competitive. Few strips are introduced in any given year and then often only when an existing feature is dropped. It is therefore very tempting for cartoonists whose strips or panels are accepted by a syndicate to sign the first contract offered.

The syndicated cartoon field is undergoing major changes, long overdue. A number of well-known cartoonists are negotiating or renegotiating contracts with major syndicates on terms more favorable to the artist. Cartoonists who are offered a syndicate contract should keep these changes in mind.

Because syndicated cartoonists' earnings are based on the number of newspapers carrying their strips or panels and the circulation level of the papers, the assumption is that syndicates use fairly standard contracts. Syndicate contracts, however, are complicated and vary considerably among the major firms.

Cartoonists owe it to themselves and their creations to prepare as well as they can and thoroughly negotiate all terms. Experience proves that there is no substitute for knowledgeable counsel in contract negotiations. It is important to get the best legal representation possible. A lawyer with expertise in cartooning, visual arts, copyright and/or literary property contracts is recommended.

Foremost among the terms that are changing in the field are the monetary split between the syndicate and the artist, ownership of the feature, and the length of the contract. The split is no longer fixed at the customary 50-50, although it is still common. Syndicates used to routinely demand ownership of the feature, but artists benefit so much economically and artistically from retaining ownership that it has become an important item in negotiations.

Contracts which used to run for 20-year terms are negotiated to be renewable in much less time (5-7 years), and cartoonists are seeking unconditional termination of the contract rather than a renewal that is conditional on the feature's performance. Such flexibility benefits the cartoonist, whose worth may increase considerably over the contract period and may therefore be able to negotiate an even more beneficial renewal.

Other terms being negotiated include the artist's share of merchandising income, quality control over products or animated versions of the feature and the ability to leave an unsatisfactory contract relationship. All terms of a contract are negotiable.

If a syndicate offers a contract for a particular strip, it indicates serious interest. However reluctantly, the syndicate will probably be willing to negotiate terms. And if one syndicate recognizes that a strip is marketable, chances are good that other syndicates will also like it. Therefore, it may be worth "walking away" from an unsatisfactory contract offer to seek another syndicate as your partner.

Progressive changes in syndicated contract terms reflect the importance of cartoon licensing in today's market and a decision by individual cartoonists to fight for more control of their creations. Cartoonists who sharpens their negotiating skills can protect their income and art for the future rather than churn out work for 20 years under unfavorable terms negotiated when the artist was a relative beginner.

Licensing and merchandising

Cartoon character licensing and merchandising continues grow rapidly. When characters such as *Snoopy, The Simpsons* or *Teenage Mutant Ninja Turtles* are licensed for a range of products from toys and apparel to designer sheets and stationery, their creators stand to earn considerable additional income *if* they retain all or a significant percentage of the subsidiary rights in the property.

It is sometimes assumed that only nationally known syndicate characters are sought by licensing agents or manufacturers. With the tremendous growth in this area, however, there are now possibilities for cartoonists to develop characters specifically for product use. Cartoonists interested in pursuing this potentially lucrative application of their work should consult an attorney specializing in this field to assure adequate copyright protection *before* presenting work to licensers or manufacturers.

Trade shows for character licensing and merchandising are held several times a year around the country. They provide a place for creators, licensors, syndicates and manufacturers to explore business opportunities.

Editorial cartooning

Editorial cartoonists are usually salaried staff artists on individual daily newspapers. Salaries vary greatly with the circulation and status of the paper and the reputation and experience of the cartoonist.

Some editorial cartoonists are syndicated nationally, while remaining on staff with their base papers. Usually their papers require that they do two locally oriented cartoons per week, and the syndicates want at least three cartoons a week relating to national issues. As with comic strips, the earnings received by editorial cartoonists from syndication depend on their contract and the number and size of the newspapers using their work regularly. (See *Syndication*, above).

Sometimes freelance cartoonists sell their work to major daily newspapers op-ed pages or to weekly news magazines. Rates vary, but generally are based on the column width of the work used and whether the drawing is an original or reprint. It is best to check with individual papers regarding their interest in freelance contributions before sending work for consideration.

Original cartoon books or collections

In addition to collections of the published work of one or more cartoonists, there has been a recent trend toward publishing original cartoon books.

Book contracts vary as much as syndication contracts, so it is advisable to consult a qualified literary agent or lawyer. In fact, book publishers prefer to negotiate terms with a knowledgeable author's representative. Cartoonists should expect an advance against royalties at contract signing. A first time cartoonist-author may expect an advance ranging from a minimum $3000 up to $10,000. Please refer also to the "Syndication" and "Children's Book Illustration" sections.

Comic books

With average monthly sales of over 200,000 per title per month, comic books are extremely popular products. Some titles average twice that amount, and on occasion a book will break sales records, as do Todd McFarlane's *Spider-Man*, selling 800,000 to 1,000,000 copies per month. According to *The New York Times* industry executives say comic book sales are growing 10 to 20 per cent annually. Major entertainment industry companies like *Time-Warner* (DC Comics), *MCA-Matsushita* (Harvey Comics Entertainment, Inc.) and financiers like Ronald O. Perelman (Marvel) are buying comic book companies on the hope that a billion-dollar character star may emerge.

Each monthly comic book (averaging 22 pages) is produced in 21 days to meet distribution deadlines. These high-pressure conditions are the reason that comic books are mass-produced in assembly line fashion. Publishers divide comic book labor among individuals with special skills who complete a specific component in the process and then pass the work on to the next stage of production. The specializations in comic books generally include: writers, pencil artists (pencillers), lettering artists (letterers), ink artists (inkers) and coloring artists (colorists). Further divisions include "background art." The trend in the last decade seems to indicate a greater number of comic book artists who write, draw and ink their own stories, but even for specialists, the rigors of the 3-week deadline requires severe discipline.

Cinematic in style, comic book publishing often mimics film production. Writers will conceive a story and develop a script, often indicating specific views of the action to be portrayed. The writers (and sometimes the pencillers) will lay out the action on 8 1/2" x 11" page storyboards consisting of 6 to 44 panels. Following the writer's script directions, the pencil artist will "breakdown" (loose sketches on art board) the concept sketches on 10" x 15" bristol board. The penciled board is passed on to the letterer, who letters the balloon captions in ink. The board is then passed on to the inker, who inks the figures and backgrounds on each panel.

The boards are then reduced to 6" x 9" on 8 1/2" x 11" finch paper, which are passed on to the colorist, who color codes the art for printing and hand colors photocopies of all 22 pages of the book. The boards, coded reductions and the colored photocopies are then sent to the printer for manufacture.

Freelance artists working in this industry are expected to meet minimum production quotas, and are paid a page rate for each page completed. Page rates vary according to the specialization.

Since comic books are paid on the "piece work" system, the faster an artist works, the more an artist will earn. However, to meet production deadlines, artists are expected to complete a minimum number of pages in each production cycle. Letterers, for example, are expected to complete at least 66 pages in a three week period, but strive to complete ten pages per day, five days a week. Many artists must work ten hours a day, six days a week in order to make a living wage.

Comic book publishers will generally pay artists a lesser page rate for reprinting an original publication. However, this seems to apply only to domestic reprinting; not to foreign editions, from which the artists receive no compensation.

If a comic book's net domestic sales exceed 75,000 copies, a royalty on the excess is usually paid to the writer, penciller (or other layout artist) and inker. Royalties are graduated according to the degree of creative input and the number of sales, but generally range from one-half per cent to two per cent of the cover price. Those artists who perform more than one function will receive a larger royalty; if more creators are involved in a project they will share the royalties.

Freelance agreements with the major comic book publishers provide for the return of original art. The artist(s) may assign, sell or transfer ownership only of the physical original. However, the artists do not retain any of the copyrights in the work as the contracts usually contain a work-for-hire clause.

Two major problems in the comic book industry, in the view of the Graphic Artists Guild, are: (1) comic books are not a collective work as defined in the Copyright Act of 1976. Therefore, comic books are not eligible to be work for hire; and (2) freelance artists working in the comic book industry may actually be conventional employees, not independent contractors. While this would mean that all work created by them is work-for-hire, it also entitles the artists to at least the minimum benefits and entitlements afforded to any conventional employee, including unemployment, disability, workers compensation insurance and the right to organize for the purposes of collective bargaining. For more information on "Employment issues," please refer to the chapter on *Professional Issues.*

All prices for illustration in the *Guidelines* are based on a nationwide survey that was reviewed by a special committee of experienced professionals through the Graphic Artists Guild. These figures, reflecting the responses of established professionals, are meant as a point of reference only and do not necessarily reflect such important factors as deadlines, job complexity, reputation and

experience of a particular cartoonist, research, technique or unique quality of expression and extraordinary or extensive use of the finished cartoon. Please refer to related material in other sections of this book, especially under *Business & Legal Practices for Commissioned Artwork* and *Standard Contracts.*

The prices shown represent only the specific use for which the cartoon is intended and do not necessarily reflect any of the above considerations. The buyer and seller are free to negotiate, taking into account all the factors involved.

Comparative fees for original cartoons in consumer magazines

Single panel	B&W	Color
1 column	$150	$250
2 or more columns	300	375
Full page	400	650

Multipanel		
1 column	$225	$375
2 or more columns	375	500
Full page	450	750

Comparative fees for original cartoons in trade magazines

Single panel	B&W	Color
1 column	$150	$225
2 or more columns	275	350
Full page	500	600

Multipanel		
1 column	$225	$300
2 or more columns	300	400
Full page	550	650

Comparative fees for original cartoons in non-syndicated newspapers

Panel	B&W	Color
Quarter page or less	$125	$250
Half page or less	225	300

Strip		
Quarter page or less	$275	$400
Half page or less	350	600

Comparative monthly gross income from syndicated cartoon strips*

Daily	$1200
Daily and Sunday	1800

*Figures shown reflect an average syndication of 50 newspapers. Gross income is split 50-50 with syndicate.

Comparative fees for cartoon reprints in consumer magazines

Single panel	B&W	Color
1 column	$130	$200
2 or more columns	225	250
Full page	400	450

Multipanel		
1 column	$200	$225
2 or more columns	250	300
Full page	400	550

Comparative fees for cartoon reprints in trade magazines

Single panel	B&W	Color
1 column	$125	$175
2 or more columns	200	225
Full page	350	400

Multipanel		
1 column	$125	$150
2 or more columns	225	250
Full page	250	350

Comparative fees for cartoon reprints in books

Textbooks	B&W	Color
Cover	$400	$800
Full page	300	600
Half page	200	400
Quarter page	150	250

Hardcover books		
Cover	$300	$500
Full page	250	400
Half page	200	300
Quarter page	150	225

Paperback books		
Cover	$250	$400
Half page or less	200	250
Quarter page	175	200

Comparative fees for cartoon reprints in cartoon anthologies (various artists)

	B&W	Color
Cover	$200	$400
Full page	175	300
Half page	150	200
Quarter page	100	150

Comparative page rates for comic book art

Original publication

Writers *(plot and script)*	$75
Layouts	35
Breakdowns	30 - 95
Pencil art*	55 - 120
Ink art*	45 - 95
Ink on overlays	55 - 105
Lettering	18 - 27
Lettering on overlay	20 - 29
Background art	10 - 25
Coloring art	12 - 22

*Add 20% to the above fees for cover art.

Computer generated art

The use of computers to create still or moving images spans the full spectrum of image-making techniques. Computers are gaining acceptance as an effective and versatile tool to aid artists and designers in their creative processes. Contrary to conventional wisdom, art created on computers is not necessarily quicker or less expensive than art created with traditional media.

Computer use is growing more in the fields of design, where it is especially suited to developing concepts, but is growing more slowly in the field of illustration because computers are just another medium that illustrators use to achieve certain results.

A computer is not a "self-functioning" tool. Like pencils, airbrushes and other graphics tools, computers do not generate work of and by themselves. *Any computer generated art is the product of the artist's talent, skill, experience and understanding of the technological application.* But, unlike other traditional tools, the computer does bring with it at least three additional concerns. First is the cost of maintaining and upgrading the hardware and software with faster programs or enhanced features; second is the learning curve that is required to keep abreast of the latest applications available; and third is the difficulty in protecting computer generated artwork from unauthorized alteration and use.

With computers, the investment in capital and education is a continual, ongoing and necessary process. Some computer graphic applications also require engineering and programming skills to implement these advances into existing hardware/software configurations.

Work done on computers remains in the digital format produced by the computer. Unlike traditional art media, digital information can be copied easily without loss of quality. If work is copied without authorization, it may be impossible to identify the original source of the artwork. If turning the digital information over to a client, the artist should use a Job Order Form specifying the authorized use of the art. To avoid potential abuse, artists should add the following into their contract when transferring their work in digital form (on disk or transmitted through a modem):

Disk may only be used for the following purposes: _____
All other use(s) and modification(s) is prohibited. This disk may not be copied without the artist's permission and must be returned after use.

Because of the great potential for abuse, artists will normally not relinquish their art in digital form via disk or modem; rather, art will be delivered as hardcopy output.

Acceptable quality of hardcopy output will depend upon the client's needs, stage of completion of the art (comps or finished art), associated costs, compatibility and accessibility of peripheral equipment, aesthetics, timing and the intended purpose of the hardcopy. Many artists who work for traditional (i.e., non-computer oriented publications) have had their work published using the following kinds of hardcopy:

Photographic output:
35mm slides shot off both curved and flat monitors, by cameras which record the information digitally or by less expensive cameras that have internal miniature monitors built into them that shoot the image in three passes using red, green, and blue filters. This produces a lower quality but frequently acceptable commercial hardcopy image.

Polaroid prints from a camera designed to interface with a computer. For comp purposes Polaroid prints can be shot directly off the screen.

Printer output:
Ink jet printout; Thermal printout; Laser printout; Laser color photocopy of color inkjet art. This is more permanent because some inks can smear and fade.

High quality black-and-white copy of inkjet prints to increase the contrast and improve the quality of the image. For example, artists may ask for high quality copy from a Xerox 9900.

Linotronic output is available on a rental basis from service bureaus (as are other types of printouts), and can be generated as reproduction quality paper or printer-ready film.

Mixed media:
Many artists combine traditional media with any of the output listed above to create a finished work of art. For example, artists may add color to a black-and-white Macintosh print with colored pencils and markers. Some artists transfer computer images to traditional printmaking media like silkscreens or etchings. Other artists use the

computer as a sketch tool to develop an idea which is then executed in a traditional media such as oil paint on canvas.

There are a variety of ways that artists are using computers both as a pure digital technology and as a medium combined with more traditional tools. As computers become more available as a business item, differences in the price and power between workstations and personal computers will diminish. Consequently, more applications for computer generated art and graphics are being developed and defined.

Computer generated artwork (referred to as computer graphics), presents a new level of options for artists and clients. It can speed up the design process, create photorealistic images, and enhance client communications. Designers using computers report that this technology allows for more design solutions to be evaluated in a shorter period of time and results in faster client approval of projects.

Among the many varieties of work done on a computer are: TV station logos, weather and news graphics, 3-D models, interactive presentations, color retouching, automatic plate make-up and design, high resolution presentation graphics, desktop publishing, desktop video, simulated models for scientific applications, and technical illustration. As the computer graphics industry matures, the applications and uses continue to increase and evolve.

Copyright

Artwork completed on a computer is copyrighted as any other work of visual art or audiovisual work. It is also possible to copyright the source code as text, protecting the work as it is expressed in fundamental computer language. For more information on copyright, please refer to the *Professional Issues* and *Business Management* chapters.

The contract for computer generated art in the *Standard Contracts* chapter is applicable to software, electronic pre-press, desktop publishing, electronic information systems and others. The contract is designed to be a starting point which can be adapted and amended as technology and industry practices change.

Applications for computer generated art

Animation uses a rapid sequence of individual frames across time (30 frames per second in video, and 24 frames per second in film), to represent and display objects in motion. High-end computer systems have been used to create special effects in the motion picture industry, such as spinning logos for broadcast television and animated characters in commercials. High-end capability is currently filtering down to the personal computer level, and personal computers are being used as a viable platform for the production of industrial videos, computer animated presentation and interactive moving graphic displays.

CAD (computer aided design) is a quickly expanding part of the computer graphics industry. CAD programs are used for engineering and architectural, industrial, fashion and package design. Models can be drawn two-dimensionally (2-D) as schematics or as a three-dimensional (3-D) wire frame to design, conceptualize, and test a product concept. Some CAD programs can add surface attributes and photorealistically render the design. This helps in design evaluation and as a presentation tool for client approval of projects.

CAM (computer aided manufacturing): Models created in a CAD program can utilized by a CAM program to create drafts, process plans, prototypes, and finally the finished product. The entire CAD/CAM production cycle begins with a design and ends with a final three-dimensional product. The cycle includes analysis, modeling, visualization, simulation, drafting, process planning, production, quality control, and job tracking for accounting purposes.

Computer generated architectural/ interior design/rendering: A large number of architectural firms have incorporated computers into their design process. Computers are used to assist in the planning, design, landscaping, detailing and the specifications of sites, buildings and interior spaces. Sophisticated software programs can correlate designs for the various subsystems of a building (lighting and electrical, plumbing, heating, ventilation and air conditioning). Once the design is finalized and approved by the client, an itemized list of material specifications can be generated and sent to contractors for bids. In addition to creating the plans and working drawings (blueprints) of the building, 3-D models can be generated with surface attributes to photorealistically simulate the actual site, building or interior. When plotted, the 3-D model can be professionally rendered and composited with an actual photograph of the location for design or presentation purposes. The model can be animated to simulate a walk through the site, building or space, to gauge a design's mass and scale. When furnishings or other decorative details are added, the animated walk-through is an effective presentation tool.

Computer generated business graphics include charts and maps, graphs and diagrams for business presentations. A large segment of the computer graphics industry creates business graphics for both slide, video and printed company presentations. Systems like *Genigraphics, Autographics,* and *Videoshow* specialize in this application, but personal computers (IBM and Macintosh) also have software programs available to take numerical information and convert it to maps, charts and graphs, create slide shows or animate these elements for film output or computer viewing.

Computer generated graphic design With a personal computer, the appropriate software and a printer, graphic designers can create and present concepts and designs to clients for approval. Comps done on a computer are more realistic and finished, and since changes to a design can be made quickly, finished designs can often be created in less time than using traditional methods, especially when a designer is showing variations of a single theme. Graphic designers are using computers in all graphic design markets, including corporate, environmental graphic design and signage, publication, advertising and collateral, among others.

Computer generated illustration (general): Illustration systems can mix colors, be used for freehand drawing and for sizing and positioning of visual elements. Finished output ranges from black-and-white illustrations executed on personal computers, to full-color illustrations executed on High Definition Television (HDTV) high-end paint systems. Computer generated illustration is used in publishing, broadcast, advertising, corporate and educational markets.

Computer generated illustration (technical): Because of the high degree of accuracy required, many technical illustrators are relying on computers to create works for product renderings for advertising or manuals, medical and pharmaceutical illustration for advertising and education, architecture and scientific research.

Computer generated industrial design is the design of three-dimensional objects for both consumers and industry. Computers are used to design products and to set up the process of manufacturing them. Industrial design applications may include such products as appliances or automobiles.

Computer generated pre-production art shows the composition of shots in a moving sequence. Storyboards are used by advertising agencies, video production houses, and film companies to visualize the positioning of elements and the action in a television commercial or motion picture. Personal computers are now being used to create storyboards for concept presentation and client approval of sequences to be shot in film and video. These individual storyboard panels can then be turned into animatics by adding camera movement and transition effects to create a sense of the action. Animatics are used to test television commercials and animated graphics.

Computer generated package design is a two-part process. First, the volume and shape of a container can be created with the surface information. Second, the two-dimensional illustration, typography, and layout can be created and mapped onto the three-dimensional shape. Computers can simulate the final product for design testing and market research.

Computer generated scientific visualization is the converging fields of computer graphics, image processing, computer vision, computer aided design, signal processing and user interface studies. Scientific visualization acts as a catalyst between scientific computation and scientific insight. It came into existence as the result of a need to visualize dense scientific data models, like wind and storm information. Artists and scientists are working together in this area to help visualize complex scientific information, making it easier to interpret and understand.

Computer generated surface design: Surface, apparel and fashion designers use computers to design works on several levels. Some surface designers use standard paint programs to design and test patterns. At the higher end of the spectrum, apparel and fashion designers may use complete CAD/CAM programs that blend fabrics, mix patterns, drape designs on models, visualize product lines, and send the information to the mills for production. Most CAD/CAM programs available are still very costly and tend to run proprietary software.

Desktop publishing is an electronic process that combines text, graphics and photographs to produce professional quality documents. These publications can be produced with a personal computer and a laser printer, or documents created on a personal computer can be sent to a service bureau for camera-ready quality reproductions or film, which is then sent to a commercial press.

Desktop video is a term used to describe the ability of personal computers to view video sequences; add titles, graphics and other overlays; edit and add sound and assemble the result into a finished product. As computer and video technologies merge, inexpensive desktop video editing and production systems are becoming available at the personal computer level.

Electronic information services are banks of information that can be accessed by a personal telephone line. These services charge a fee to access the information. Some of these services are beginning to use graphics and illustrations as a part of their displays.

Electronic pre-press uses digital technology to create text, design graphics, layout pages, and scan photographs. A complete electronic pre-press system can digitally pass information through the pre-production printing process from copy initially created in a word processing program to the final film separations that are used for printing the actual piece.

Electronic retouching (photo & illustrative): Recent advances in technology allow electronic scanning and manipulation of images (including global color correction, cloning a subject, distorting or enhancing an image, and preserving an image without disintegration of the dyes). As a time factor, electronic retouching dispenses with the intermediate step of a dye transfer and the time necessary to recreate a facsimile of the original artwork. However, when compared to hand work, computer retouching does not necessarily provide better quality or cheaper rates. Electronic retouching can do very subtle things (e.g. defining individual hairs in a hairdo or create subtleties in skin tones). Electronic retouching is improving, but the colors of printed pieces that were electronically retouched may vary from the colors displayed on the screen, although those with the expertise can correct or allow for them. Electronic retouching is convenient; it has a justified compatibility with the mechanics of the pre-press process. As these technologies become more widely available, scanning and output fees will drop significantly.

Image processing techniques on the computer modify images to enhance image visibility and to creatively alter the image. Images can be either photographs that are scanned into the computer or synthetically generated through processes like ray-tracing. Image processing computer programs manipulate the images rather than create them. One use for this technique is to enhance medical or scientific photographs to clarify or highlight areas of the pictures that are difficult to see.

Interface design is a new area of design that has evolved as a result of the computer revolution. Interface design is used in human-computer interaction; it is how people communicate with computers. The current interface trend is to use Graphical User Interfaces (GUIs). This combines graphic icons and text to execute commands on the computer. Interface design requires a combination of graphic design and programming skills. Systems like the Macintosh have very specific guidelines that developers must follow in designing the interface for programs to run on the Macintosh.

Pagination is an integration of paste-up and stripping into a digital computer process that allows both applications to be done on one computer system. As it combines pictures and text into a whole page, it eliminates the need for hand done mechanicals. Output can be in the form of camera-ready reproductions or film with registration marks that are ready for printing. Work done on a personal computer can be sent to a Linotronic machine for high quality reproduction. Service bureaus are available to convert data stored on PC disks to camera-ready art for printing.

Systems administration: Computers are a complex technology. It is the responsibility of the systems administrator to keep the computers running and information flowing. When dealing with graphics, a systems administrator needs an extensive knowledge of computer technology and a background in graphic applications.

Three-dimensional (3-D) modeling defines three-dimensional objects in a computer with points, lines, planes, and volumes. This includes perspective drawing, determining visible surfaces, textures, and shading. Generally, an object is modeled in a three-dimensional wire frame within a representational space which can then be rendered with defined surface attributes to create a photorealistic image of an object. Three-dimensional modeling is similar to constructing an actual object in terms of shape and volume, but computer objects are virtual representations in a computer environment. Some three-dimensional programs can send the information to CAM systems to create the final finished product.

Training: Another way computer graphic artists earn extra income is to train other people to use computers. A good computer designer requires a strong background in art and design, as well as a comprehensive understanding of the computer as an artistic medium. Artists who meet these qualifications are in demand to train other artists and designers.

Two-dimensional (2-D) modeling graphic programs include freehand drawing, color mixing, contrast expansion, and working with picture elements (PIXELS), to create or manipulate an image. The images exist on a two-dimensional surface in the computer.

These applications combine a variety of design, production and programming skills. In some computer graphics applications, for example, the artist must also be an engineer. The computer is changing traditional job functions and the role of the artist/designer. The artist/designer must still be expert within a particular discipline, but must also be able to understand and use a variety of technical software programs and hardware platforms. As use of this technology grows in all disciplines of the graphic arts, traditional handwork will diminish. Many talented and skilled artists and designers are now faced with the need to learn and use computer technology to be competitive in the job market.

Computer graphics for video

The use of computers in the making of moving imagery is extensive and spans a full spectrum of approaches, including rotoscoping and hand drawn effects, motion graphics and three-dimensional modeling and choreography and compositing. From the fine arts to commercial television, the applications for these artistic styles are becoming more widespread.

Computer imagery for commercial videos always requires a designer or art director to effectively communicate the information visually. The designer may act independently as an art director and be responsible for the production of the animation elements at a computer/video facility, or be hired by the facility directly. In either case, the visual translation of information is critical and should not be underestimated in terms of the designer's time and efforts.

Computer graphics for the video industry fall into three categories: industrial, advertising and broadcast. When computer graphics are used in video for either animation or other special effects, they are usually part of a larger work and are frequently combined with live footage and traditional techniques. This can make pricing a little more complicated than when art is being commissioned as the whole project.

Computer graphics for commercial videos normally are not done by individuals, but by animation/video companies. These companies range from small studios, which do animation and art on computer only, to large studios that provide full video services as well as full film services, handling total production for a project. Even the larger companies frequently contract freelance artists on special jobs and/or rent special equipment from other facilities.

Because of equipment costs, it is unusual for individual artists to be able to provide all of these services for a client. Even large companies do not always own all of the video equipment necessary for a particular job.

Some of the more popular systems on which video graphic artists and broadcast designers work include *Wavefront* and/or *Alias* programs (for 3-D), *Quantel Paintbox* (for illustration, graphics, backgrounds, textures and sparingly for storyboards and design). *Quantel Harry* with a digital video effects device (D.V.E.) like *Encore* or *Kaleidoscope* (for compositing, sequencing and effects) and other paint systems by *Digital F/ X* or *Color Graphics.*

Industrials are usually 3/4" (or 1/2" *Beta*) videos used for non-broadcast purposes such as training films, video newsletters or brochures, sales videos, video catalogs and how-to's for the home VCR market. These videos are also referred to as non-theatrical releases.

Computer graphics account generally for only a percentage of the total video/film, with growth charts, location maps and logos (sometimes including animation) being the most likely applications.

The choice of visual concepts for industrial use affects the final price of a job. In some cases, more than one computer graphics system may have to be used to produce the desired effect. The job may, therefore, end up being produced in more than one location on more than one piece of equipment. Pricing should reflect this factor as well as post-production costs for special techniques.

Pre-production consultation is vital in determining the price and for describing to the client the best and most efficient processes for arriving at the final product.

Broadcast: This category is usually

produced in formats like 1" *D2* (composite digital) or *Beta* and includes title sequences (station I.D.'s and promos), educational films and maps and charts (such as weather maps). Many of the same factors in determining prices for industrials apply to this section as well. The creation of title sequences will generally be priced higher than maps and charts because the designs are more complex and more editing time is required.

Advertising: These jobs are usually done by medium to large-sized animation studios who have large permanent staff and who occasionally hire freelance artists for special projects. Fees for this type of work are not only determined by usage, but also by time, complexity and type of equipment needed, including the use of outside equipment.

Pricing computer graphics

Art produced by computer is like any other area of the graphic arts as far as pricing and business practices are concerned. In pricing computer generated art, the final application of the work is determinate: that is, the price will depend, in part, on whether the art will be used as illustration, text design, graphic design elements, broadcast graphics, etc. And, like pricing for other forms of artwork, consideration is made for the ways in which the art will be used. The applications covered here are primarily for work done on personal computers and workstations. As the price of workstations decreases and the power of personal computers increases the distinction between these two platforms is disappearing. Art that was traditionally done on high-end systems is now filtering down to personal computers on the desktop. Furthermore, as applications and environments become transparent, artwork created on a personal computer can be networked to higher level platforms to create a higher quality end product.

Factors to be considered when pricing computer graphics include:

Time: A job done on a computer may be more efficient or may take longer than art produced with traditional media. Unlike traditional approaches, using computers allows for data created during the design phase of a project to be stored in a data base and transferred through the design process to create a final product. Comps produced on a computer can be rendered into a finished product upon demand. Time can be saved in making alterations and in multiple uses or applications. For illustrators and designers who create their own databases, or libraries of images and layouts, time can be saved when opportunities arise to modify or reuse those images and layouts .

Extra expenses: Post-production costs for service bureau output (such as video, 35mm slides, transparencies, film development), delivery services, rental of peripheral equipment, purchase of specific software to meet a job requirement, etc., will add expense(s) to the cost of the art. Other expenses to be reimbursed by the client typically include subcontractors' fees, supplies, travel, long-distance phone calls, overnight couriers and messenger services. The markup for these typically range from 15 to 20 per cent, with the standard based on the advertising agency markup of 17.65 per cent. The markup reimburses the computer graphic artist for supervisory and handling time and insures that all work is done to specifications and standards for quality. In short, all additional expenses related to a job, including conversion to hardcopy, are accounted and billed to the client as part of the service rendered.

Graphic artists working in the personal computer environment must initially invest an average of $22,000 to $30,000 in hardware and software to meet their client's needs effectively. Some, depending on the specific services they provide, have invested $100,000 or more for the tools they require. Significantly greater than the capital investments made by other graphic artists, these investments do not include the time needed for continued training, learning curves, the ongoing need to upgrade equipment and software and the time required to "debug" unexpectedly complex problems with equipment and software programs.

To remain competitive, computer graphic artists must recoup their investments over a period of time. One way that graphic artists may charge an equipment usage fee is to form a separate company and bill computer time as a separate service. Forming separate companies for the express purpose of renting equipment may obligate its principals to collect sales tax. It is important therefore, for artists to discuss this method with an accountant or lawyer.

Most computer artists will recoup their investments of time and capital by factoring those costs into their hourly or project fees, or by adding an equipment fee in addition to their creative fees. Artists should discuss all estimated costs with the client before starting the job, and it is important for an itemized list of those costs to be presented to the client on the invoice as additional expenses.

The pricing formula for computer graphics below is designed as a guideline for calculating total fees.

Pricing formula for computer graphics in normal print media

Creative fee[1] $+$ computer equipment fee[2] $+$ expenses[3] $=$ Total computer graphics fee

[1]See appropriate specialty.

[2]Hardware and software rental and/or operator fees. It is customary and usual for computer artists to charge a rental fee for the use of his or her equipment. Equipment fees will vary according to the systems used, and currently range from $50-100 per hour above and beyond the creative fee.

[3]Expenses include, but are not limited to, the cost of output services such as 35mm slides, Linotronic services, type cost, color separations or any other hardcopy output. A markup will generally be added to all billable expenses

---

Trade Practices

The following trade practices are accepted as standard:

1. The intended use of the computer graphic must be clearly stated in a contract, purchase order, or letter of agreement stating the price and terms of sale.

2. If a computer graphic is to be used for other than its original purpose, the price should be negotiated as soon as possible. The secondary use of computer graphics may be of greater value than the primary use. Although there is no set formula for reuse fees, a reuse fee ranging from 25-50 per cent of the fee that would have been charged had the computer graphics been originally commissioned for the anticipated usage is a fairly typical charge.

3. Graphic artists and designers should negotiate reuse arrangements with the original commissioning party with speed, efficiency and all due respect to the client's needs.

4. Return of original artwork, computer disks or mechanicals to the graphic artist or designer is automatic unless otherwise negotiated.

5. The use of art or design always influences the price. If the work is to be featured over an extensive area or is an all-rights sale, fees will be significantly higher than when used locally or within a selected area.

6. Fees for rush work will be higher than the figures listed here. Regular overtime figures are one and one-half times to two times the usual rate.

7. A cancellation fee should always be agreed upon in the event a job is cancelled through no fault of the designer. Depending upon the stage at which the job is terminated, the fee paid should reflect all work completed or hours spent, including research time, artwork, billable expenses and compensation for lost opportunities resulting from an artist or designer refusing other offers to make time available to a specific commission.

8. A rejection fee should be agreed upon if the assignment is cancelled because the preliminary or finished work is found not to be reasonably satisfactory. The rejection fee should be equal to the number of hours spent, depending on the reason for rejection.

9. Work done on speculation does not conform to industry trade practices and is contrary to the Joint Ethics Committee's Code of Fair Practice, because of its exploitive nature.

10. The Graphic Artists Guild is unalterably opposed to the use of work-for-hire contracts, in which authorship and all rights that go with it are transferred to the commissioning party and the independent graphic artists or designer is treated as an employee for copyright purposes only. The independent graphic artist or designer receives no employee benefits and loses the right to claim authorship or profit from future use of the work forever. Additional information on work for hire can be found on page 15.

All prices for design in the Guidelines are based on a nationwide survey that was reviewed by a special committee of experienced professionals through the Graphic Artists Guild. These figures, reflecting the responses of established professionals, are meant as a point of reference only and do not necessarily reflect such important factors as deadlines, job complexity, reputation and experience of a particular designer, research, technique or unique quality of expression and extraordinary or extensive use of the finished art or design. Please refer to related material in other chapters of this book, especially under *Business & Legal Practices for Commissioned Artwork* and *Standard Contracts*.

The price ranges listed below do not constitute specific prices for particular jobs.

They are guidelines to be considered along with other factors specific to the commissioned work under consideration. Please refer to related material in other sections of this book, especially the pricing sections in the chapters on *Illustration Prices and Trade Customs, Graphic Design Prices and Trade Customs* and *Animation Prices and Trade Customs*.

Comparative hourly creative fees for computer artists and designers*

Desktop publishing	Per hour
Art direction	$50
Charts and graphs	45
Consultation	70
Graphic design	45
Illustration	70
Layouts	45
Photo retouching	145
Production	35
Training	70
Typesetting	40

Audiovisual/multimedia (including broadcast, industrial and advertising)	Per hour
2-D animation	$45
3-D animation	125
3-D images	130
Audiovisual design	60
Consulting	100
Editing	150
Editing (Harry with Encore or Kaleidoscope)	400 - 600
Illustration	75
Interactive design	100

Interface design	65
Paintbox with artist	200 - 300
Paintbox and Harry with artist	400 - 600
Slide production	50
Storyboards	75
Titles	65

*For staff salaries, see the chapter on *Salaried Prices and Trade Customs*.

Comparative fees for desktop publishing projects for advertising

Computer illustration	B&W	Color
Full page	$2,000	$3,000
Half page	1,000	1,500
Quarter page	500	1,000
Spot	375	500

Computer generated newsletter design		$200 per page

Charts and graphs	B&W	Color
Simple	$125	$350
Complex	250	700

Comparative fees for desktop publishing projects for advertising (continued)

Computer generated collateral advertising*	1 color	4 color
One page	$750	1,500
12 pages	3,500	9,000

*Brochures and flyers, (with one or two folds). Prices are largely dependent on size of company, complexity of design, number of images (photographic or illustrative) per page, copy length, audience, etc.

Computer generated logos	$750

Simple computer photo retouching	$1,000

Comparative fees for computer generated audiovisual/multimedia graphic art projects for advertising

AV concept and design	Per slide	Per second
Single projector	$125 - 250	-
Multiple projector	-	85

Computer generated storyboards	$35 per frame

Computer generated animation (per second)	2-D	3-D
Animatics	$250	$1,500
Industrial	500	2,800
Broadcast	1,000	3,000

Computer generated 3-D object	Simple	Complex
	$500	$850

Interactive graphics project (50 screens)	$100,000

Comparative fees for desktop publishing for corporate business projects

Computer illustration	B&W	Color
Full page	$1,000	$2,000
Half page	600	1,250
Quarter page	400	750
Spot	350	600

Computer generated newsletter design	$175 per page

Charts and graphs	B&W	Color
Simple	$125	$300
Complex	200	500

Computer generated collateral advertising*	1 color	4 color
One page	$750	1,500
12 pages	3,500	9,000

*Brochures and flyers, (with one or two folds). Prices are largely dependent on size of company, complexity of design, number of images (photographic or illustrative) per page, copy length, audience, etc.

Computer designed graphics standards manual	$75 per page

Computer designed educational booklets	$25 per page

Comparative fees for computer generated audiovisual/multimedia for corporate business projects

AV concept and design	Per slide	Per second
Single projector	$100 - 200	-
Multiple projector	-	85

Computer generated storyboards $35 *per frame*

Computer generated animation *(per second)*	2-D	3-D
Animatics	$250	$1,500
Industrial	500	2,000
Broadcast	1,000	3000

Computer generated 3-D object	Simple	Complex
	$350	800

Interactive graphics project *(75 screens)* $100,000

Courseware design project *(25 screens)* $20,000

Comparative fees for desktop publishing for graphic design studio projects

Computer illustration	B&W	Color
Full page	$1,200	$2,000
Half page	600	1,000
Quarter page	475	500
Spot	350	375

Computer generated newsletter design $200 - 375 *per page*

Charts and graphs	B&W	Color
Simple	$150	$500
Complex	300	1,000

Computer generated collateral advertising*	1 color	4 color
One page	$750	1,500
12 pages	3,500	9,000

*Brochures and flyers, (with one or two folds). Prices are largely dependent on size of company, complexity of design, number of images (photographic or illustrative) per page, copy length, audience, etc.

Computer generated catalogs *(per page)*

With typesetting	$250
Import type	200

Computer generated logos	$3,500
Customized type logo	$4,500

Comparative fees for audiovisual/multimedia projects for graphic design studios

AV concept and design	Per slide	Per second
Single projector	$100	-
Multiple projector	-	75

Computer generated storyboards	
	$15 per frame

Comparative fees for desktop publishing for publishing and editorial projects

Computer illustration	B&W	Color
Full page	$1,000	$2,000
Half page	750	850
Quarter page	600	750
Spot	350	500

Charts and graphs		
Simple	$125	$500
Complex	300	1,000

Computer generated collateral advertising*	1 color	4 color
One page	$750	1,500
12 pages	3,500	9,000

*Brochures and flyers, (with one or two folds). Prices are largely dependent on size of company, complexity of design, number of images (photographic or illustrative) per page, copy length, audience, etc.

Computer generated logos	$250

Customized type logo	$500

Comparative fees for desktop publishing for medical imaging and scientific visualization projects

Computer color illustration	Medical	Scientific
Full page	$3,000	$2,500
Half page	1,500	1,000

Computer Graphics Glossary

ASCII
American Standard Code for Information Interchange. This code gives specific numbers to alphabetic characters and is one of the few ways in which different computers can exchange information.

binary
A numbering system based on 2's rather than 10's, which uses only the digits 0 and 1.

bit
Binary digit - a single piece of binary data.

buffer
Temporary data-storage device, often used to store a single image.

byte:
A sequence of binary digits operated on as a unit, e.g., an 8-bit or 16-bit byte.

CAD/CAM
Computer Aided Design/Computer Aided Manufacture - used to design and test parts, machinery, generate schematics, calculate manufacturing specifications, etc.

chip
A miniature electrical circuit etched from silicon.

color map/palette
Synonym for the range of colors from which an artist/operator chooses the particular colors used in an individual image.

CPU
Central Processing Unit - hardware which performs the main calculations of the computer.

cursor
A position indicator on a computer screen indicating where data will be entered.

data
A general term for the basic elements of information, alphanumeric or graphic, which can be processed by a computer.

digital
A way of representing information (words, pictures, music, etc.) in discrete numerical values.

documentation file
A stored collection of data treated as a unit.

hardcopy
Any non-electronic version of what is viewed on the computer screen, e.g. black-and-white or color print-outs, slides or photographic prints.

hard disk/floppy disk
A means for storing both computer programs and the data created with those programs (i.e., drawings, animations, novels, etc.). Both are record-like disks coated with magnetic material. Hard disks are faster, have a greater capacity and generally stay with the computer system, while floppy disks can be easily transported. The implication is that an artist's work is less vulnerable to copyright infringement if saved on a floppy disk over which the artist maintains control.

hardware
The physical components of a computer system.

jaggies
The saw-toothed, stair-stepped quality of a line produced by most computer programs.

image-processing
Manipulation of an image (usually video scanned), i.e., enhancement, colorizing or distortions.

input
Information or data entered into a computer's memory; the act of doing so; devices enabling the data to be entered.

menu
A list of functions of a particular program from which the operator chooses the specific action desired. In graphic program, it is usually displayed on the screen or on the graphic tablet.

output
Computer results, devices which accept and display these results.

pixel
Picture element, the individual dots on the display device, arranged in a grid, that comprise the image.

RAM/ROM
Random Access Memory/Read Only Memory - types of internal computer memory. RAM can hold changing data such as programs and the data created with the programs and is erased when the power is shut off. ROM cannot be changed by the user and holds various instructions used by the computer to do its work.

Raster system
A graphics system which draws shapes pixel by pixel.

resolution
The absolute number of pixels across and down on a display device. This determines the fineness of detail available, much as grain in a photograph.

RGB
Red-green-blue. The primary colors of light and, therefore, of video screens. Also describes a type of high quality monitor where the signal for each color is handled as a separate electronic signal.

software
Programs for the operation of the computer.

terminal
An input/output device that may look like a microcomputer, but does not do the computations. Many terminals may be connected to a single large computer.

time-sharing
Renting time on a computer that is at a different

location other than the terminal from which the work is being done, usually accomplished through telephone lines or a special data communication network.

vector system
A graphics system that draws shapes in line segments rather than pixel by pixel. Many high-resolution drawings or presentation programs operate on vector systems.

GRAPHIC DESIGN PRICES

AND TRADE CUSTOMS

Graphic design

Graphic designers are professionals who practice visual communications. As trained graphic artists, they use the elements of design and production (such as color, type, illustration, photography and printing techniques) to organize ideas visually in order to convey the appropriate visual impact and message. In addition to aesthetic judgment and project management skills, the professional graphic designer is experienced in evaluating and developing effective communication strategies which enhance the company's image, service or product.

Graphic design is effectively applied to all sorts of visual communications; not only to printed materials like magazines and books, but also to three-dimensional packaging and products, and to the identity systems and sales campaigns of business and industry through logos and collateral promotion (including annual reports, catalogs, brochures, press kits and direct mail packages).

To achieve the desired results, graphic designers generally work with or may hire other graphic designers, illustrators, production artists or photographers on a salaried or freelance basis. Almost all graphic designers buy *and* sell art.

Graphic designers who handle many different projects within a range of industries refer to themselves as general graphic designers. General graphic designers work for corporate clients, publishers, advertising agencies, retailers, manufacturers and entrepreneurs. Specialized areas of design are described on the following pages. Trade customs and practices for these areas have been noted. Otherwise, the standards noted under general design apply.

Graphic designers may be freelance, employed by a company as a staff designer or may be employed by a design firm. A small design firm has one to nine employees, a medium-sized firm has 10 to 49 employees and a large design firm has over 50 employees. The vast majority of design firms in the U.S. are small or medium-sized. Because the overhead expense and the level of experience of a design practice can vary considerably, graphic design is one of the most difficult areas for which to establish pricing guidelines.

Graphic designers and their clients

Graphic designers are often invited by clients to provide creative direction for a project and coordinate all the details of its production. As professional consultants, graphic designers can assess the feasibility of a project by incorporating their knowledge of the market and the resources available. Clients sometimes choose to develop projects and *then* bring in a designer. This is often inefficient since many decisions may have been made about which a designer should have been consulted, resulting in unnecessary delays, additional costs and inadequate design solutions. The sooner designers are called in to consult on a project, the easier it is for them to help steer the project to the best graphic solution.

Some of the factors that affect a client's decision to hire a designer include:

(1) *Talent/expertise:* The client's project(s) demand sufficient proficiency and/or talent to achieve the desired results. Talent, however, may be difficult to quantify, especially for corporate clients who must rely on measurable standards to conduct their business. Clients will often judge (and sometimes misjudge) design talent based on perceptions of the designer's appearance, ability to effectively communicate an understanding of the client's needs or the positive chemistry between them;

(2) *Capacity:* The scope and scale of the client's project(s) may dictate the size of the design firm commissioned to execute it, or whether it is technologically equipped to accommodate a client's special needs;

(3) *Location:* Proximity to the client, which may facilitate better communication or delivery of work.

A client may wish to choose a graphic designer with whom a long-term relationship can be established. This is particularly appropriate when a series of projects is planned needing design continuity. With such an ongoing relationship, a designer may be retained during the early stages of a project as a consultant to help plan, schedule and budget.

To better convey a company's philosophy, identity and goals, graphic designers use initial meetings to determine the client's targeted audience, desired response and the overall effect or feeling to be achieved. Responsible clients clearly communicate at the beginning of a project any limitations such as budget, deadlines and elements to be provided, like text, photographs or charts.

Based on initial discussions, designers will "walk through" a project step by step, calculating the time needed for every activity and multiplying that time by the appropriate rate(s). Or, if the situation warrants, the designer may evaluate a project's fee based on market conditions and/or the value the client expects to derive from the work. For example, a company desiring top talent to develop a new identity program may pay a substantially higher fee than if calculated according to time. Conversely, a designer may design a greeting card for a long-term client for substantially less than if billed hourly, as a client accommodation.

Whether based on estimated hourly billings or project fees, this design proposal estimating fees, expenses and schedules is generally presented to the client before work on a major project begins. The proposal reflects many of the following factors: (1) objectives and requirements of the project; (2) research; (3) art and/or copy that will be developed by the designer; (4) typography and other production services; (5) printing requirements; (6) intended use of the printed piece; and (7) schedule. Additionally, designers frequently prepare documents explaining subcontractor (such as illustrator or photographer) relationships, billing procedures and contract terms. For more information, please refer to the "Writing a proposal" section in the *Standard Contracts* chapter of this book.

It is customary for project descriptions and cost proposals to be submitted to clients as a complimentary service, although any fees and expenses incurred thereafter on a client's behalf and with the client's consent are billable. If the client accepts the proposal, the terms and conditions expressed in writing are signed by the client and the designer. When signed by both client and designer, a proposal is legally binding as a contract.

Once the agreement is signed, the designer begins researching the project and exploring design alternatives which will best achieve the client's goals. With one or more design concepts in mind, the designer may prepare a presentation that shows the general direction and format of the design. Depending on the needs of the client and the understanding between the client and the designer, the presentation may be "tight" or "loose." These preliminary renderings or "comps" represent concepts which show the layout of the piece and are presented to the client for approval. Once approved, the designer begins assembling the elements and

services necessary to carry out the project within the client's budget.

The designer makes key decisions on size, length, color, visuals (e.g. illustration or photography), paper, printing methods and the specific "look" of the piece or package. Any alterations or additions at this point are relatively easy and inexpensive to execute. This is the last step before the designer commissions illustration or other work and begins to produce the finished art which will be used by the printer or other production source. It is important to note that changes that come after approval of the layouts are considered author's alterations (AA's), and are billable. AA's can be expensive to the client and increase the difficulty of completing the project within the time scheduled.

Since many clients commissioning designers don't buy art on a regular basis, the designer negotiates with individual artists on the client's behalf within the scope of the client's approved art budget. Designers often assume the responsibility to educate the client on the intent, content and ethics of trade customs and copyright law.

The agreement

Since graphic designers work with so vast an array of graphic resources, it is important that all conditions and expectations be spelled out before the work begins. The following points should be considered:

Payment: For larger projects, the standard schedule for payment is one-third upon agreement, one-third upon approval of design comprehensives, and one-third within thirty days of delivery of mechanicals or printed pieces.

Rights: Most contracts include a section specifying how, when, where and the duration for which the design will be used. The extent of use determines which rights of copyright the client needs and may be a factor in establishing appropriate fees. Graphic designers are entitled to credit and copyright, unless another arrangement is negotiated. Often, designers contract freelance illustrators, designers and photographers on a limited-use basis for specific projects. Unless specified in writing, it is assumed the individual creator owns the copyrights in the work, not the client. It is not uncommon therefore, for copyrights to be held by several different contributors to a project, who may all deserve the same acknowledgement and rights on the piece or package of pieces.

In addition to copyright concerns, the

terms and conditions are clearly outlined in writing and are generally reviewed prior to the first commission. These standard customs are contained in the contract, letter of agreement or confirmation of engagement form (see the *Standard Contracts* chapter).

Expenses: In addition to the designer's fee, expenses reimbursed by the client typically include subcontractors' fees, typesetting, supplies, photostats, travel, long-distance phone calls, overnight couriers and messenger services. The markup for these typically range from 15 to 20 per cent, with the standard based on the advertising agency markup of 17.65 per cent, accepted by many design firms. The markup reimburses the designer for supervisory and handling time and ensures that all work is done to the designer's specifications and standards for quality. Reimbursable expenses are billed monthly, upon completion of project phases or upon completion of the project.

Consultation fees: When a graphic designer is called in by a client to advise on a project or design decision, a consultation fee is charged according to an hourly rate. Consultation fees normally range from $75 to $200 per hour.

Trade practices

The following trade practices are accepted as standard:

1. The intended use of the design must be clearly stated in a contract, purchase order or letter of agreement stating the price and terms of sale.

2. If a design is to be used for other than its original purpose, the price should be negotiated as soon as possible. Since the secondary use may be of greater value than the primary use, there is no formula for reuse fees.

3. Designers should negotiate reuse arrangements with the original commissioning party with speed, efficiency and all due respect to the client's needs.

4. Return of original artwork, mechanicals or computer disks to the designer is automatic unless otherwise negotiated.

5. Fees for rush work will be higher than the figures listed here. Rush deadlines may increase the original fee by an additional 50 to 100 per cent.

6. A cancellation fee should always be agreed upon in the event a job is cancelled through no fault of the designer. Depending upon the stage at which the job is terminated, the fee paid should reflect all work completed or hours spent.

7. A rejection fee should be agreed upon if the assignment is terminated because the preliminary or finished work is found not to be reasonably satisfactory. The rejection fee should be equal to the number of hours spent, depending on the reason for rejection.

8. Work done on speculation does not conform to industry trade practices and is contrary to the Joint Ethics Committee's Code of Fair Practice, because of its exploitive nature.

9. The Graphic Artists Guild is unalterably opposed to the use of work-for-hire contracts, in which authorship and all rights that go with it are transferred to the commissioning party and the independent designer is treated as an employee for copyright purposes only. The independent designer receives no employee benefits and loses the right to claim authorship or profit from future use of the work forever. Additional information on work for hire can be found on page 15.

Note: Corporate logo designs are ineligible as "work for hire," but "all-rights" transfers to the client are common.

10. No new or additional designer or firm should be hired after a commission begins without the original designer's knowledge and consent. The original designer may then choose to resign the account or agree to collaborate with the new design firm.

All prices for design in the *Guidelines* are based on a nationwide survey that was reviewed by a special committee of experienced professionals through the Graphic Artists Guild. These figures, reflecting the responses of established professionals, are meant as a point of reference only and do not necessarily reflect such important factors as deadlines, job complexity, reputation and experience of a particular designer, research, technique or unique quality of expression and extraordinary or extensive use of the finished design. Please refer to related material in other chapters of this book, especially under *Business & Legal Practices for Commissioned Artwork* and *Standard Contracts.*

Comparative average billable hourly rates

	Per hour	*Overtime*
Principal	$125	$250
Project designer	100	150
Junior designer	75	110
Production	50	75

Corporate graphic design

*C*orporate graphic designers specialize in the design of corporate communications and identity programs, signage, internal and promotional publications and/or annual reports.

These designers often work in an office that may include a principal of the firm, a production manager, a copywriter, and possibly an account executive. The nature of projects that corporate design offices are commissioned to handle often involve long-term research and development. Many corporate design offices work on a retainer basis, acting as design consultants in peripheral areas besides their main projects. Consequently, corporate designers are often brought in at the early stages of a project and may be integrally involved in directing that project to fruition.

Project proposals

The project begins once a client accepts the design proposal outlining the scope of the project, its budget, schedule and the terms under which it will be executed. Most design projects are typically quoted and billed by phase, with an initiating fee representing 10-30 per cent of total estimated fees and reimbursable expenses.

Phase 1, programming: This phase is concerned with gathering information and establishing design criteria, and often requires spending a great deal of time with the client to define the needs and problems that are to be solved.

Phase 2, concept development: After the designer and client have reached an agreement concerning the basic program, visual solutions are pursued that solve the stated problems. Much of this phase results in a presentation showing *only* those ideas that the design team feels are viable, appropriate and meet the prescribed criteria.

Phase 3, design development: At this stage, the design team refines the accepted design, which may include the grid, selected typefaces and other elements, and the assignment of illustration and/or photography. A final presentation may be made explaining the applications. Once the client and designer have chosen a definite direction, any changes in budget and/or schedules are agreed upon.

Phase 4, design implementation: Decisions on all related art direction including commissioned illustrations and photography;

typography; copywriting; mechanicals and all other elements are final at this point. Any changes made by the client after this point are billable as "author's alterations" (AA's), although designer errors or printer errors (PE's), are not.

Phase 5, production: Depending on the end product(s) a design firm has been commissioned to produce, this phase may be a matter of going on press and/or supervising the fabrication or manufacturing of products. Supervision is the key to this phase since so much depends on the precision and quality achieved in this final step. After the end product is approved, the project is considered billable. The client can make changes to the mechanical and on press only through the designer. Conversely, the designer can only execute any design alterations on both the mechanicals and on press only with the client's final approval.

Billing

Billing expenses and fees may be handled in a number of ways. During the first phase, the studio may arrange to bill on an hourly or project basis. If clients prefer to be billed on an project basis, they will usually establish an acceptable "cap" on the total amount billed. (See the chapter on *Business Management* for establishing hourly rate formulas).

Expenses are always estimated and billed with handling charges or markups included, except for costs incurred for client-approved travel. Sales tax and freight are never included in estimates and are normally billed periodically or at the end of the project along with client alterations (AA's), which are billed at a predetermined senior designer's or principal's hourly rate.

The printing or manufacturing part of the project may be billed by the studio or directly to the client. This depends on the practice of the studio principals. The printer and all other professionals working with the designer are accountable to the designer and are ethically bound to follow the designer's direction while working on the project, regardless to whom the invoice is sent. This, of course, becomes a matter of practicality since the designer is orchestrating many elements and must control them all to ensure consistency.

Corporate identity

The objective of a properly executed *corporate identity* program is the accurate visual presen-tation of an organization's unique personality. Although the client's initial focus may be on the development of a new graphic mark or logo, a complex procedure that involves several phases and a wide range of expertise is required in order to furnish a professional level of service.

A contract, often in the form of a design proposal, outlines the services that will be performed. The client may cancel the project upon completion of any phase of work agreed to and must pay for all work completed and expenses incurred by the design firm.

A typical, three-phase program would include the following:

Phase 1, orientation: This phase of the program is concerned with gathering information and establishing design image criteria. A significant sampling of visual materials is collected and evaluated. Interviews are conducted with the various and relevant audiences. Communication objectives, a plan of action and a nomenclature system are established.

Phase 2, design development: In this creative phase, design ideas for the logo or other primary identification device are developed. Applications to stationery and signage must also be designed in order to demonstrate the specific advantages of each design. Recommendations are also made regarding color schemes and secondary typography. The design selection process should be made according to the approved image criteria, not individual taste or subjective preference.

Phase 3, implementation: This phase of the program is unquestionably the most important. Sufficient application formats must be developed in order to visually demonstrate the nature of the corporate identification system. Guidelines, usually in the form of a graphics standards manual, establish the management-endorsed design policy and implementation procedures. Rules governing proper usage of the program's design elements and formats are presented, which include reproduction materials for graphics and colors.

Finally, organizations that have made the most effective use of Corporate Identity have either contracted for a long-term consulting agreement with a qualified design firm, established a properly administered in-house communications department, or both.

The pricing ranges listed below do not constitute specific prices for particular jobs. They are guidelines to be considered along with other factors specific to the commissioned work under consideration. Please refer to related material in other sections of this book.

Comparative fees for comprehensive corporate identity design projects*

$100 million+ corporation	$250,000
$50 - 100 million corporation	125,000
$10 - 50 million corporation	75,000
Small corporation	30,000

*Based on services that include research, consultation and a comprehensive design audit; design of an integrated identity system including links to divisions and affiliates; presentation of three to six schematic applications; final applications to stationery and other corporate formats; implementation guidelines (standards manual) and client consultation. Production of mechanicals and all reimbursable/out-of-pocket expenses incurred to produce sketches, comps and mechanicals are billed separately.

Comparative fees for corporate logo design projects*

$100 million+ corporation	$100,000
$50 million corporation	50,000
Small corporation	12,000

*Based on research, original concepts and design of primary logo identity; presentation of three to six schematic applications; final application to stationery; implementation guidelines and client consultation. Production of mechanicals and all reimbursable/out-of-pocket expenses incurred to produce sketches, comps and mechanicals are billed separately.

Comparative design for restaurant identity*

Major franchise	$100,000
Regional chain	50,000
Independent restaurant	10,000 - 25,000

*Based on research, design and presentation of up to three logo concepts showing format and comprehensive layout; application to signage, stationery and forms, menus, placemats, napkins, matches and tent cards. Production of mechanicals and all reimbursable/out-of-pocket expenses incurred to produce sketches, comps and mechanicals are billed separately.

Comparative design project for stationery system using existing logo*

Large company	$12,000
Small company	5,000
Personal	1,600

*Based on research and redesign of letterhead, envelope and card only; presentation of up to three comprehensive layouts showing format. Production of mechanicals and all reimbursable/out-of-pocket expenses incurred to produce sketches, comps and mechanicals are billed separately.

Comparative rates for corporate annual reports*

Large company (Fortune 500 companies)	$150,000+
Medium company (100 million + in sales)	$50,000
Small company (up to 20 million in sales)	25,000

*Based on research and design of 8 pages of financial and 24 pages of text; presentation of up to three layouts showing format and comprehensive layout; supervision of photography or illustration. Production of mechanicals and all reimbursable/out-of-pocket expenses incurred to produce sketches, comps and mechanicals are billed separately.

Comparative creative fees for corporate newsletter prototype design*

Large company (Fortune 500 companies)	$25,000 - 30,000
Medium company ($100 million +)	20,000
Small company (up to $20 million in sales)	15,000

*Based on research and design of twelve-page newsletter, including presentation of up to three layouts showing format and comprehensive layout and final layout, implementation and client consultation, supervision of photography, illustration or printing and corrections. Some adjustments in fees will occur among 2-color and 3-color graphic designs, full-color spot design, and full-color bleed art. Production of mechanicals and all reimbursable/out-of-pocket expenses incurred to produce sketches, comps and mechanicals are billed separately. *Design and production of subsequent issues are negotiated separately.*

Chart and map design

C hart and map designers, like other designers, use design skills to visually solve a client's specific problems. But to execute those solutions, they rely upon the pictorial abilities of illustrators. The chart or map designer is frequently works from raw data provided by the client's research, and is seldom required to provide that research themselves.

There is a difference between the term "map design" and the traditional task of cartography. Map design generally consists of the editing, combining and restyling of data from pre-existing maps. Cartography includes these tasks, but also requires independent confirmation and correction of data on existing maps and raw data. Both map design and cartography require an understanding of projections (reproductions of spatial objects like the earth upon flat or curved surfaces) and their significant implications, but more so for cartographers. Map designers often begin with a projection provided by the client.

Chart design ranges from the whimsical and highly illustrative to the scientific and highly technical. On the editorial end, the map or chart designer is treated much like a traditional illustrator. The designer is asked to provide artwork to fit a prescribed space, and prices for such work are comparable to pricing for illustration in similar markets. Larger works of map and chart design usually command higher fees than traditional illustration because they can be highly complex, requiring considerable detail and accuracy.

Other uses include advertising and collateral, corporate literature and technical publications. Often, the designer is treated as an integral part of the project by the project directors and art directors working on it. This involvement can include page layout, determination of style, size, content, color and even the printing method. Prices generally increase with the designer's involvement. In these circumstances, it is generally recognized that map and chart design is not illustration per se, and projects are therefore priced on a fee plus expenses basis. Expenses include everything required, from messengers and miscellaneous art supplies to typography and Linotronic paper or film output.

The map or chart designer's responsibilities usually include provision of a tight sketch in color and all typography in position; a revision, if necessary; and finished artwork. This finished artwork can be in almost any form, including full-color artwork for separation, mechanical artwork, disk, film provided by a computer program and Linotronic output, traditional illustration, or any combination.

The price ranges listed below do not constitute specific prices for particular jobs. They are guidelines to be considered along with other factors specific to the commissioned work under consideration. Please refer to related material in other sections of this book.

Comparative fees for map and chart design
(ranges represent simple to complex projects)

	Spread	Full page	Half-page	Quarter-page
Corporate/advertising	$2,500 - 5,000	$1,700 - 3,500	$1,000 - 1,500	$800 - 1,200
Corporate in-house	1,500 - 3,500	1,200 - 2,000	700 - 1,200	600 - 750
Editorial	1,500 - 2,500	1,000 - 1,500	500 - 800	250 - 500

Environmental graphic design

Environmental graphic designers plan, design and specify sign systems (signage) and other forms of visual communication in the built and natural environment.

These designers come predominantly from the fields of graphic design, architecture, interior design and landscape design. They work closely with architects, real estate developers and individual clients on projects that vary widely in scale and size. Consequently, environmental graphic designers have extensive knowledge of building design and construction and their practice conforms to standards established by the Construction Specifications Institute (CSI), the American Institute of Architects (AIA), and the Society of Environmental Graphic Designers (SEGD).

Environmental graphic designers often work in a firm that may include a principal of the firm, a project designer and assistant designers. Projects that environmental design offices are commissioned to handle often involve long-term research and development. Many environmental graphic design offices work on a retainer basis, acting as design consultants in peripheral areas besides their main projects. Consequently, environmental designers are often brought in at the early stages of a project and may be integrally involved in directing that project through fruition.

Project proposals

The project begins once a client accepts the design proposal outlining the scope of the project, its budget, schedule and the terms under which it will be executed. Most environmental graphic design projects are typically quoted and billed by phase, with an initiating fee representing 10-20 per cent of total fees and reimbursable expenses.

Phase 1, programming: This phase is concerned with gathering information and establishing design criteria, and often requires spending a great deal of time with the client to define the needs and problems that are to be solved.

Phase 2, schematic design: After the designer and client have reached an agreement concerning the basic program, visual solutions are pursued that solve the stated problems. Much of this phase is concept development, which results in a presentation showing *only* those ideas that the design team feels are viable, appropriate and meet the prescribed criteria.

Phase 3, design development: At this stage, the design team refines the accepted design and a final presentation is offered explaining the applications. Once the client and designer have chosen a definite direction, any changes in budget and/or schedules are also agreed upon.

Phase 4, contract documentation: Decisions are final at this point. The project is fully documented for implementation; which includes preparing working drawings, specifications, and reproducible artwork where appropriate. Any changes made by the client after this point become billable as "author's alterations" (AA's), although designer errors are not.

Phase 5, production: Depending on the end product(s) a studio has been commissioned to produce, this phase may mean supervising the manufacturing of products. Supervision is the key to this phase since so much depends on the precision and quality achieved in this final step. After the end product is approved, the project is considered billable. The designer normally retains the right to execute any design alterations, corrections and fabrication.

Billing

Billing expenses and fees may be handled in a number of ways. The designer arranges to bill on an hourly or project basis during the first phase. If clients prefer to be billed on an project basis, the client will usually establish an acceptable "cap" on the total amount billed. (See the chapter on *Business Management* for establishing hourly rate formulas).

Expenses are always estimated and billed with handling charges or markups included, except for costs incurred for client-approved travel. Sales tax and freight are never included in estimates and are normally billed periodically or at the end of the project along with client alterations, which are billed at a predetermined studio or principal's hourly rate currently ranging between $75 and $250.

Depending on the practice of the studio principals, the printing or manufacturing part of the project may be billed directly to the client. The fabricator and all other professionals working with the designer are accountable to the designer and are ethically bound to follow the designer's direction while working on the project, regardless of who is invoiced. This, of course, becomes a matter of practicality since the designer is orchestrating many elements and must control them all to ensure consistency.

The pricing ranges listed below do not constitute specific prices for particular jobs. They are guidelines to be considered along with other factors specific to the commissioned work under consideration. Please refer to related material in other sections of this book.

Comparative fees for commercial building signage and graphics*

Large project	$75,000
Small project	20,000

*Based on research and design of *exterior and interior* signage system, excluding tenant signage; presentation of up to three rough tissue layouts showing format and comprehensive layout; final art and design. Production of mechanicals and all reimbursable/out-of-pocket expenses incurred to produce sketches, comps and mechanicals are billed separately.

Comparative fees for internal signage system*

Large hotel	$50,000
Small hotel	20,000

*Based on research and design of *interior* signage system, including directories, service and back-of-house areas, dining, ballroom and banquet areas; presentation of up to three rough tissue layouts showing format and comprehensive layout; final art and design. Production of mechanicals and all reimbursable/out-of-pocket expenses incurred to produce sketches, comps and mechanicals are billed separately.

Comparative fees for exterior supergraphic*

Large client	$20,000
Small client	12,000

*Based on research and design for thirteen-story midtown building, 150 feet wide including creation of image and placement of logo; presentation of up to three rough tissue layouts showing format and comprehensive layout; final art and design. Supervision of execution and billable expenses are billed separately.

Comparative fees for exhibit design*

Large project for large company	$70,000
Small project for small company	12,500

*Based on research and consultation of exhibit covering 2,500 square feet, including all structural forms and organization of illustrative, photographic and editorial material; presentation of up to three rough tissue layouts showing format and comprehensive layout; final art and design. Supervision of execution and billable expenses are billed separately.

Advertising and promotion design

A dvertising designers must have a sophisticated knowledge of marketing, sales and advertising print production, as well as design expertise. Because these designers have expertise in a variety of disciplines, they can successfully coordinate a company's identity and its marketing. Consequently, more and more of these designers are being asked by clients to replace advertising agencies. In these cases, the designers often apply for agency status to be able to place advertising with magazines and newspapers in order to capture all or some part of media conditions.

When a client signs on with an advertising agency, the fees the agency charges the client usually bears a relationship to the total advertising budget, historically a 15-20 per cent commission for creative and media placement, with 17.65 per cent the accepted standard for advertising agencies. In today's marketplace, this fee is usually negotiated even by large agencies.

Several agencies pitch the client (i.e., the account), presenting ideas for their upcoming advertising campaigns on speculation. The investment and risk are accepted by the agencies since the agency that wins the account stands to generate revenue commensurate with the risks involved. This is contrary to the practice of general graphic designers, who consider work on speculation to be unethical because of its exploitative nature.

In an agreement with an advertising agency, the client is committing to work with the agency for at least the length of the entire advertising campaign, which is a long-term rather than project-based relationship. The fees of most graphic design firms, however, are normally based on hourly or per project estimates, not calendar projections.

The investment clients make in advertising is often sizeable. Risks must be calculated because of the value of advertising relative to the sales it produces. This puts limits on the creative input that designers might have, sometimes to the *detriment* of the client. The designer's role is to work as part of a team comprised of a copywriter, possibly an account executive and/or public relations professional. The proposal given to the client should present a strategy as well as a design solution.

When a design firm or individual designer is hired instead of an agency, one of many arrangements may be agreed upon. For example, the designer may handle only the creative work but not the placement; in these cases a starting point in negotiations might be to charge 10 per cent of the total advertising budget for the duration of the campaign. The designer may also negotiate to be hired on a retainer basis. Or the designer may be hired to create only a single ad and negotiate a price based on the type of placement (i.e., a full color, full page advertisement in *Rolling Stone* magazine would command a higher fee than a small black and white ad in a limited run trade publication). See the chapter on *How Artwork is Priced* for further discussion on "Page rate pricing."

This method of pricing differs from other methods since it relates less to the amount of time the ad would take to design than to the client's investment in placing the ad.

Graphic designers who specialize in advertising and promotion design often handle posters, billboard and press kits besides the design and placement of magazine and newspaper advertising. Since they hire other graphic artists on a freelance basis and purchase art and photography on behalf of their clients, they must have a good working knowledge of advertising illustration and photography, including the trade customs that govern both.

The price ranges below assume limited use of the advertising design up to five insertions within a specified media for one year. Unlimited usage within the same media will increase the fees by 40 per cent. Unlimited use in any media will increase the fees by 75 per cent. A complete transfer of copyrights will increase fees by 90 per cent. Please note the price ranges listed below do not constitute specific prices for particular jobs. They are guidelines to be considered along with other factors specific to the commissioned work under consideration. Please refer to related material in other sections of this book.

Comparative fees for print advertising design*

National campaign	$10,500
Regional campaign	7,500
Local campaign	4,000

*Based on concept and design of an advertisement of at least 3 different sizes and shapes; maximum of three layouts plus final comp layout for each unit using the elements of photography or illustration, headline, subhead, body copy and company logo or sign off. Production of mechanicals and all reimbursable/out-of-pocket expenses incurred to produce sketches, comps and mechanicals are billed separately.

Comparative fees for magazine advertising design*

	Cover	Spread	Full page	Half page	Quarter page
National consumer	$3,500	$3,000	$1,750	$1,000	$750
Regional consumer	3,000	2,750	1,500	1,000	750
Trade publication	2,750	2,000	1,250	1,000	750
Specialized audience	2,500	1,750	1,000	750	750
In-house magazine	2,000	1,250	750	750	750

*Based on concept and design of up to 3 layouts and final comprehensive layout using the elements of photography or illustration, headline, subhead, body copy and company logo or sign off. Production of mechanicals and all reimbursable/out-of-pocket expenses incurred to produce sketches, comps and mechanicals are billed separately.

Comparative fees for newspaper advertising design*

	Supplement or insert	Full page	Half page	Less than half page
National advertising campaign	$2,700	$2,300	$1,500	$800
Regional advertising campaign	2,300	1,700	1,000	500
Weekly newspaper	1,700	1,300	800	500

*Based on concept and design of up to 3 layouts and final comprehensive layout using the elements of photography or illustration, headline, subhead, body copy and company logo or sign off. Production of mechanicals and all reimbursable/out-of-pocket expenses incurred to produce sketches, comps and mechanicals are billed separately.

Comparative fees for television advertising design*

National advertising campaign	$14,000
Regional advertising campaign	9,000
Local advertising campaign	6,000

*Based on the development of a 30 second spot including several approaches, finished storyboards and client consultation. Production of mechanicals and all reimbursable/out-of-pocket expenses incurred to produce sketches, comps and mechanicals are billed separately.

Comparative fees for outdoor advertising*

Billboards

Large company	$5,000
Small company	3,000

Public transportation

Large company	$4,500
Small company	2,000

*Based on concept and design of up to three rough tissue layouts and final comp; client consultation. Production of mechanicals and all reimbursable/out-of-pocket expenses incurred to produce sketches, comps and mechanicals are billed separately.

Comparative fees for political campaigns*

National campaign	$25,000
Regional campaign	15,000
Local campaign	9,500

*Based on creation of a complete marketing program to apply logo design and concept to a number of items including; posters, bumper stickers, direct mail packages, buttons, banners, outdoor advertising and brochures. Production of mechanicals and all reimbursable/out-of-pocket expenses incurred to produce sketches, comps and mechanicals are billed separately.

Comparative fees for package design*

	General consumer market	Specialized consumer market
Food	$25,000	$10,000
Consumer goods	10,000	6,000

*Based on concept and design including rough tissue layouts; finished comp layout; supervision of photography or illustration. Production of mechanicals and all reimbursable/out-of-pocket expenses incurred to produce sketches, comps and mechanicals are billed separately.

Comparative fees for shopping bag design*

	Two color	Three color
Large company or extensive use	$3,000	$4,000
Small company or limited use	1,600	2,200

*Based on concept and design including rough tissue layouts and comprehensive layouts. Production of mechanicals and all reimbursable/out-of-pocket expenses incurred to produce sketches, comps and mechanicals are billed separately.

Comparative fees for recording artist tour campaign*

World tour	$15,000
National tour	10,000

*Based on concept and design of a consistent visual look to include album cover(s), point of purchase displays, merchandising material (souvenir books, T-shirts, tour jackets, and/or posters). Production of mechanicals and all reimbursable/out-of-pocket expenses incurred to produce sketches, comps and mechanicals are billed separately.

Comparative fees for album design*

Major label	$6,500
Other	3,700

*Based on concept and design of compact disc (CD), LP and/or audiocassette including up to 3 rough tissue layouts; one finished comp layout; supervision of photography or illustration. Production of mechanicals and all reimbursable/out-of-pocket expenses incurred to produce sketches, comps and mechanicals are billed separately.

Collateral advertising design

Graphic designers who specialize in collateral material handle the design of catalogs, packaging, brochures, press kits and direct mail packages.

While clients generally retain advertising agencies to handle major campaigns for products and/or services, clients will often commission or retain a design firm to furnish their collateral material.

Like advertising designers whose work is targeted to elicit a specific response, collateral designers must have a sophisticated awareness of advertising, marketing and sales.

These designers are often supplied with art and photography by the client, so it is important to know the rights that are transferred with those visuals. If additional rights must be purchased, they should be negotiated *before* the design or production stage. It is standard for designers to sell specific uses to the client, for example, first time print runs.

The price ranges listed below do not constitute specific prices for particular jobs. They are guidelines to be considered along with other factors specific to the commissioned work under consideration. Please refer to related material in other sections of this book.

Comparative fees for collateral and direct response design*

Product and service catalog

Four color, 8 pages	$9,000 - $12,000
One color, 8 pages	4,500 - 6,000

Brochures

Four color, 12 pages	6,000 - 9,600
One color, 12 pages	3,600 - 6,000

*Price ranges are largely dependent on size of company, complexity of design, number of images (photographic or illustrative) per page, copy length, audience, etc. Fees reflect research and consultation; presentation of up to 3 rough tissue layouts showing format and final comprehensive layout. Production of mechanicals and all reimbursable/out-of-pocket expenses incurred to produce sketches, comps and mechanicals are billed separately.

Comparative fees for direct mail package design*

Two color	$5,000 - 15,000
Four color	7,500 - 20,000

*Creative fees are largely dependent on size of company, complexity of design, number of images (photographic or illustrative), copy length , audience, etc. Fees reflect design of a basic package including envelope, personalized letter, brochure, reply card and return envelope; research and consultation; presentation of up to 3 rough tissue layouts showing format and final comprehensive layout. Production of mechanicals and all reimbursable/out-of-pocket expenses incurred to produce sketches, comps and mechanicals are billed separately.

Comparative fees for press kit or media kit design*

Two color	$5,000 - 15,000
Four color	7,500 - 20,000

*Creative fees are largely dependent on size of company, complexity of design, number of images (photographic or illustrative), copy length, audience, etc. Fees reflect design of a basic kit including cover or folder. Letterhead for text and formatting for other insert material; research and consultation; presentation of up to 3 rough tissue layouts showing format and final comprehensive layout. Production of mechanicals and all reimbursable/out-of-pocket expenses incurred to produce sketches, comps and mechanicals are billed separately.

Display and novelty design

Display and novelty design is often handled by graphic designers, surface designers and illustrators, although some artists specialize in this field. Display and novelty design includes posters, greeting cards, gift or boutique-type items, holiday decorations, eyeglass covers and similar items.

Since manufacturing materials, resources and requirements for production of these items often limit the type of display and design, research into those factors can be an important part of an assignment of this type. The resourcefulness of artists in combining these limits with creative design is often the key to a successfully marketed display or novelty item.

Some specialists in this field will often develop their own self-initiated designs and attempt to license their work to manufacturers and receive royalties on gross sales ranging between 5 and 10 per cent. For commissioned work, flat fees are commonly negotiated considering the client, the intended use and other market conditions. For additional information, please reference the "Greeting card design" section in the chapter on *Illustration Prices and Trade Customs.*

The price ranges listed below do not constitute specific prices for particular jobs. They are guidelines to be considered along with other factors specific to the commissioned work under consideration. Please refer to related material in other sections of this book.

Comparative fees for point-of-purchase display material design*

	Extensive use	Limited use
Counter cards	$2,000	$1,500
Counter display	1,500	1,000
Posters	2,700	1,800
Banners	1,000	750

*Based on design and concept including rough tissue layouts and a final comprehensive layout. Production of mechanicals and all reimbursable/out-of-pocket expenses incurred to produce sketches, comps and mechanicals are billed separately.

Publication design

Publication designers create the formats and "look" of magazines or tabloids. These publications have an editorial point of view and often contain advertising.

While most publication design is done on staff within a parent company, there are freelance publication designers. There are also independent offices that produce magazines and/or tabloids on a periodic basis, but they are not the norm in this field.

For staff design information, please refer to the chapter on *Salaried Prices and Trade Customs*.

A publication designer may, on a freelance basis, design the format for a magazine or tabloid, and be retained as a consultant for periodic oversight of the publication. In this case, the role filled by the publication designer is called art director. An art director may work with one or more associate art directors, assistant art directors, and/or designers and production artists.

At the planning stages for each issue of the publication, the key editorial staff (most often the editor-in-chief, section editors and key writers for the issue) meet with the art director and appropriate staff to hold a story and cover conference. During this session, the strategy for several issues is mapped out, with major focus on the current issue. A direction is established and concepts may be determined at this time. From this point on, the art director commissions art for the issues within the yearly budget constraints. However, editors of a publication have approval over dummies and storyboards, since they are accepted as the authority for the publication. In all instances the publisher has final approval over the package.

Freelance artists who are commissioned to work on publications are often expected to sell on an all-rights or work-for-hire basis. These types of contracts limit the pool of talent available to publications, since work-for-hire and all-rights are unacceptable terms for many artists.

Frequently, freelance or independent designers are commissioned to redesign an existing magazine and continue on as consultants, either on retainer or fee based on an estimated number of hours per issue.

Since logos are the anchors of most magazines, logos are the anchor of most magazine design work. Consequently, fees for magazine design are front-loaded towards the logo. Designers are never called upon to design or redesign a "spread" of a magazine all by itself. If no logo design is required (i.e., an existing magazine wishes a new design without changing its logo), then the design fee would be weighted toward cover rather than logo design.

Standard procedure is to bill the design and development fee in segments, no matter what the size or cost of the job. A typical arrangement for a larger project is to bill one-third of the fee at the beginning, one-third at midpoint, and one-third at the conclusion. For a smaller project the arrangement might simply be one-half at the outset and the balance upon submission of finished layouts. Billable expenses and production charges are billed regularly, usually weekly or monthly, in order to minimize the designer's outlay.

Possible fees for editorial design vary as widely as the magazines themselves. Some of the factors affecting price are: the size (number of pages) of the magazine; the numerical and geographical circulation of the magazine; its production values and capacity (black and white vs. color, printing methods, etc.); whether the publisher is an individual, corporation, low-end or high-end; the size and stature of the designer or design firm; the urgency of the schedule; and others. The complexity of the work involved is *always* an element. The lower end of a fee range is appropriate for a redesign that only requires the designer to demonstrate one or two covers and a few inside pages. A higher fee will be in order if the client requires a full-blown dummy issue in order to demonstrate every possible variation that might occur in an issue of the magazine.

With such factors in mind, the fee for designing (based on concept and design; rough tissue layouts and comprehensive layouts; and client consultation) a small-circulation, black-and-white magazine might range from $3,000 to $15,000. Production of mechanicals and all reimbursable/out-of-pocket expenses incurred to produce sketches, comps and mechanicals are billed separately.

The lower fee could apply to an freelance designer working out of his or her home to modernize a modest local publication. The higher fee might be charged by a prestigious national design firm working on a very sophisticated but limited-circulation publication.

Similarly, the possible fee for a national, four-color magazine will vary from about $15,000 to as much as $75,000. Again, the lower figure could cover one designer freelancing for an inexpensive, celebrities-on-newsprint magazine; the higher fee might apply to a glossy, mass-circulation publication like *Time* or *McCall's* being redesigned by a large national design firm.

These price ranges do not constitute specific prices for particular jobs. They are guidelines to be considered along with other factors specific to the commissioned work under consideration. Please refer to related material in other sections of this book.

Comparative fees for editorial magazine design*

Small circulation, black and white	$3,000 - $15,000
Large circulation, Four color	15,000 - 75,000

*Ranges depend upon complexity, number of pages, circulation, production values, the client, the designer and the urgency of the schedule. Low ranges may reflect a redesign demonstrating one or two covers and a few inside pages. High ranges may reflect a new design requiring a full-blown dummy of the magazine. Production of mechanicals and all reimbursable/out-of-pocket expenses incurred to produce sketches, comps and mechanicals are billed separately.

Book jacket design

ook jacket designers are graphic artists who create the look of the jacket or cover of a book, or series of books using the graphic elements of typography, illustration, photography and/or designed letterforms.

After terms and fees are agreed upon by the publishing house's art director and the designer, one comprehensive (comp) is prepared for presentation. If additional comps are required, it is customary for an additional fee to be paid. Once the comp is approved, the designer proceeds to execute or commission illustration, lettering, or other graphic elements used in the finished art.

Generally, the comp is as close as possible in appearance to the finished piece. Such tight comps often entail expenses for typesetting, photostats, or color keys to achieve a finished look. All out-of-pocket expenses in the sketch and finished stages are billable to the client.

Because of the nature of publishing, there is a high rate of rejection on comp presentations. This is accepted as a risk by designer and publisher. A rejection fee reflecting the amount of work completed at the time of termination of the project is always paid, and any incurred expenses are additional.

Copyright and credit for the designer should be agreed upon before work begins. If other creative elements (e.g., illustration or lettering) appear on the cover, they should be credited as well. If the publisher is preparing the flaps of the jacket or the back cover where the copyright will appear, all credit should be noted on the mechanical but outside of the reproduction area. When the rest of the jacket or cover is set in type, the credit will naturally be added; otherwise, it is easily overlooked. In any event, when confirming a job and on the invoice, book jacket designers should specify that artwork is prepared only for the named edition and title.

Designers usually sell one-time reproduction rights. The designer should receive additional payment for use of the art by other domestic or foreign publishers and book clubs, by film or television, or other sources of media.

Production costs such as (but not necessarily limited to) photographic processing, type, mechanically reproduced lettering, and photostats should be billed by the designer over and above the design fee, or such costs can be directly assumed by the client.

It is customary for a 15 to 25 per cent handling fee (markup) be applied to expenses incurred (type, photostats, etc.) by the designer for a jacket design, when the publisher does not pick up these costs directly.

Additional rights for use of the finished art by the original client are usually limited to advertising and promotion of the original book in the edition initially contemplated. If any other rights are covered, a statement of those rights should appear on the designer's bill. Any bill should also state that all other rights are reserved by the designer and that original art should be returned to the designer.

Comparative fees for hardcover book jacket design concepts*

	One concept	Additional concepts (per sketch)	Concept followed by voluntary termination (% of fee)
Mass market	$1,500	$700	50%
Major trade	1,200	550	50%
Minor trade	750	350	50%
Textbook	1,200	550	50%
Young adult	800	400	50%

*Based on design and presentation of finished front cover and spine. Some adjustments in fees will occur among 2-color and 3-color graphic designs, full color spot design, and full color bleed art. *Fees for wraparound book jackets will range from 50% to 75% more than the basic design fees above.*

Comparative fees for paperback cover design*

	One concept	Additional concepts (per sketch)	Concept followed by voluntary termination (% of fee)
Mass market	$1,600	$800	50%
Major trade	1,300	650	50%
Minor trade	800	400	50%
Textbook	900	450	50%
Young adult	800	400	50%

*Based on design and presentation of finished front cover and spine. Some adjustments in fees will occur among 2-color and 3-color graphic designs, full color spot design, and full-color bleed art. *Fees for wraparound book covers will range from 50% to 75% more than the basic design fees above.*

Book design

Book designers are graphic artists who develop the style and visual flow of a book by using the graphic elements of typography, illustration and photography. The functions of book designers range from highly creative to purely mechanical.

The basic design fee

A basic fee includes an initial consultation with the publisher to discuss the project, analysis of manuscript or representative sample pages, cast off, preparation of tissue layouts and composition order (detailed type specifications), manuscript mark-up, and presentation of completed design. When sample pages are to be set, the basic fee includes "specing" (writing design specifications or codes on) the sample manuscript and a review of sample pages after they have been set.

If a publisher requests minor changes in the design, revisions will be included in the basic design fee. If major changes are requested, the design fee may have to be renegotiated, or changes billed at the designer's hourly rate.

The prices following are based on preparation of as many layouts as the designer feels are necessary to show major design elements. When the client wishes to see highly detailed layouts showing elements which could just as easily be communicated to the compositor by typemarking of the sample manuscript pages, an increase of the fee is in order. Any additional considerations (such as a book in two or more colors) should also be reflected in an increase in the fee.

Before the designer can tackle the creative aspects of a job, it is necessary for someone — either the publisher or the designer — to analyze the project in order to prepare a design brief that includes the information outlined below.

The design brief

The *design brief* includes: (1) a copy of the manuscript, and/or a selection of representative copy for sample pages and a summary of all typographic problems, copy areas, code marks, etc.; (2) the compositor's name, method of composition and a listing of type-

faces; and (3) a description of the proposed physical characteristics of the book (e.g. trim size, page length, number of columns, number of colors, if more than one). The publisher should also indicate whether any particular visual style is expected.

The design brief may be prepared either by the publisher or by the freelance book designer. Pricing in the book design categories is based on the preparation of the design brief by the publisher. When the designer's assignment includes this responsibility, it should be reflected by an increase in the design fee.

Design

After the fee is agreed upon by the publisher and the book designer, the designer prepares layouts for chapter openings, title page and double-page spreads of the text that include all typographic elements, and treatment of illustrations or photographs. These typical examples of pages clearly show the design to the publisher and are used as a guide in production. Designers usually provide a "composition order" (comp order) for a typesetter that indicates all type specifications in detail based on the layouts. Since each publisher often has different preconceived ideas of what a comp order should include and look like, it is best that the designer request the publisher's guidelines (if available) and/or samples of previous comp orders. Designers may also mark up all or part of the manuscript.

Most publishers use in-house or compositor's production facilities to take the book from sketches to page makeup. Designers should check galleys and page proofs to make sure the compositor has followed all design specifications. With complicated layouts, the publisher may request that the book designer dummy the book. *Dummying* is taking actual copies of galleys and stats or photocopies of art and photographs, sizing them and placing them in position on dummy sheets. The dummy may then be used by the production staff or designer to prepare the mechanicals for the printer, if this method is utilized.

Dummy fee

The dummy fee currently ranges between $6.00 and $15.00 per page (depending on the complexity of the design), and covers the cutting up of galleys, layout, sizing art and photo inserts and presenting the final dummies to the publisher; it does not include a design check. If the dummier also checks the galleys or page proofs to insure the designer's specifications were followed, then an additional $2.00 to $3.00 per page will be charged. These checks however, can either be a separate function performed by a "page checker," who is a freelance source, or a member of the publisher's staff. Dummiers will sometimes cast off the manuscript (estimate the typeset length or the number of pages), but this is normally the responsibility of the publisher, and is done in-house by the editorial department, production department, the designer or the composition house (typesetter). When a publisher asks the dummier or the typesetter to cast off a book, an hourly fee of approximately $20 - $40 will be charged.

Mechanical fee

Advances in new technologies which can generate camera-ready output or film are making preparation of master mechanical boards less necessary than in the past. Please refer to the chapter on *Computer-generated art* and the "Production" section for more discussion. However, if a publisher is using traditional production methods, a mechanical fee will cover the preparation of mechanical boards, finished art for ornaments, maps, etc. and the final corrections made by the publisher.

Extra charges

Supervision of an art program, including hiring of and coordination with illustrators or photographers; extra conference time and trips to the publisher; time spent handling stats or type, or other production work are billed at the hourly design rate (though the cost of type, stats and other supplies are billable expenses).

Book packaging

Occasionally, a writer and book designer may collaborate to create a package for presentation to a publisher. Such a package includes camera-ready mechanicals or pasteups, relieving the publisher of these production responsibilities. This way of working is generally used when the idea of the book originated with the writer or designer.

Book design categories:

There are some unusual projects or books for small presses that may not fit easily into the categories below. In these cases, designers sometimes use their hourly rates as the basis for a fee. If the design is to be used for a series of books, a reuse fee should be negotiated.

Trade books
    Simple: A straightforward book such as a novel or short book of poetry. Design includes a layout showing a title page, a chapter opening, and a double spread of text and spreads for front matter. These simple books are generally done in-house, but may be given to a freelance designer if the publisher is small and does not have an in-house design department.
    Average: Nonfiction trade books, cookbooks, poetry or drama, anthologies or illustrated books that are designed on a grid system. Design may include front matter (halftitle, ad card, title, copyright, dedication, acknowledgements, preface, contents, list of illustrations, introduction), part opening, chapter opening, text comprising from three to six levels of heads, tabular matter, extracts, footnotes, and simple back matter such as bibliographies and indexes. The design, exclusive of the front matter, may be set into sample pages by the publisher, to be approved before typesetting of the complete manuscript begins.
    Complex: These are books such as workbooks, catalogs, and elaborate art or picture books, requiring special treatment of each page; two-color basic texts, cookbooks, or other books of greater complexity than in the previous category. Like the other categories, fees for complex book design projects are generally negotiated as a flat fee. Current ranges for complex book design projects are $2,000 to $3,500.

Textbooks
    Simple: Mostly straight text with up to three levels of heads, simple tables and/or art.
    Average: Up to six levels of heads, tables, extract, footnotes, and use of illustrations, diagrams and/or photographs in a grid system.
    Complex: Foreign language texts, two, three or four-color texts, complicated workbooks, catalogs or illustrated books that require special treatment of each page. Design fees for complex textbooks currently range from $3,000 to $5,000.

The price ranges listed below do not constitute specific prices for particular jobs. They are guidelines to be considered along with other factors specific to the commissioned work under consideration. Please refer to related material in other sections of this book.

Comparative fees for book design*

Mass market	$800 - $2,300
Trade	750 - 1,500
Each additional trade book in series	40% - 50%
College textbook	1,200 - 2,500
Each additional textbook in series	50% - 50%
El-hi textbook	1,500 - 5,000
Young adult trade	600 - 750
Each additional young adult book in series	50%
Dummy fee (per page)	6 - 15

*Ranges reflect complexity of design. Ranges do not reflect preparation of a design brief. If designer's assignment includes this responsibility, it should be reflected by an increase in the design fee.

Lettering and typeface design

Lettering artists create original letterforms, modify existing typefaces or design typefaces. Lettering is used in all areas of the communications industry: advertising; corporate identity and promotion; publishing and institutional. Many letterers are also graphic designers or illustrators. In fact, it is rare to find a graphic artist who does lettering only.

The work of lettering artists is similar to that of illustrators. Upon agreement of the terms and fee for the project, a letterer prepares a sketch or sketches of possible solutions to a specific problem. Upon acceptance of the comp or sketch, finished art is prepared for reproduction.

In built-up lettering and typeface design, the outline of the letter is drawn first and then filled in. Much of this work is now being done on computer. In calligraphy, the letters are formed directly from the broad-edged pen.

Calligraphy is personalized and not often created for purposes of reproduction. Calligraphers' work is usually used on envelopes, invitations, award certificates and illuminated scrolls. Prices for calligraphy are usually a flat rate per line or per piece.

The recent and dramatic development of computer software with type manipulation capabilities as well as photo and film lettering has made it necessary to restructure the pricing concepts for professional letterers and type designers. Among the many factors affecting the prices of lettering are the following: (1) intended uses and distribution; (2) amount of time allowed to complete the project; (3) amount of design work involved; (4) size and complexity of the original art; (5) surface upon which it is to be executed (matte or glossy paper, glass or can); and (6) number of comps required.

The prices below reflect the average letterer's fee. All expenses are additional. The prices to a client may be higher if the lettering is being commissioned through a designer or art director because the end price must accommodate their additional participation.

Typeface design

Typeface design, involving the creation or styling of complete families of fonts (or portions thereof), is complicated and time-consuming. New designs of fonts may require up to eight sets of finished drawings, reflecting looks (roman and italic), weights (normal, condensed and bold) and upper and lower cases for entire character sets. Designers may also approve kerning for proper fit. Kerning modified or redesigned typefaces requires similar effort.

Computers have dramatically changed business practices in this market. Finished art is digitized, usually by a typeface manufacturer, or by the few designers who have access to the necessary equipment. The designer's kerning specifications are also programmed for use on the computer, and is matched to the font software.

Pricing for this field can be complex; fees to clients will reflect the investments of time and capital necessary to complete the work. Generally, designers will license their designs to manufacturers for an advance for each weight drawn plus a royalty on manufacturer's sales. Corporations that commission the design of a unique font will generally be licensed to use the typeface design; otherwise, payments upwards of $35,000 might be required for exclusivity.

In the past, typographers would commission or purchase typeface designs to add to their libraries, however, due to advances in computer technology, most typographers rely on manufacturers to build their libraries. Please see the chapter on *Computer generated art* for more information.

Typeface designers commissioned by individual clients will not relinquish the computer disks containing their designs. Rather, photo or laser copies of the work is sent to the art director for approval, and then finished output is generated and delivered. In these cases, the typeface designer assumes the role of typesetter.

The price ranges listed below do not constitute specific prices for particular jobs. They are guidelines to be considered along with other factors specific to the commissioned work under consideration. Please refer to related material in other sections of this book.

Comparative fees for lettering

Publication headlines
(one comp, one finish, for article)

	Average	Complicated
Major magazine	$1,000	$1,800
Specific audience	500	850
Corporate in-house	450	750

Publication title heading
(three comps, one finish; unlimited rights)

Major magazine	$7,500	$12,500
Specific audience	3,000	6,000
Corporate in-house	1,000	1,500

Logos
(three comps, one finish; unlimited rights)

Corporate	$6,000 - $10,000 and up*	
Individual	1,000	2,500

*The range reflects the value the client derives from the uses intended for the logo.

Hardcover book jacket lettering*
(as a design solution component)

	Average	Complicated
Mass market	$1,000	$2,000
Trade	750	1,250

Paperback cover lettering*
(as a design solution component)

	Average	Complicated
Mass market	$850	$1,500
Trade	650	900

*Based on one comp, one finish; one-time rights limited to the specific edition involved.

Comp lettering	$50 per hour
Finished built-up lettering	60 per hour
Type modification	60 per hour

Comparative fees for calligraphy*
(per piece)

	Average	Complicated
Invitation to corporate functions	$150	$250
Invitation to a wedding	70	150
Certificate fill-ins (one name line)	3	10
Award certificates	150	300
Envelopes (three lines)	3	8
Scrolls (illuminated)	250	750

*Fees do not reflect transfer of reproduction rights.

Comparative fees for typeface design*

	Flat fee	Advance	Royalty
Simple (based on one look, one weight; either new design or modification)			
Manufacturer	-	$1,000	10-20%
Magazine (depending on intended use)	6,500+		
Complicated (based on 2 looks, 4 weights each; new design or modification)			
Manufacturer	25,000 and up	8,000	10-20%
Magazine (depending on intended use)	7,500+		

*Production of mechanicals and all reimbursable/out-of-pocket expenses incurred to produce sketches, comps and mechanicals are billed separately.

Retouching

Retouchers are graphic artists who alter, enhance, or add to a photograph by using bleaches, dyes, brush, airbrush or electronic techniques. The resulting image usually appears untouched. This "invisible art" requires a highly skilled hand and eye in order to be successful. Therefore, the retoucher most often specializes in one area of retouching and concentrates on the skills and technical knowledge of that area.

Computers vs. hand work

Recent advances in technology allow electronic scanning and manipulation of images (including global color correction, cloning a subject, distorting or enhancing an image, and preserving an image without disintegration of the dyes). As a time factor, electronic retouching dispenses with the intermediate step of a dye transfer and the time necessary to recreate a facsimile of the original artwork. However, when compared to hand work, computer retouching does not necessarily provide better quality or cheaper rates. Computer retouching in New York, for example, can cost $400-$700 per hour, compared to $200 per hour for a top retoucher who works by hand.

Electronic retouching can do very subtle things (e.g. defining individual hairs in a hairdo or create subtleties in skin tones), but so can hand retouching. Electronic retouching is getting better, but the colors of printed pieces that were electronically retouched may vary from the colors displayed on the screen, although those with the expertise can correct or allow for them. For the time being, large businesses and advertising agencies are returning to hand work. And the traditional techniques of bleach, dye and airbrush are still used on black and white, as there is no point to using the expensive computer technology unless color is involved.

On the other hand, electronic retouching is convenient; it has a justified compatibility with the mechanics of the pre-press process; and it is crafted by artists as accomplished as conventional retouchers. As these technologies become more widely available, scanning and output fees will drop significantly. Please see the chapter on *Computer generated art* for further discussion.

Pricing

When pricing a retouching project, many factors come into play:

Surface: Most color work of high quality is done on transparencies, chromes or dye transfers because of the subtleties that can be achieved on these surfaces. A retoucher uses dyes and bleaches when working on a chrome. Because of the extreme detail that C-prints can represent, they are often used for presentation purposes, but are limited to being painted with airbrush opaques. C-prints require approximately an hour to retouch, including drying.

Dye transfers are a bleeding process and are less sharp than C-prints, but are extremely dependable for printers to reproduce, as are chromes. Dye transfers may require 18 hours to retouch; they require a test print, an adjustment, another test print, and finally the retouching.

Brush, pencil, dyes, bleaching, etching, and airbrush techniques are used in retouching on all surfaces. In black-and-white retouching, photographic prints of high quality are most commonly used as a surface to be retouched.

Complexity: Retouching can run the gamut of change in the photo, from simply adding a few highlights to actually creating photorealistic, hand-wrought backgrounds, shapes or figures, or stripping two or more photos together to create a montage.

Expenses: Typography, photography, props and other out-of-pocket expenses are considered to be additional, billable expenses.

Overtime: Retouching, by its nature, should not be a last-minute project. It's important, therefore, to know how the retoucher charges for extraordinary time requirements. Normal timing for any average-size project is three days. Overtime rates for less than three days' turnover are figured at: *two days:* 50 per cent more; *one day:* 100 per cent more (rush job status). If the job requires evening, weekend or holiday time, there is often a 100 per cent overtime charge.

Rights: Unlike other graphic artists, retouchers always work on an existing piece of art and are usually not entitled to copyright or reuse fees. The fee that they charge initially represents the total income from that project, unlike artists who work on the basis of selling future rights.

Studio: A retouching studio has full equipment and staff to provide multiple talents, flexibility in handling larger projects, and accessibility. Studio rates are higher than freelance rates.

Freelance: Freelance retouchers handle each project themselves and generally work out of their own studios. They rarely work on the client's premises.

Comparative fees for retouching

Advertising	Color	B&W
National	$1,800-$3,500	$750-$1,800
Trade	1,000-2,500	600-1,500
Editorial		
National	1,000-2,400	600-1,500
Trade	1,000-1,800	
Pharmaceutical	1,200-2,400	600-1,800

Notes: Ranges reflect average to extensive projects. Time is a major factor in pricing. Two-day service is 150% of the normal fee. One-day service is 200% of the normal fee. Overtime for holidays and weekends is 150%-200% of the normal fee.

Comparative hourly rates for retouching

Color chromes or dye transfers	$75-$200
C-prints (comp retouching)	80-150
Black and white prints	75-150
Electronic	300-500 *(includes scanning fees)*

Production

Production artists are graphic artists who execute the finished mechanical or pasteup for a graphic designer or art director to their layout specifications. Production artists, in short, make the project camera ready for the printer. The subtle decisions and interpretations that production artists must make on the board determine the final product. The details are critical.

Advanced production artists are adept at keyline ruling, overlays, and all other complicated production techniques.

Some of the considerations production artists use in determining the cost of producing a mechanical or pasteup are: (1) conditions of the job and tightness of the layout; (2) extent of responsibility in gathering materials for the job; (3) location of job (on site or in own studio); (4) complexity of style; (5) urgency of schedule (amount of overtime involved); and (6) last minute decision-making responsibilities in regards to design or layout.

Pasteups are simpler than mechanicals and require only a modest positioning of type and other elements. Mechanicals require more complex shifting of elements including type and photostats and may also include the drawing of graphs, charts and overlays.

The advent of new technologies, however, has had a tremendous impact on this market. Many graphic designers who use the computer as a tool can now produce the equivalents to pasteups and mechanicals with more speed and accuracy; in many cases eliminating the need for production artists. Obviously, graphic designers with computer expertise have an competitive edge over those who do not. Please refer to the chapter on *Computer generated art* for more information.

Most production artists base their fees on hourly rates, although page-rate prices are occasionally negotiated. The following rates do not reflect the hourly rates for computer use; please refer to the chapter on *Computer generated art* for more information.

Comparative hourly rates for preparing camera-ready art

Pasteups

Corporate	$17-20
Publishing	15-20
Advertising	20-25

Mechanicals

Corporate	25-30
Publishing	20-25
Advertising	25-30

Ranges reflect volume of work, complexity and urgency of schedule.

Illustration

Illustrators are graphic artists who create artwork for any of a number of different markets. Most illustrators are freelance artists who maintain their own studios and work for a variety of clients as opposed to salaried staff artists working for one company. While some artists have representatives to promote their work to art buyers, many do their own promotion and marketing.

Illustrators use a variety of techniques such as pen and ink, airbrush, acrylic and oil painting, watercolor, collage, three-dimensional and computer-generated work. Most specialize in one signature style, while some are sought for their versatility. Illustrators are responsible for knowing the technical requirements of separation and printing necessary to maintain the quality of the final printed piece.

Illustration is sold primarily on the basis of usage and reproduction rights, but other factors are important. The price quoted on a project is based on its intended usage and intended market as well as such standard factors as deadline, research, complexity of the assignment, the artist's reputation, complexity of style and overhead costs.

Original artwork, unless sold separately, remains the property of the illustrator.

Usage rights are generally sold based on the client's needs. Other uses for a work may be sold as long as they are non-competitive or do not compromise the commissioning client's market. It is recommended that clients only buy rights particular to the project, as it is uneconomical to pay additionally for rights that are not needed and that will not be used.

Advertising illustration

In the advertising market, illustrators work with art directors, account executives, copywriters and creative-group heads of agencies to illustrate products or services for specific advertising needs. Agencies often ask illustrators to work in a specific style represented in their portfolios and to follow a sketch supplied by the agency and approved by the client. The terms and fee for the art are normally negotiated with the agency's art director or art buyer by the illustrator or the artist's representative.

Premium prices for illustration are paid in the advertising field, where the highest degree of professionalism and performance is expected from artists working within unusually strict time demands. Changes and last-minute alterations are not uncommon. Illustrators may need to please several people of varying opinions, since many advertisements are created by committee.

Advertising illustration prices are negotiated strictly on a use basis, with extra pay added for sale of residual or all rights, complexity of style or tighter deadlines.

Advertisements are usually thought of in terms of multiple appearances. Therefore, in advertising, a sale of usage rights may refer to limited or unlimited use in a specific area within a specified time period, for example, "limited for 1-5 insertions in consumer magazines for one year." The media and time period for which advertising rights are being sold must be made clear and the price agreed upon before the project starts

Trade practices

The following trade practices are accepted as standard:

1. The intended use of the art must be clearly stated in a contract, purchase order or letter of agreement stating the price and terms of sale.

2. Artists normally sell rights to 1-5 insertions of their artwork within a given media for one year from date of first use, unless otherwise stated.

3. If artwork is to be used for other than its original purpose, the price should be negotiated as soon as possible. The secondary use of an illustration may be of greater value than the primary use. Although there is no set formula for reuse fees, a reuse fee ranging from 25-50 per cent of the fee that would have been charged had the illustration been originally commissioned for the anticipated usage is a fairly typical charge.

4. Illustrators should negotiate reuse arrangements with the original commissioning party with speed, efficiency and all due respect to the client's position.

5. Return of original artwork to the artist is automatic unless otherwise negotiated.

6. Fees for rush work will be higher than the figures listed here. Rush deadlines may increase the original fee by an additional 50 per cent.

7. A cancellation fee should be agreed upon if a job is cancelled through no fault of the artist. Depending upon the stage at which the job is terminated, the fee paid should cover all work done, including research time, sketches, billable expenses and compensation for lost opportunities resulting from an artist's refusing other offers to make time available for a specific commission. In addition, clients who put commissions "on hold" or withhold approval for commissions for longer than 30 days should secure the assignment by paying a deposit.

8. A rejection fee should be agreed upon if the assignment is terminated because the preliminary or finished work is found not to be reasonably satisfactory. The rejection fee for finished work should be upwards of 50 per cent of the full price depending on the reason for rejection and complexity of the job. When the job is rejected at the sketch stage, a fee of one-third the original price is customary. This fee may be less for quick, rough sketches and more for highly rendered, time-consuming work.

9. Work done on speculation does not conform to industry trade practices and is contrary to the Joint Ethics Committee's Code of Fair Practice, because of its exploitive nature.

10. The Graphic Artists Guild is unalterably opposed to the use of work-for-hire contracts, in which authorship and all rights that go with it are transferred to the commissioning party and the independent artist is treated as an employee for copyright purposes only. The independent artist receives no employee benefits and loses the right to claim authorship or profit from future use of the work forever. Advertising is not eligible to be work for hire, as it does not fall under any of the eligible categories defined in the law. Additional information on work for hire can be found on page 15.

11. Expenses such as unusual props, costumes, model fees, travel costs, production costs, consultation time and so on, should be billed to the client separately. An expense estimate should be included in the original written agreement or as an amendment to the agreement.

All prices for illustration in the *Guidelines* are based on a nationwide survey that was reviewed by a special committee of experienced professionals through the Graphic Artists Guild. These figures, reflecting the responses of established professionals, are meant as a point of reference only and do not necessarily reflect such important factors as deadlines, job complexity, reputation and experience of a particular illustrator, research, technique or unique quality of expression and extraordinary or extensive use of the finished art. Please refer to related material in other sections of this book, especially under *Business & Legal Practices for Commissioned Artwork* and *Standard Contracts*.

The prices shown represent *only the specific use for which the illustration is intended* and do not necessarily reflect any of the above considerations. The buyer and seller are free to negotiate, taking into account all the factors involved.

Comparative fees for illustration used in magazine advertising

National consumer magazines	B&W	Color
Full page	$4,000	$6,000
Half page	3,000	4,000
Spot - quarter page	2,000	2,500
Regional consumer magazines		
Full page	$2,500	$4,000
Half page	2,000	3,000
Spot - quarter page	1,200	1,800
Limited audience consumer magazines		
Full page	$2,200	$3,300
Half page	1,600	2,200
Spot - quarter page	1,200	1,200

Comparative fees for illustration used in magazine advertising (continued)

Mass trade magazines	B&W	Color
Full page	$3,000	$4,500
Half page	2,000	2,500
Spot - quarter page	1,000	1,200

Specific trade and limited audience magazines

	B&W	Color
Full page	$2,000	3,500
Half page	1,800	2,000
Spot - quarter page	1,200	1,400

Notes:
National magazines have circulations greater than 1,000,000.

Regional magazines have circulations from 500,000 up to 1,000,000.

Local and limited audience magazines have circulations less than 500,000.

Mass trade magazines have circulations over 35,000.

Specific trade magazines have circulations under 35,000.

Comparative fees for illustration used in newspaper advertising

National or major metro area newspapers	B&W	Color
Full page	$4,000	$5,000
Half page	3,000	3,400
Quarter page	2,200	2,400
Spot	1,600	1,800

Small to midsized city newspapers

	B&W	Color
Full page	$2,500	$3,000
Half page	1,600	2,000
Quarter page	1,400	1,600
Spot	1,000	1,200

Magazine supplements for major metro area newspapers

	B&W	Color
Full page	$3,500	$4,000
Half page	2,500	3,000
Spot - quarter page	1,600	1,800

Magazine supplements for small to midsized city newspapers

	B&W	Color
Full page	$2,000	$3,000
Half page	1,200	2,000
Spot - quarter page	800	1,000

Notes:
Major market newspapers have circulations over 100,000.

Regional market newspapers have circulations from 10,000 to 100,000.

Local market newspapers have circulations under 10,000.

Comparative fees for illustration used in collateral and direct mail*

Print runs over 100,000 pieces

	B&W	Color
Cover	$2,800	$4,500
Full page	2,000	2,500
Half page	1,500	2,000
Spot	1,000	1,200

Print runs from 10,000 to 100,000 pieces

	B&W	Color
Cover	$2,200	$3,000
Full page	1,600	2,500
Half page	1,200	1,750
Spot	900	1,000

Print runs under 10,000

	B&W	Color
Full page	$2,000	$2,500
Half page	1,200	2,000
Quarter page	1,000	1,500
Spot	700	800

*Color posters, brochures, catalogs, flyers, direct mailers and hand-outs.

Comparative fees for illustration used in advertorials*

National consumer or mass trade publications	B&W*	Color
Spread	$2,800	$4,500
Opening page	2,500	3,800
Full page	1,800	3,000
Half page	1,500	2,500
Spot - quarter page	1,000	1,500

Regional or specific trade publications	B&W*	Color
Spread	$2,500	$4,000
Opening page	2,000	2,800
Full page	1,700	2,500
Half page	1,500	2,000
Spot - quarter page	1,000	1,300

*Special advertising sections added into magazines and newspapers.

Comparative fees for illustration used in point of purchase advertising

Over 5,000 pieces	B&W*	Color
Poster	$4,000	$6,000
Medium	3,000	4,000
Small	2,500	3,000

Under 5,000 pieces		
Poster	$3,000	$5,000
Medium	2,500	3,800
Small	1,800	2,500

*Posters, counter cards, shelf signs. Add 35% to the above black and white fees for each color overlay.

Comparative fees for illustration used in displays and exhibits

One show use	B&W	Color
Large	$3,500	$5,000
Medium	3,000	4,000
Small	2000	3,000

One year use		
Large	$4,500	$6,500
Medium	3,500	4,500
Small	2,500	3,500

Comparative fees for illustration used in outdoor advertising

Bus and car cards	B&W*	Color
Major campaign, large	$2,500	$6,000
Major campaign, small	2,000	3,500
Regional campaign, large	2,000	4,000
Regional campaign, small	1,500	3,000
Local campaign, large	1,500	3,000
Local campaign, small	1,200	2,500

Station posters		
Major campaign	$3,500	$4,500
Regional campaign	3,000	4,000
Local campaign	2,500	2,500

Billboards (add 25% for 3-D or extensions)	B&W	Color
Over 40 installations	-	$7,500
From 10-40 installations	-	6,500
From 1-10 installations	-	5,500

*Add 25% to black and white prices for each color overlay.

Comparative fees for illustration used in packaging*

Product	Simple color	Complex color
National distri- bution or extensive product life	$4,500	$6,000
Limited distribution, short product life or test run	2,500	4,000

Software	Color
Business	$4,400
Educational	2,500
Games	3,000

* Add 25% to black and white prices for each color overlay.

Notes:
Most purchasers of product packaging require extensive rights for use of the artwork due to the unpredictable nature of the market. Royalty arrangements have been made, but are fairly unusual; higher fees, reflecting these additional usages, are more often negotiated in advance.

Comparative fees for illustration used in motion picture posters

Major distribution	Color
Produced poster	$15,000
Finished art unused	7,500
Comp sketch only	3,000

Limited distribution or low budget film	
Produced poster	$7,000
Finished art unused	4,500
Comp sketch only	2,000

Note:
In most film poster assignments, the art is usually commissioned in three stages: (1) sketch, (2) a highly rendered comp and (3) the finished poster art. Separate fees are usually arranged for each stage of completion.

Comparative fees for illustration used in theater and event advertising*

	B&W	2 or 3 color	4 color
Large production	$3,800	$4,000	$6,000
Small production	2,500	3,500	5,000

*See station posters, above

Comparative fees for illustration used in television commercial styling*

	Simple	Complex
30 second	$2,500 - 3,500	$4,000 - 6,500
60 second	5,000 - 7,000	8,000 - 14,000

*Ranges will depend on number of key illustrations and backgrounds specified.

Pre-production art (comps, animatics, storyboard illustration, TV and audiovisual illustration)

Artists who specialize in pre-production art service the advertising, television and motion picture industries and are usually called upon to produce high-caliber professional work within tight deadlines. Although some artists tend to specialize, nearly all are engaged in three areas of pre-production art: comps (formerly called "comprehensives"), storyboards and animatics.

Comps are visual renderings of proposed advertisements and folders (print media only) including headlines, body text and a "visual," which is the rendering of the illustration or photo to be used in the finished piece.

A *storyboard* is a visual presentation of a proposed television commercial or program, or a feature film using a limited number of sequential frames usually drawn on a telepad, although larger format images are common.

In advertising, storyboards are generally used in-house (within an agency), to present the concept of the proposed commercial to the client. A key frame is a large single frame used in concert with other frames to establish the overall mood or to portray the highlight or key moment of the commercial. It must be given extra attention and compensation as it carries most of the narrative burden.

Storyboard rendering for feature films or television are relied upon by producers to realize creative concepts and to evaluate a concept's visual qualities and continuity. Used most often as reference to an accompanying script, the storyboards and text are filmed as a "photoplay;" a critical element in determining a property's value as entertainment and its value as a visual production. Storyboards are the visual blueprint producers rely upon for budgeting and to help avoid cost overruns.

Storyboard fees for television programming or feature-film production depend upon the production's budget and its intended distribution. Fees for high-budget productions, which usually require more complex storyboard rendering, will generally be higher than fees for low-budget productions. The break point between a low- or-high-budget television production is $500,000. For feature films, the break point between low and high budget is $2,000,000.

An *animatic* is a limited-animation film using camera movements, a select number of drawings, some animation and a sound track. An animatic is usually produced to test a proposed "spot" or TV commercial. The need for animatics has risen due to the increased desirability of test marketing for advertisers. An animatic must "score" well on audience recall, etc., in order to go into full production. Video storyboards are becoming commonly used in other markets as well, especially in the motion picture for television market because of the wider availability of relatively inexpensive video equipment.

Some agencies, production companies, producers and individuals may request artists to work in-house and sign nondisclosure or non-compete agreements to protect trade secrets and creative properties for specified periods. These conditions may severely restrict an artist's opportunities for future work and is a factor that should be seriously considered when negotiating fees.

Video storyboards use storyboard art only (no moving parts) and movement is achieved with simple camera moves. Often a tighter style than normal is required and the fee should be approximately 25 per cent higher than for regular storyboards.

In pricing animatics, one background illustration and one to one-and-one-half cut-out figures comprise one frame. Two figures and their moving parts can constitute one frame when backgrounds are used for several scenes. Pre-production artists generally receive taped copies of their work from production houses so that they can compile a reel of sample commercials for their portfolios.

Fees in this field depend on job complexity including factors such as the degree of finish required, the number of subjects in a given frame, the type of background required and so on.

Artists must know ahead of time whether film or videotape will be used since each has its own special requirements. A good grasp of current TV commercial styles is crucial to success in this field. Some agencies will also request that artists work in-house and that fact should be taken into account when establishing a fee.

Rush work is billable at a minimum of 25 per cent more than the regular fee. Hourly rates, while not encouraged, range between $75 and $150 per hour. Flat per-frame rates reflect more accurately all the factors involved in the job, although these hourly rates can apply for consultation time if the artist participates on the design of the scene or sequences.

Trade practices

The following trade practices are accepted as standard:

1. The intended use of the art must be clearly stated in a contract, purchase order or letter of agreement stating the price and terms of sale.

2. Artists normally sell only first reproduction rights unless otherwise stated.

3. If artwork is to be used for other than its original purpose, the price should be negotiated as soon as possible. The secondary use of an illustration may be of greater value than the primary use. Although there is no set formula for reuse fees, a reuse fee ranging from 25-50 per cent of the fee that would have been charged had the illustration been originally commissioned for the anticipated usage is a fairly typical charge.

4. Illustrators should negotiate reuse arrangements with the original commissioning party with speed, efficiency and all due respect to the client's position.

5. Return of original artwork to the artist is automatic unless otherwise negotiated.

6. Fees for rush work will be higher than the figures listed here. Rush deadlines may increase the original fee by an additional 50 per cent.

7. A cancellation fee should be agreed upon if a job is cancelled through no fault of the artist. Depending upon the stage at which the job is terminated, the fee paid should cover all work done, including research time, sketches, billable expenses and compensation for lost opportunities resulting from an artist's refusing other offers to make time available for a specific commission. In addition, clients who put commissions "on hold" or withhold approval for commissions for longer than 30 days should secure the assignment by paying a deposit.

8. A rejection fee should be agreed upon if the assignment is terminated because the preliminary or finished work is found not to be reasonably satisfactory. The rejection fee for finished work should be upwards of 50 per cent of the full price depending on the reason

for rejection and complexity of the job. When the job is rejected at the rendering stage, a fee of one-third the original price is customary. This fee may be less for quick, rough sketches and more for highly rendered, time-consuming work.

9. Work done on speculation does not conform to industry trade practices and is contrary to the Joint Ethics Committee's Code of Fair Practice, because of its exploitive nature.

10. The Graphic Artists Guild is unalterably opposed to the use of work-for-hire contracts, in which authorship and all rights that go with it are transferred to the commissioning party and the independent artist is treated as an employee for copyright purposes only. The independent artist receives no employee benefits and loses the right to claim authorship or profit from future use of the work forever. Additional information on work for hire can be found on page 15.

11. Expenses such as unusual props, costumes, model fees, travel costs, production costs, consultation time and so on, should be billed to the client separately. An expense estimate should be included in the original written agreement or as an amendment to the agreement.

All prices for illustration in the *Guidelines* are based on a nationwide survey that was reviewed by a special committee of experienced professionals through the Graphic Artists Guild. These figures, reflecting the responses of established professionals, are meant as a point of reference only and do not necessarily reflect such important factors as deadlines, job complexity, reputation and experience of a particular illustrator, research, technique or unique quality of expression and extraordinary or extensive use of the finished art. Please refer to related material in other sections of this book, especially under *Business & Legal Practices for Commissioned Artwork* and *Standard Contracts.*

The prices shown represent only the specific use for which the illustration is intended and do not necessarily reflect any of the above considerations. The buyer and seller are free to negotiate, taking into account all the factors involved.

Comparative fees for pre-production art for television commercials

Animatics	Simple	Complex
Per frame	$325	$500

Television storyboards (per frame)	Simple	Complex
Miniboards*	$40	$55
Telepads†	40	55
4 x 5 inches	95	130
5 x 7 inches	145	225
8 x 10 inches	250	275
9 x 12 inches	300	350

*Miniboards are less than 2 - 3/4 x 3 - 3/4 inches.
†Telepads are 2 - 3/4 x 3 - 3/4 inches.

Comparative fees for illustration used in television programming storyboards

Minor productions (budgets less than $500,000)	Line	Tone*
4 x 5 inches	$40	$55
5 x 7 inches	75	90

Major productions (budgets greater than $500,000)	Line	Tone*
4 x 5 inches	$80	$110
5 x 7 inches	135	175

*Tone drawings may be either color or black and white.

Comparative fees for feature illustration used in film production storyboards

Minor productions (budgets less than $2,000,000)	Line	Tone*
2 x 5 inches	$115	$150
4 x 10 inches	225	275
8 x 20 inches	325	375
Major productions		
2 x 5 inches	$175	$250
4 x 10 inches	375	450
8 x 20 inches	750	850

*Tone drawings may be either color or black and white.

Comparative fees for comp illustration for print

Major campaign	Line	Tone*
Spread	$1,125	$800
Full page	675	725
Minor campaign	Line	Tone*
Spread	$625	$500
Full page	350	400

*Tone drawings may be either color or black and white.

Comparative fees for audiovisual pre-production (per slide)

	Simple	Complex
Transparencies	$150	$300

Corporate and institutional illustration

An illustrator creating corporate or institutional art works with a graphic designer or art director to create illustrations for annual reports, in-house publications and other material targeted to internal audiences. The assignment is generally editorial in nature and the illustrator is often called upon to determine the concept and design of the art. In annual reports particularly, illustrations are "think pieces" which contribute substantially to enhancing the corporation's or institution's public image.

Corporations and institutions include Fortune 500 companies, educational institutions, government agencies and other businesses and not-for-profit entities. Not-for-profit entities consist of groups and associations that organize for purposes other than private profit. However, this does not mean these organizations operate at a deficit. Some of these organizations, like the American Association of Retired Persons (AARP) with over 32.5 million members, have enormous resources available. Other examples of not-for-profits include trade associations, unions and philanthropic, charitable or educational organizations. Whether a client is for profit or not-for-profit, pricing in this area will vary according to its size and resources.

Annual reports

An annual report, the yearly fiscal report by the corporation to its stockholders and the financial community, is an important vehicle for the company's self-promotion. Designers of annual reports often seek thoughtful, provocative illustration that will offset the written and financial material while effectively and powerfully projecting the company's public image.

Fees for illustration are relative to the size of the corporation and the nature of the annual report and are usually negotiated on a one-time use basis only.

Corporate calendars

Prices for illustration for company calendars can vary greatly. The fee is usually dependent on the size of the company and the complexity of the subject. Another important factor determining the fees for corporate calendars is the intended use. Fees for calendars designed only for internal use will generally be less than those for calendars distributed to consumers as a promotion or by sale. Current fees for color calendars range from $1,200 to $2,500 per illustration.

Trade practices

The following trade practices are accepted as standard:

1. The intended use of the art must be clearly stated in a contract, purchase order or letter of agreement stating the price and terms of sale.

2. Artists normally sell only first reproduction rights unless otherwise stated.

3. If artwork is to be used for other than its original purpose, the price should be negotiated as soon as possible. The secondary use of an illustration may be of greater value than the primary use. Although there is no set formula for reuse fees, a reuse fee ranging from 25-50 per cent of the fee that would have been charged had the illustration been originally commissioned for the anticipated usage is a fairly typical charge.

4. Illustrators should negotiate reuse arrangements with the original commissioning party with speed, efficiency and all due respect to the client's position.

5. Return of original artwork to the artist is automatic unless otherwise negotiated.

6. Fees for rush work will be higher than the figures listed here. Rush deadlines may increase the original fee by an additional 50 per cent.

7. A cancellation fee should be agreed upon if a job is cancelled through no fault of the artist. Depending upon the stage at which the job is terminated, the fee paid should cover all work done, including research time, sketches, billable expenses and compensation for lost opportunities resulting from an artist's refusing other offers to make time available for a specific commission. In addition, clients who put commissions "on hold" or withhold approval for commissions for longer than 30 days should secure the assignment by paying a deposit.

8. A rejection fee should be agreed upon if the assignment is terminated because the preliminary or finished work is found not to be reasonably satisfactory. The rejection fee for finished work should be upwards of 50 per cent of the full price depending on the reason for rejection and complexity of the job. When the job is rejected at the rendering stage, a fee of one-third the original price is customary. This fee may be less for quick, rough sketches and more for highly rendered, time-consuming work.

9. Work done on speculation does not conform to industry trade practices and is contrary to the Joint Ethics Committee's Code of Fair Practice, because of its exploitive nature.

10. The Graphic Artists Guild is unalterably opposed to the use of work-for-hire contracts, in which authorship and all rights that go with it are transferred to the commissioning party and the independent artist is treated as an employee for copyright purposes only. The independent artist receives no employee benefits and loses the right to claim authorship or profit from future use of the work forever. Additional information on work for hire can be found on page 15.

11. Expenses such as unusual props, costumes, model fees, travel costs, production costs, consultation time and so on, should be billed to the client separately. An expense estimate should be included in the original written agreement or as an amendment to the agreement.

All prices for illustration in the *Guidelines* are based on a nationwide survey that was reviewed by a special committee of experienced professionals through the Graphic Artists Guild. These figures, reflecting the responses of established professionals, are meant as a point of reference only and do not necessarily reflect such important factors as deadlines, job complexity, reputation and experience of a particular illustrator, research, technique or unique quality of expression and extraordinary or extensive use of the finished art. Please refer to related material in other sections of this book, especially under *Business & Legal Practices for Commissioned Artwork* and *Standard Contracts.*

The prices shown represent only the specific use for which the illustration is intended and do not necessarily reflect any of the above considerations. The buyer and seller are free to negotiate, taking into account all the factors involved.

Comparative fees for illustration used in employee publications

Large corporation or large print run	B&W*	Color
Cover	$2,500	$4,500
Full page	2,000	3,000
Half page	1,400	1,800
Spot - quarter page	750 - 1,000	1,200

Medium corporation or medium print run		
Cover	$2,000	$3,000
Full page	1,500	2,500
Half page	900	1,600
Spot - quarter page	400 - 600	750 - 1,200

Small corporation		
Cover	$2,000	$2,500
Full page	1,200	1,800
Half page	1,000	1,200
Spot - quarter page	500 - 750	1,000

*Add 25% to black and white prices for each color overlay.

Comparative fees for illustration used in corporate annual reports

Large corporation or large distribution	B&W*	Color
Cover	-	$6,500
Full page	3,000	3,500
Half page	1,500	2,000
Spot - quarter page	750 - 1,200	800 - 1,500

Medium corporation or medium distribution		
Cover	-	$4,000
Full page	2,000	2,500
Half page	1,200	1,400
Spot - quarter page	650	800

Small corporation		
Cover	-	$2,600
Full page	1,400	2,000
Half page	1,000	1,250
Spot - quarter page	600	800

*Add 25% to black and white prices for each color overlay.

Comparative fees for corporate audiovisual illustration

Presentation slides	Frame
Advertising	$300
Promotional/corporate	250
Educational	200

Book jacket illustration

Book jacket illustration or design is the second most important ingredient in the promotion and sale of a book, superseded only by the fame and success of the author.

The publishing business has undergone a tremendous growth and change in the last decade. Most well-known publishing houses have been acquired by multinational conglomerates here and abroad. Publishing is flourishing, as indicated by the increased number of titles published each year. Prices for book jacket and paperback cover illustration have risen accordingly as marketing considerations play a more and more important role.

The book publishing market is a complex area with respect to illustration pricing, so attention should be paid to all the factors involved. Romance, science fiction and other genre paperback covers generally command higher fees than hardcover jackets because the paperback audience is much larger. Artists who design and illustrate jackets may have a somewhat different business structure and should also refer to the Book Jacket Design section.

Often, illustrators who are specially selected for occasional cover assignments will receive higher fees than illustrators who specialize only in the book jacket field. In addition, artists recognized for their painterly, highly realistic or dramatic studies may command much higher fees than those whose styles are more graphic and design oriented. Although this practice is prevalent in the entire illustration field, it is particularly evident in publishing.

Some paperback publishers give very specific instructions on assignments, sometimes including the art director's rough notes from a cover conference. If an illustrator is required to read a lengthy manuscript in search of illustrative material and then produce sketches subject to approval by editors, this factor should be taken into account when negotiating the fee.

Other factors requiring additional fees include: (1) changes in approach and direction after sketches are completed, requiring new sketches; (2) additional promotional uses that are above and beyond what is the common trade practice (e.g., using the art separately from the cover without the title or author's name); (3) extremely tight color comps done for sales meetings and catalogs. All of these contingencies should be understood and negotiated by buyer and seller before the assignment is confirmed.

Trade practices

The following trade practices are accepted as standard:

1. The intended use of the art must be clearly stated in a contract, purchase order or letter of agreement stating the price and terms of sale.

2. Artists normally sell only first reproduction rights unless otherwise stated.

3. If artwork is to be used for other than its original purpose, the price should be negotiated as soon as possible. The secondary use of an illustration may be of greater value than the primary use. Although there is no set formula for reuse fees, a reuse fee ranging from 25-50 per cent of the fee that would have been charged had the illustration been originally commissioned for the anticipated usage is a fairly typical charge.

4. Illustrators should negotiate reuse arrangements with the original commissioning party with speed, efficiency and all due respect to the client's position.

5. Return of original artwork to the artist is automatic unless otherwise negotiated.

6. Fees for rush work will be higher than the figures listed here. Rush deadlines may increase the original fee by an additional 50 per cent.

7. A cancellation fee should be agreed upon if a job is cancelled through no fault of the artist. Depending upon the stage at which the job is terminated, the fee paid should cover all work done, including research time, sketches, billable expenses and compensation for lost opportunities resulting from an artist's refusing other offers to make time available for a specific commission. In addition, clients who put commissions "on hold" or withhold approval for commissions for longer than 30 days should secure the assignment by paying a deposit.

8. A rejection fee should be agreed upon if the assignment is terminated because the preliminary or finished work is found not to be reasonably satisfactory. The rejection fee for finished work should be upwards of 50 per cent of the full price depending on the reason for rejection and complexity of the job. When the job is rejected at the sketch stage, a fee of one-third the original price is customary. This fee may be less for quick, rough sketches and more for highly rendered, time-consuming work.

9. Work done on speculation does not conform to industry trade practices and is contrary to the Joint Ethics Committee's Code of Fair Practice, because of its exploitive nature.

10. The Graphic Artists Guild is unalterably opposed to the use of work-for-hire contracts, in which authorship and all rights that go with it are transferred to the commissioning party and the independent artist is treated as an employee for copyright purposes only. The independent artist receives no employee benefits and loses the right to claim authorship or profit from future use of the work forever. Additional information on work for hire can be found on page 15.

11. Expenses such as unusual props, costumes, model fees, travel costs, production costs, consultation time and so on, should be billed to the client separately. An expense estimate should be included in the original written agreement or as an amendment to the agreement.

All prices for illustration in the *Guidelines* are based on a nationwide survey that was reviewed by a special committee of experienced professionals through the Graphic Artists Guild. These figures, reflecting the responses of established professionals, are meant as a point of reference only and do not necessarily reflect such important factors as deadlines, job complexity, reputation and experience of a particular illustrator, research, technique or unique quality of expression and extraordinary or extensive use of the finished art. Please refer to related material in other sections of this book, especially under *Business & Legal Practices for Commissioned Artwork* and *Standard Contracts*.

The prices shown represent only the specific use for which the illustration is intended and do not necessarily reflect any of the above considerations. The buyer and seller are free to negotiate, taking into account all the factors involved.

Mass market and trade books

Mass market books have large print runs and appeal to a wide audience. They include "blockbuster" novels, mysteries, spy stories, gothics, fantasy and science fiction, historical and modern romance novels. Trade books target a specialized audience and include poetry, serious fiction, biography, how-to books and more scholarly works that appeal to a special audience.

Because of their larger print runs and higher gross sales, mass market books normally pay higher fees. When pricing work in these areas, the size of the print run should be taken into account.

A hardcover assignment might also include paperback rights, for which a minimum of 50 per cent of the original fee is customarily charged. A considerably larger paperback printing could amount to 100 per cent of the original fee, and possibly more.

Domestic book club rights are usually included in the original hard cover fee. All other residual rights, especially movie and television rights, are reserved by the artist. Transfer of those and all other rights are negotiated by the artist and the client.

Comparative fees for paperback book cover illustration*

	Front cover	Wrap-around
Mass market	$3,500	$5,000
Trade		
Major distribution	3,000	3,500
Minor distribution	2,000	2,750
Young adult	1,500	2,000
Textbook	1,900	-

*Mass market books have large print runs and appeal to a wide audience. Trade books have limited print runs and/or appeal to a specialized audience.

Comparative fees for hardcover book jacket illustration

	Front cover	Wrap-around
Mass market	$3,000	$4,500
Trade		
Major distribution	2,500	3,500
Minor distribution	2,000	2,800

Book illustration

Book illustrators work with editors, art directors or book designers to create illustrations for trade or textbooks. Illustrations have long been recognized as an important ingredient in the editorial and marketing value of a book. Book illustration varies from simple instructional line drawings to full color spread illustrations for textbooks, young adult books, picture books and special reprints of classics.

The text and its related elements (illustration, design and type), are considered a package. The importance of illustration to a specific book may be significant or limited, depending on needs determined by the publisher.

Children's picture books and storybooks are paid by an advance against royalties. Interior illustrations for all other categories normally are paid with a one-time flat fee.

Rights to reprint the artwork in later editions and to use the art in promotional material may affect the fees and/or the royalties. Other factors affecting fees in this complex area include:

1. The type of book and the importance of the author;

2. The artist's reputation and record of commercial success;

3. The size of the print order;

4. Color separations (overlays). Artists should be paid as much or more for separations than the price of full-color illustrations since they are doing the engraver's work, thereby reducing engraving expenses;

5. Length of time estimated for the total project. Long projects may require payment to the illustrator as work progresses. For example, one-third the total fee is customarily paid upon approval of sketches, one-third upon delivery of finished art and the remainder within thirty days of delivery of finished art.

Trade practices

The following trade practices are accepted as standard:

1. The intended use of the art must be clearly stated in a contract, purchase order or letter of agreement stating the price and terms of sale.

2. Artists normally sell only first reproduction rights unless otherwise stated.

3. If artwork is to be used for other than its original purpose, the price should be negotiated as soon as possible. The secondary use of an illustration may be of greater value than the primary use. Although there is no set formula for reuse fees, a reuse fee ranging from 25 - 50 per cent of the fee that would have been charged had the illustration been originally commissioned for the anticipated usage is a fairly typical charge.

4. Illustrators should negotiate reuse arrangements with the original commissioning party with speed, efficiency and all due respect to the client's position.

5. Return of original artwork to the artist is automatic unless otherwise negotiated.

6. Fees for rush work will be higher than the figures listed here. Rush deadlines may increase the original fee by an additional 50 per cent.

7. A cancellation fee should be agreed upon if a job is cancelled through no fault of the artist. Depending upon the stage at which the job is terminated, the fee paid should cover all work done, including research time, sketches, billable expenses and compensation for lost opportunities resulting from an artist's refusing other offers to make time available for a specific commission. In addition, clients who put commissions "on hold" or withhold approval for commissions for longer than 30 days should secure the assignment by paying a deposit.

8. A rejection fee should be agreed upon if the assignment is terminated because the preliminary or finished work is found not to be reasonably satisfactory. The rejection fee for finished work should be upwards of 50 per cent of the full price depending on the reason for rejection and complexity of the job. When the job is rejected at the sketch stage, a fee of one-third the original price is customary. This fee may be less for quick, rough sketches and more for highly rendered, time-consuming work.

9. Work done on speculation does not conform to industry trade practices and is contrary to the Joint Ethics Committee's Code of Fair Practice, because of its exploitive nature.

10. The Graphic Artists Guild is unalterably opposed to the use of work-for-hire contracts, in which authorship and all rights that go with it are transferred to the commissioning party and the independent artist is treated as an employee for copyright purposes only. The independent artist receives no employee benefits and loses the right to claim authorship or profit from future use of the work forever. Additional information on work for hire can be found on page 15.

11. Expenses such as unusual props, costumes, model fees, travel costs, production costs, consultation time and so on, should be billed to the client separately. An expense estimate should be included in the original written agreement or as an amendment to the agreement.

All prices for illustration in the *Guidelines* are based on a nationwide survey that was reviewed by a special committee of experienced professionals through the Graphic Artists Guild. These figures, reflecting the responses of established professionals, are meant as a point of reference only and do not necessarily reflect such important factors as deadlines, job complexity, reputation and experience of a particular illustrator, research, technique or unique quality of expression and extraordinary or extensive use of the finished art. Please refer to related material in other sections of this book, especially under *Business & Legal Practices for Commissioned Artwork* and *Standard Contracts*.

The prices shown represent only the specific use for which the illustration is intended and do not necessarily reflect any of the above considerations. The buyer and seller are free to negotiate, taking into account all the factors involved.

Children's books

The illustrator's contribution to a children's book can cover a wide range, from a jacket illustration and a few inside drawings for a young adult novel to the entire contents of a wordless picture book. For pricing purposes, the possibilities fall into two categories: a flat fee, for books in which the illustrator's contribution is substantially less than the author's; and a royalty contract, in which the contributions of author and illustrator are comparable or in which the illustrator is also the author.

Publishers' flat-fee contracts tend to ask for all possible rights in the art in return for a one-time fee. However, the illustrator can negotiate to retain some of the rights or to provide for additional payment for additional uses, such as the sale of the paperback rights. Retaining rights to the illustrations can be more easily negotiated in cases where the author has also retained rights.

Some children's books meant for an older age level are illustrated for a flat fee, as are most young adult books. A typical flat-fee book includes the execution of a full-color jacket and from 8 to 14 black-and-white interior illustrations of various sizes.

In most children's picture books, storybooks and mid-level books, an advance against royalties is paid. If the author and the artist are not the same person, a full royalty of the book's list price is split between the two creators, commonly 50-50 in the case of a picture book. The royalty and amount of the advance are based on the illustrator's reputation, experience and desirability.

The advance is designed to reflect the anticipated earnings of the book, and will rarely exceed the royalty due on the sales of the book's entire first printing. 50 per cent of the advance is frequently paid on signing the contract and the remaining 50 per cent is paid on delivery of the artwork. Or advances may be paid in thirds on signing, on delivery of rough sketches and on delivery of the finished art.

An appropriate advance will be earned back within two years after publication. If the advance is earned back after only three months of release, either the advance was too low or the book was an unexpectedly good seller. It is to the illustrator's advantage to obtain as large an advance as possible, since considerable time can pass before the book is published and royalties are actually paid.

An advance against royalties should always be paid; otherwise the work is considered to be speculative in nature. Care should be taken to determine whether the contract requires the advance to be refunded in the event sufficient numbers of books are not sold to earn it back. It is to the illustrator's advantage to secure nonrefundable advances only.

Royalty contracts are complicated and vary from publisher to publisher. Actually "boilerplate" author's contracts, they are rarely written with artists in mind, and are difficult to comprehend. The Graphic Artists Guild strongly recommends that an attorney review any contract with which the illustrator is unfamiliar or if it contains terms about which the illustrator is uncertain, especially if it is the artist's first book contract.

Publisher's "boilerplate contracts," however, are not carved in stone and can be changed if the changes are agreeable to both parties. Among those sections of a royalty contract that are often negotiated are the lists of the royalty percentages for the publisher's uses of the work ("Publishers direct sales")

and for the sale of subsidiary rights. Please refer to the table at the end of this section for the comparative children's book illustration royalties for uses beyond the original hardcover edition.

The basic provisions of a children's book royalty contract are:

1. Grant of rights: The illustrator grants to the publisher the right to use the art as specified within the contract.

2. Delivery: Sets deadlines for finished art and sometimes for rough sketches.

3. Warranty: A representation that the illustrator has infringed on no copyrights nor broken any other laws in granting rights to the publisher.

4. Indemnity: The illustrator shares the cost of defending any lawsuit brought over the art. An artist who is found to have broken the terms of the warranty bears the entire cost of the lawsuit and any damages that may result. This clause might present more risk than the illustrator is willing to accept, but without an attorney it is difficult to counter effectively. An illustrator can request to be indemnified by the publisher for any suits arising from a request on the publisher's part, such as making a character look like a famous person.

5. Copyright: The publisher agrees to copyright the work in the artist's name.

6. Agreement to publish: The book will be published within a specific period of time, usually eighteen months from receipt of finished art.

7. Advance and division of royalties: The main points were discussed above and are reflected in the table following this section. Additional points to consider are:

(a) Paperback advance: Whether an advance against royalties will be paid for the original publisher's own paperback reprint should be negotiated at the time of the original contract. The royalty rate will usually be less than for the hardcover edition.

(b) Escalation: For trade books, royalties totaling 10% (for author and illustrator combined) often escalate to 12 1/2% after sales reach 20,000 copies. Mass market books have lower royalty rates, which can also escalate.

(c) De-escalation: Some publisher's contracts allow for royalty rates to decrease dramatically under two conditions: when high discounts are given to distributors or other buyers; or when book sales from a low-quantity reprint are slow. Not all publishers include these clauses in their contracts; the Graphic Artists Guild recommends attempting to strike, or at least to alter them.

There may be some justification for the illustrator to accept a lower royalty in a book whose sales are vastly increased by a high discount (50% or more). However, this clause should reduce the royalty gradually rather than allow the sudden cuts which occur if the royalty is based on amounts received rather than on the list price.

It is also desirable to ensure that this deep discount is not a part of the publisher's normal business practice. This could mean that publishers are using these discounts to gain sales at the expense of the artist and/or author.

By accepting a decrease in royalty for a slow-selling reprint, the illustrator may give the publisher incentive to keep the book in print. But the terms of the decrease should have limitations. For example, the book should have been in print at least two years, be in a reprint edition of 2,500 or fewer copies and have sales of less than 500 copies in one royalty period. Under these conditions, the royalty might drop 50 to 75 per cent of the original rate.

8. Author's copies: Publisher's contracts usually provide ten free copies of the book to the author, but twenty free copies are often negotiated. Most publishers offer the artist a 40 per cent discount off the list price on purchases of their book, but some will give 50 per cent off. Some publishers will pay royalties on these sales, while others, ungenerously, do not.

9. Schedule of statements and payments: This defines when and how accounting will be made. In this section a useful clause found in many contracts allows access by the artist or a designated accountant to examine the publisher's books and records. If, in a given royalty period (usually six months), errors of 5 per cent or more are found in the publisher's favor, the publisher will correct the underpayment and pay the cost of the examination up to the amount of the error.

Another provision that is often negotiated is a "pass-through clause," which takes effect when the illustrator's share of a subsidiary sale exceeds $1,000. The publisher will then send payment within thirty days of receipt rather holding it for the semi-annual royalty reporting date.

10. Remaindering: If the book is to be remaindered, the publisher should allow the illustrator to buy any number of copies at the remaindered price.

11. Termination of agreement: Provides that if a work is not or will not be available in any edition in the United States, it is out of print. At that time, the illustrator may request in writing that all rights return to the artist. The publisher will usually have six months to declare an intent to reprint and a reasonable amount of time in which to issue a new edition. Failing this, the agreement terminates and all rights return to the artist.

In some boilerplates, "out-of-print" is defined too narrowly, or the time allowed the publisher can be unreasonably lengthy. Some contracts also grant the illustrator the right to purchase any existing film, plates, die stamps, etc., within thirty days after termination.

Occasionally, a provision is added to contracts which allow the illustrator to consult on the design of the book and to view blues, color separations and proofs while corrections can still be made. However, a good working relationship and an informal agreement with the art director is probably as good a guarantee of this actually occurring.

Many of these contractual points may not add up to much money for any one book, or even a lifetime of books. But in order for the illustrator to retain the most control over the work, it makes sense to attempt to negotiate the best possible contract, not merely the best possible advance.

Young adult picture books

Advances or royalties are normally not paid in this category. Books are done for a straight fee. A typical book includes a full-color wraparound jacket and from 8 to 14 black-and-white interior illustrations of various sizes.

Juvenile workbooks

Most workbooks are given out through brokers or agents who work directly with the publisher on pricing for each book. Brokers and agents specializing in this field represent many illustrators who work in varied styles. Workbooks usually are priced out per page, per half page or per spot. Although fees are quite low, an entire workbook can add up to a considerable amount of work. Artists who are able to turn out this kind of artwork at a fast rate may find this type of assignment quite lucrative and feel secure in knowing that months of work lie ahead. Often, a single book needing a considerable amount of illustration is divided up among several illustrators in order to meet publishing deadlines.

Budgets for workbooks vary considerably depending on the size of the publisher, locality, publication schedules and experience of the artist.

Comparative fees for illustrations used in book interiors

Young adult, major publisher or large distribution

	B&W*
Spread	$1,000
Full page	500
Half page	400
Spot - quarter page	300

Young adult, small publisher or limited distribution

	B&W*
Spread	800
Full page	400
Half page	350
Spot - quarter page	300

Adult hardcover, major publisher or large distribution

	B&W	Color
Spread	$1,800	$2,000
Full page	1,000	1,600
Half page	600	1,000
Spot - quarter page	400	600

Adult hardcover, small publisher or limited distribution

	B&W	Color
Spread	$1,500	$1,500
Full page	1,000	1,200
Half page	600	700
Spot - quarter page	300	300

College textbooks

	B&W*	Color
Spread	$750	$1,500
Full page	600	1,200
Half page	400	750
Quarter page	275	400
Spot	175	250

El - hi textbooks (elementary through high school levels)

	B&W	Color
Spread	$600	$1,200
Full page	400	1,000
Half page	350	700
Quarter page	200	400
Spot	100	150

*Add 25 per cent for each color overlay.

Juvenile workbook illustration

	B&W*	Color
Full page	$500	$800
Half page	350	500
Quarter page	200	300
Spot	100	150

Notes:
A spot illustration is one animal, one person or on inanimate object. Necessary research should be supplied by the publisher otherwise additional compensation is warranted.

* Add 25% to black and white prices for each color overlay.

Comparative fees for children's picture book illustration*

	Advance	Royalty	Royalty escala-tion
Illustrations only	$9,500	5 - 7.5%	6.25 - 10%
Text and illustrations	13,500	10%	12.5%

*Based on a 32-page picture book. For illustrations only, royalties escalate after sales of 18,500 copies. For text and illustrations, royalties escalate after sales of 14,000 copies.

Comparative royalties for children's picture books used beyond the original hardcover edition*

Publisher's direct sales	Percentage of receipts†
Publisher's own paperback edition	6% of list price
Canadian sales	10% (may escalate to 12 - 1/2%, or 2/3 to 1/2 of regular royalty)
Consumer sales	5%
Remainder sales	10%

Subsidiary rights sales

Foreign publisher, translation or English language edition	75%
First serial, dramatic TV, motion picture	90%
Domestic reprint, paperback, book club, digest, serial or anthology, merchandising, audiovisual, sound recording	50%

*For rights not reserved by the artist. Rights most commonly reserved include dramatic, TV, motion picture adaptation and merchandising

†For two creators, this figure would (as is the basic royalty), be divided between them.

Editorial illustration

Illustrators creating editorial art work with art directors and editors of consumer and trade magazines and newspapers to illustrate specific stories, covers, columns or other editorial material. Often, the art director, editor and illustrator discuss the slant and intended impact of a piece before sketches are prepared. If necessary, illustrators might prepare several sketches to explore a range of approaches to the problem. Editorial art is usually commissioned under tight deadlines, especially in news publications and weekly magazines.

Fees for editorial illustration are often considerably lower than fees in advertising. This is generally true for all creative services in the editorial field, including salaries or fees paid to editors, photographers and writers. Despite inflation, increasing advertising revenue (per page sold) and large increases in other production costs (paper stock, printing and binding, mailing), current fees paid by many national magazines are often compa-rable to fees for the same work commissioned twenty years ago. On the positive side, the editorial area continues to provide a showcase for illustrators just entering the field and usually offers greater creative freedom to experienced illustrators than does advertising illustration.

Trade practices

The following trade practices are accepted as standard:

1. The intended use of the art must be clearly stated in a contract, purchase order or letter of agreement stating the price and terms of sale.

2. Artists normally sell only first reproduction rights unless otherwise stated.

3. If artwork is to be used for other than its original purpose, the price should be negotiated as soon as possible. The secondary use of an illustration may be of greater value than the primary use. Although there is no set formula for reuse fees, a reuse fee ranging from 25-50 per cent of the fee that would have been charged had the illustration been originally commissioned for the anticipated usage is a fairly typical charge.

4. Illustrators should negotiate reuse arrangements with the original commissioning party with speed, efficiency and all due respect to the client's position.

5. Return of original artwork to the artist is automatic unless otherwise negotiated.

6. Fees for rush work will be higher than the figures listed here. Rush deadlines may increase the original fee by an additional 50 per cent.

7. A cancellation fee should be agreed upon if a job is cancelled through no fault of the artist. Depending upon the stage at which the job is terminated, the fee paid should cover all work done, including research time, sketches, billable expenses and compensation for lost opportunities resulting from an artist's refusing other offers to make time available for a specific commission. In addition, clients who put commissions "on hold" or withhold approval for commissions for longer than 30 days should secure the assignment by paying a deposit.

8. A rejection fee should be agreed upon if the assignment is terminated because the preliminary or finished work is found not to be reasonably satisfactory. The rejection fee for finished work should be upwards of 50 per cent of the full price depending on the reason for rejection and complexity of the job. When the job is rejected at the sketch stage, a fee of one-third the original price is customary. This fee may be less for quick, rough sketches and more for highly rendered, time-consuming work.

9. Work done on speculation does not conform to industry trade practices and is contrary to the Joint Ethics Committee's Code of Fair Practice, because of its exploitive nature.

10. The Graphic Artists Guild is unalterably opposed to the use of work-for-hire contracts, in which authorship and all rights that go with it are transferred to the commissioning party and the independent artist is treated as an employee for copyright purposes only. The independent artist receives no employee benefits and loses the right to claim authorship or profit from future use of the work forever. Additional information on work for hire can be found on page 15.

11. Expenses such as unusual props, costumes, model fees, travel costs, production costs, consultation time and so on, should be billed to the client separately. An expense estimate should be included in the original written agreement or as an amendment to the agreement.

All prices for illustration in the *Guidelines* are based on a nationwide survey that was reviewed by a special committee of experienced professionals through the Graphic Artists Guild. These figures, reflecting the responses of established professionals, are meant as a point of reference only and do not necessarily reflect such important factors as deadlines, job complexity, reputation and experience of a particular illustrator, research, technique or unique quality of expression and extraordinary or extensive use of the finished art. Please refer to related material in other sections of this book, especially under *Business & Legal Practices for Commissioned Artwork* and *Standard Contracts.*

The prices shown represent only the specific use for which the illustration is intended and do not necessarily reflect any of the above considerations. The buyer and seller are free to negotiate, taking into account all the factors involved.

Magazines

Fees for editorial assignments are usually tied to the magazine's circulation and geographic distribution, which in turn determine its advertising rates and thus its income. Several categories of consumer magazines are presented below. However, magazines don't always fall into one exact category. For example, *Time, Reader's Digest* and *Family Circle* are high-circulation, national magazines. Although *Forbes* is distributed nationally, it falls into the regional or medium category because of its relatively lower circulation. It is, however, a highly successful publication which experienced tremendous growth during the aggressive business climate of the 1980's. *Popular Mechanics* is also distributed nationally but falls into the local or small category because of its specialized audience and relatively lower circulation. *New York* magazine is primarily local in readership but has a circulation large enough to place it in the regional or medium category.

For editorial assignments in trade publications, figures on circulation and readership are the most accepted basis for judging the proper categories for publications. Occasionally the type of readership can influence the level of quality of the publication and fees paid for commissioned artwork. Circulation and distribution information is usually available from advertising and subscription departments of magazines.

Spot illustrations are usually one column in width and simple in matter. Although quarter-page illustrations are not spots, some magazines (particularly those with lower budgets) make no distinction between the two. Judging the complexity of the assignment can help determine if a spot rate is appropriate. There is a tendency in recent years to call any illustration that is less than three-quarter or one-half page a spot illustration. This practice is unacceptable as it fails to accurately describe the commissioned illustration and undermines established trade practices to the detriment of the artist.

Spread illustrations occupy two facing pages in a publication. In the event a spread illustration occupies only one-half of each page, a basis for fee negotiation could be based on the addition of the partial page rates below. However, if only the title or very little text is used on the spread, it could be interpreted as a full spread illustration. In these cases, discretion should be used.

Newspapers

Some city newspapers like *The New York Times* and *Washington Post* are considered large-circulation, national publications for pricing purposes. They carry national and international news and are distributed both nationally and internationally. Medium-circulation newspapers generally are regional in nature, sell outside the city where they are published, often carry national news and publish four-color supplements and weekend magazines. Local newspapers, naturally, have the lowest circulation. However, even in this category the size of readership varies widely and must always be taken into account when determining fees. It is worth noting that this is one of the lowest-paying fields of illustration and has its value mostly as a trade-off for the excellent exposure that large daily newspapers provide, especially for new and emerging talent. Still, the Guild maintains that the prevailing fees in this market are low and that wide exposure is a poor exchange.

Comparative fees for magazine editorial illustration

National consumer, mass trade or large circulation	B&W*	Color
Cover	-	$4,000
Spread	-	3,000
Full page	-	2,000
Half page	900	1,200
Spot - quarter page	500 - 800	600 - 900

Regional consumer, specific trade or medium circulation		
Cover	-	$2,800
Spread	-	2,600
Full page	-	1,800
Half page	750	1,000
Spot - quarter page	400 - 600	500 - 750

Limited audience or small circulation		
Cover	-	$2,400
Spread	-	2,200
Full page	1,000	1,400
Half page	700	800
Spot - quarter page	350 - 500	400 - 700

*Add 25% to black and white prices for each color overlay.

Comparative fees for newspaper editorial illustration

National or major metro area	B&W
Section opener	$1,500
Half page	900
Quarter page	600
Spot	300-500

Small city	B&W
Section opener	$1,000
Half page	800
Quarter page	500
Spot	300

Comparative fees for magazine supplements for newspapers editorial illustration

National or major metro area	B&W	Color
Front cover	-	$2,000
Full page	-	1,500
Half page	750	800
Spot-quarter page	350-600	400-600

Small city	B&W	Color
Front cover	-	$1,400
Full page	-	1,200
Half page	600	800
Spot-quarter page	300-450	400-600

Recording cover illustration

The demand for engaging, forceful and highly creative packaging for recordings has attracted the best of today's talented editorial and advertising illustrators, who in turn have created a new art form. Many record album covers have become collector's items. Several books have been published on record album cover art and an ongoing market has developed for collecting.

Commissions for recording cover illustration can be lucrative. Fees vary widely, however, depending on recording artists, particular label and recording company and the desirability and fame of the illustrator.

Fees for complex recording packages have gone higher than $10,000. This kind of assignment, however, requires many meetings, sketches and changes.

Most recording companies produce under different labels depending on the recording artist and type of music. The minor labels of major recording companies are usually reserved for less commercial records and re-releases of previous recordings.

Recent mergers and acquisitions in the recording industry (Sony-Columbia, BMG-RCA, Time-Warner), have all but eliminated any discernible differences in fees based on geographic location. In all cases, only record company publication rights are transferred and the original art is returned to the artist. Sometimes, tie-in poster rights are included.

Trade practices

The following trade practices are accepted as standard:

1. The intended use of the art must be clearly stated in a contract, purchase order or letter of agreement stating the price and terms of sale.

2. Artists normally sell only first reproduction rights unless otherwise stated.

3. If artwork is to be used for other than its original purpose, the price should be negotiated as soon as possible. The secondary use of an illustration may be of greater value than the primary use. Although there is no set formula for reuse fees, a reuse fee ranging from 25-50 per cent of the fee that would have been charged had the illustration been originally commissioned for the anticipated usage is a fairly typical charge.

4. Illustrators should negotiate reuse arrangements with the original commissioning party with speed, efficiency and all due respect to the client's position.

5. Return of original artwork to the artist is automatic unless otherwise negotiated.

6. Fees for rush work will be higher than the figures listed here. Rush deadlines may increase the original fee by an additional 50 per cent.

7. A cancellation fee should be agreed upon if a job is cancelled through no fault of the artist. Depending upon the stage at which the job is terminated, the fee paid should cover all work done, including research time, sketches, billable expenses and compensation for lost opportunities resulting from an artist's refusing other offers to make time available for a specific commission. In addition, clients who put commissions "on hold" or withhold approval for commissions for longer than 30 days should secure the assignment by paying a deposit.

8. A rejection fee should be agreed upon if the assignment is terminated because the preliminary or finished work is found not to be reasonably satisfactory. The rejection fee for finished work should be upwards of 50 per cent of the full price depending on the reason for rejection and complexity of the job. When the job is rejected at the sketch stage, a fee of one-third the original price is customary. This fee may be less for quick, rough sketches and more for highly rendered, time-consuming work.

9. Work done on speculation does not conform to industry trade practices and is contrary to the Joint Ethics Committee's Code of Fair Practice, because of its exploitive nature.

10. The Graphic Artists Guild is unalterably opposed to the use of work-for-hire contracts, in which authorship and all rights that go with it are transferred to the commissioning party and the independent artist is treated as an employee for copyright purposes only. The independent artist receives no employee benefits and loses the right to claim authorship or profit from future use of the work forever. Additional information on work for hire can be found on page 15.

11. Expenses such as unusual props, costumes, model fees, travel costs, production costs, consultation time and so on, should be billed to the client separately. An expense estimate should be included in the original written agreement or as an amendment to the agreement.

All prices for illustration in the *Guidelines* are based on a nationwide survey that was reviewed by a special committee of experienced professionals through the Graphic Artists Guild. These figures, reflecting the responses of established professionals, are meant as a point of reference only and do not necessarily reflect such important factors as deadlines, job complexity, reputation and experience of a particular illustrator, research, technique or unique quality of expression and extraordinary or extensive use of the finished art. Please refer to related material in other sections of this book, especially under *Business & Legal Practices for Commissioned Artwork* and *Standard Contracts.*

The prices shown represent only the specific use for which the illustration is intended and do not necessarily reflect any of the above considerations. The buyer and seller are free to negotiate, taking into account all the factors involved.

Comparative fees for recording cover illustration

	Popular and rock	Classical and jazz	Other
Major studio or distribution	$5,000	$3,000	$3,500
Small studio or distribution	3,500	2,500	3,000
Re-released recording	3,000	2,000	2,500

*Fees reflect one work of art used on LP record covers, CD covers and cassette covers.

Fashion illustration

Fashion illustrators are graphic artists who illustrate clothed figures and accessories within a certain style or "look" for retail outlets, agencies or manufacturers. Occasionally, fashion illustrators work in the editorial area for fashion magazines or newspapers.

Sometimes, these artists are required to create an illustration with only the garment for reference (i.e., the illustrator must invent the model, pose and background). Model fees, props, photography, research and special materials are some of the factors that affect pricing in this area.

Although the market for apparel and accessory illustration has declined in recent years, it has been offset in part by growth in the beauty and cosmetic areas, including package illustration.

Most apparel illustration is paid on a per-figure basis, with an additional charge for backgrounds. Model fees are always a billable expense. Most accessory illustration is paid on a per-item basis. When more than one item is shown, additional items can be charged at a lower unit price. With the exception of specialized work, accessory illustration rates are generally 50 to 75 per cent of per-figure prices.

The price ranges reflect fees for women's, men's and children's fashion illustration. These ranges do not reflect complexity of style and fees for the new, highly rendered and photographic style of fashion illustration, which commands a 50 per cent premium over the high ranges in all categories. A particular illustrator's experience and desirability is always an important factor in determining the fee.

Trade practices

The following trade practices are accepted as standard:

1. The intended use of the art must be clearly stated in a contract, purchase order or letter of agreement stating the price and terms of sale.

2. Artists normally sell only first reproduction rights unless otherwise stated.

3. If artwork is to be used for other than its original purpose, the price should be negotiated as soon as possible. The secondary use of an illustration may be of greater value than the primary use. Although there is no set formula for reuse fees, a reuse fee ranging from 25-50 per cent of the fee that would have been charged had the illustration been originally commissioned for the anticipated usage is a fairly typical charge.

4. Illustrators should negotiate reuse arrangements with the original commissioning party with speed, efficiency and all due respect to the client's position.

5. Return of original artwork to the artist is automatic unless otherwise negotiated.

6. Fees for rush work will be higher than the figures listed here. Rush deadlines may increase the original fee by an additional 50 per cent.

7. A cancellation fee should be agreed upon if a job is cancelled through no fault of the artist. Depending upon the stage at which the job is terminated, the fee paid should cover all work done, including research time, sketches, billable expenses and compensation for lost opportunities resulting from an artist's refusing other offers to make time available for a specific commission. In addition, clients who put commissions "on hold" or withhold approval for commissions for longer than 30 days should secure the assignment by paying a deposit.

8. A rejection fee should be agreed upon if the assignment is terminated because the preliminary or finished work is found not to be reasonably satisfactory. The rejection fee for finished work should be upwards of 50 per cent of the full price depending on the reason for rejection and complexity of the job. When the job is rejected at the sketch stage, a fee of one-third the original price is customary. This fee may be less for quick, rough sketches and more for highly rendered, time-consuming work.

9. Work done on speculation does not conform to industry trade practices and is contrary to the Joint Ethics Committee's Code of Fair Practice, because of its exploitive nature.

10. The Graphic Artists Guild is unalterably opposed to the use of work-for-hire contracts, in which authorship and all rights that go with it are transferred to the commissioning party and the independent artist is treated as an employee for copyright purposes only. The independent artist receives no employee benefits and loses the right to claim authorship or profit from future use of the work forever. Additional information on work for hire can be found on page 15.

11. Expenses such as unusual props, costumes, model fees, travel costs, production costs, consultation time and so on, should be billed to the client separately. An expense estimate should be included in the original written agreement or as an amendment to the agreement.

All prices for illustration in the *Guidelines* are based on a nationwide survey that was reviewed by a special committee of experienced professionals through the Graphic Artists Guild. These figures, reflecting the responses of established professionals, are meant as a point of reference only and do not necessarily reflect such important factors as deadlines, job complexity, reputation and experience of a particular illustrator, research, technique or unique quality of expression and extraordinary or extensive use of the finished art. Please refer to related material in other sections of this book, especially under *Business & Legal Practices for Commissioned Artwork* and *Standard Contracts*.

The prices shown represent only the specific use for which the illustration is intended and do not necessarily reflect any of the above considerations. The buyer and seller are free to negotiate, taking into account all the factors involved.

Comparative fees for fashion illustration in advertising

Newspapers	B&W*
Major department store, small ad	$400 - 600
Major department store, full page	500 - 1,250
Large specialty shop, small ad	400 - 600
Small specialty shop, small ad	350 - 500
Mat service, any size	75 - 500
Major advertising agency	1,500 - 3,000
Small advertising agency	750 - 1,800
Trade manufacturer	350 - 1,000

Magazines	B&W*	Color
National, full page	$750 - 1,250	$750 - 2,000
National, one - third page	600 - 900	-
Local, full page	350 - 600	500 - 750
Local, one - third page	350 - 500	-
Spot	75 - 250	-
Trade manufacturer	350 - 500	500 - 750

Other	B&W*	Color
Collateral advertising	$400 - 600	$750 - 1,000
Store catalog	200 - 400	350 - 600
Patterns	200	300 - 400
Showroom illustrations	-	75 - 250
Presentation boards	-	100 - 250
Lines sheets/sales catalog, figures	20 - 50	-
Line sheets/sales catalog, flat	10 - 25	-
Retail buying service	25 - 40	

*Add 25% to black and white prices for each color overlay.

Greeting card, novelty and retail goods illustration

The greeting card and the paper novelty fields have grown more competitive after experiencing a business boom in the 1980's. New greeting card companies and fresh card lines continue to enter—and leave—the industry, while the largest card publishers continue to hold the lion's share of the market. Since success or failure in this business is based largely on the buying responses of the public, greeting card designs lend themselves particularly well to royalty or licensing arrangements.

Artwork for retail products such as novelty merchandising, apparel, china, giftware, toys and other manufactured items is purchased thorough licensing agreements. Calendars and posters for retail sale may use licensing or royalty agreements.

Please refer to "Royalties" and "Licensing" in the chapter on *How Artwork Is Priced* and to "Book Illustration," in this chapter.

Greeting cards

Although the major companies publish mostly cards developed by staff artists, they do commission some outside work. The rest of the industry depends heavily on freelance illustration and design. Designs are generally developed to fit into everyday or seasonal lines. Everyday cards include friendship, birthday, anniversary, get well, juvenile, religious/inspirational, congratulations, sympathy and similar greetings. The vast majority of seasonal greetings are Christmas cards, making up more than one-third of all cards sold and as much as 50 to 100 per cent of some card companies' offerings. Other seasonal cards include Valentine's Day, Easter, Mother's and Father's Day, Hanukkah, and other holidays. Most greeting cards are created in full color. Special effects, such as embossed, die-cut or pop-up cards, command larger fees.

Sales in mass-market outlets such as supermarkets experienced tremendous growth over the last decade, a factor emphasizing the benefits of royalty agreements. Emphasis in the future is expected to be on addressing specific consumer audiences.

New market niches, such as cards for Hispanics, working women and seniors, are being introduced and expect some growth in sales during the next decade.

Generally, freelance graphic artists create individual designs which they sell to publishers for greeting card use. Revisions on a proposed design should not take place before reaching agreement on payment and terms. Graphic artists who base their business on greeting card designs usually develop a different style for different clients to minimize competition.

Artists whose cards sell well may propose or be commissioned to develop an entire line of cards for a company, which involves creating from 20 to 36 stylistically similar cards with a variety of greetings. In cases where an artist's cards have become top sellers and the style strongly identified with the company, the value of the artist's work to the company has been recognized with equity and other compensation.

Greeting card designs are sold on an advance against royalty basis or for a flat fee. The royalty is usually a percentage of the wholesale price. A nonrefundable advance should always be paid in anticipation of royalties, as production and distribution schedules require a year to eighteen months before a design reaches the marketplace.

Many greeting card companies purchase greeting card rights only, with the artist retaining all other rights. Limited rights are appropriate, since most cards, particularly holiday greetings, are only marketed for one year.

Royalties and the related topic of licensing are further discussed in the chapter on *How Artwork Is Priced.*

Retail products

When a design or illustration is developed for resale and marketing as a product, it is usually done under a licensing agreement. Art for T-shirts, towels, mugs, tote bags and other such items, whether developed and sold by the artist or as spin-offs from nationally known characters, is sold in this manner. Among markets that customarily use licensing agreements are novelty items, apparel, greeting cards, paper products, giftware, china, toys, posters and manufacturing.

In licensing agreements an artist, designer or owner of rights to artwork permits another party to use the art for a limited specific purpose, for a specified time, in a specified territory, in return for a fee or royalty. At the expiration of the license, the right to use the property reverts to the owner.

Payment under licensing agreements normally takes the form of royalties. When the product or artwork is to be sold commercially, royalties are usually a percentage of the retail or wholesale price or a fixed amount per item sold.

In this field a large royalty percentage is generally more desirable than smaller royalties with a larger advance. A non-refundable advance against royalties should be included in the contract and negotiating a guaranteed minimum royalty is advisable. It is advisable to consult an attorney before signing a licensing or royalty agreement, which are binding contracts.

Many graphic artists base their business on creating images for licensing to one or more markets. Recently new companies have formed that specialize in representing licensed properties. They may even plan marketing support for these products through animated movies, TV series, publishing ventures, recordings and other forms of promotion.

For a detailed discussion of licensing, please refer to the chapter on *How Artwork Is Priced.* An excellent book on licensing is *Licensing Art and Design* by Caryn Leland, published by Allworth Press (see Bibliography for ordering information). A Model Short Form Licensing Agreement appears in the chapter on *Standard Contracts*, reprinted by permission of the author.

Limited edition prints

Art for limited edition prints may be created by artists independently or under contract with a gallery or publisher. Payment is either on a commission or royalty basis, and an advance is usually included. Both the advance and the ultimate payment to the artist will vary depending on the size of the print run, the number of colors printed, the selling price and other factors. A typical arrangement of a limited edition of prints is for advance against 50 to 67 per cent of gross sales revenues (i.e., the gallery's commission is 33 to 50 per cent). If the publisher or gallery is responsible for all production costs (plate-making, etching, proofing, paper, ink, etc.) and advertising and promotion, artists will receive less.

A typical edition ranges from 100 to 250 prints. Each print is usually numbered and signed by the artist. The agreement should guarantee the artist a certain number

of artist's proofs to use in any way they wish.

Marketing can make or break a limited-edition venture. Market research should be done prior to entering into a binding agreement, making significant outlays of money or investing time in creating the art. The market for limited edition prints is regulated by law in a number of states, including New York, California and Illinois. Extensive disclosures or disclaimers may have to accompany limited edition prints sold in these states.

Trade practices

The following trade practices are accepted as standard:

1. The intended use of the art must be clearly stated in a contract, purchase order or letter of agreement stating the price and terms of sale.

2. Artists normally sell only first reproduction rights unless otherwise stated.

3. If artwork is to be used for other than its original purpose, the price should be negotiated as soon as possible. The secondary use of an illustration may be of greater value than the primary use. Although there is no set formula for reuse fees, a reuse fee ranging from 25-50 per cent of the fee that would have been charged had the illustration been originally commissioned for the anticipated usage is a fairly typical charge.

4. Illustrators should negotiate reuse arrangements with the original commissioning party with speed, efficiency and all due respect to the client's position.

5. Return of original artwork to the artist is automatic unless otherwise negotiated.

6. Fees for rush work will be higher than the figures listed here. Rush deadlines may increase the original fee by an additional 50 per cent.

7. A cancellation fee should be agreed upon if a job is cancelled through no fault of the artist. Depending upon the stage at which the job is terminated, the fee paid should cover all work done, including research time, sketches, billable expenses and compensation for lost opportunities resulting from an artist's refusing other offers to make time available for a specific commission. In addition, clients who put commissions "on hold" or withhold approval for commissions for longer than 30 days should secure the assignment by paying a deposit.

8. A rejection fee should be agreed upon if the assignment is terminated because the preliminary or finished work is found not to be reasonably satisfactory. The rejection fee for finished work should be upwards of 50 per cent of the full price depending on the reason for rejection and complexity of the job. When the job is rejected at the sketch stage, a fee of one-third the original price is customary. This fee may be less for quick, rough sketches and more for highly rendered, time-consuming work.

9. Work done on speculation does not conform to industry trade practices and is contrary to the Joint Ethics Committee's Code of Fair Practice, because of its exploitive nature.

10. The Graphic Artists Guild is unalterably opposed to the use of work-for-hire contracts, in which authorship and all rights that go with it are transferred to the commissioning party and the independent artist is treated as an employee for copyright purposes only. The independent artist receives no employee benefits and loses the right to claim authorship or profit from future use of the work forever. Additional information on work for hire can be found on page 15.

11. Expenses such as unusual props, costumes, model fees, travel costs, production costs, consultation time and so on, should be billed to the client separately. An expense estimate should be included in the original written agreement or as an amendment to the agreement.

All prices for illustration in the *Guidelines* are based on a nationwide survey that was reviewed by a special committee of experienced professionals through the Graphic Artists Guild. These figures, reflecting the responses of established professionals, are meant as a point of reference only and do not necessarily reflect such important factors as deadlines, job complexity, reputation and experience of a particular illustrator, research, technique or unique quality of expression and extraordinary or extensive use of the finished art. Please refer to related material in other sections of this book, especially under *Business & Legal Practices for Commissioned Artwork* and *Standard Contracts.*

The prices shown represent only the specific use for which the illustration is intended and do not necessarily reflect any of the above considerations. The buyer and seller are free to negotiate, taking into account all the factors involved.

Comparative fees for novelty and retail goods illustration

Greeting cards	Color
Original design, flat fee	$400 - 600
Original design, advance	350 - 500
Original design, royalty*	4 - 8%
Character licensing, advance	1,000 +
Character licensing, royalty*	7 - 10%

*Royalties are based on wholesale price. Advances and royalties may vary widely depending on the client and the distribution.

Posters	
Original design, flat fee	$8,500
Original design, advance	2,500
Original design, royalty	10%
Licensed artwork, flat fee	6,500
Licensed artwork, advance	2,500
Licensed artwork, royalty	10%

Calendars (12 illustrations plus cover)	B&W*	Full color
Flat fee only	$12,000	$24,000
Advance	2,500	5,000
Royalty	10%	10%

Products (T-shirts, gift tins, mugs, china, game boards)	Color
Original design, flat fee	$5,000
Original design, advance	2,000
Original design, royalty	5%
Licensed artwork, flat fee	2,000
Licensed artwork, advance	1,000
Licensed artwork, royalty	5 - 10%

*Add 25% for each color overlay

Medical illustration

Medical illustration is one of the most demanding and highly technical areas of the graphic arts. Medical illustrators are specially trained graphic artists who combine a ready scientific knowledge of the human body with a mastery of graphic techniques to create medical and health illustrations. The work of a medical illustrator ranges from ultra-realistic, anatomically precise pieces emphasizing instructional content, to imaginative and conceptual pieces emphasizing subjective impact.

Accuracy of content and effectiveness of visual presentation are paramount in this field. Many medical illustrators hold Master's degrees from one of five medical schools offering training in the field. Formal studies include gross anatomy, physiology, embryology, pathology, neuroanatomy and surgery, plus commercial art techniques, television and photography.

Most medical illustrators work with a wide variety of rendering techniques including pen and ink, pencil, carbon dust, watercolor, colored pencil, acrylic and, recently, computers. Many of these artists also design and construct models, exhibits and prosthetics. Some medical illustrators also specialize in techniques for film and video.

Because of their extensive backgrounds in science and medicine, medical illustrators often work directly with clients, editors and art directors in the conceptual development of projects.

A growing market for medical illustration is the legal field. Medical illustration is commissioned specifically for use in courtroom proceedings to clarify complex medical or scientific information for judges and juries.

Prices for medical illustration are based on the intended market, copyright uses purchased, project complexity, research required and the individual artist's experience and skill. For the purposes of the *Guidelines* pricing information is given for only the primary markets that commission medical art.

Trade practices

The following trade practices are accepted as standard:

1. The intended use of the art must be clearly stated in a contract, purchase order or letter of agreement stating the price and terms of sale.

2. Artists normally sell only first reproduction rights unless otherwise stated.

3. If artwork is to be used for other than its original purpose, the price should be negotiated as soon as possible. The secondary use may be of greater value than the primary use. Although there is no set formula for reuse fees, a reuse fee ranging from 25-50 per cent of the fee that would have been charged had the illustration been originally commissioned for the anticipated usage is a fairly typical charge.

4. Illustrators should negotiate reuse arrangements with the original commissioning party with speed, efficiency and all due respect to the client's position.

5. Return of original artwork to the artist is automatic unless otherwise negotiated.

6. Fees for rush work will be higher than the figures listed here. Rush deadlines may increase the original fee by an additional 50 percent.

7. A cancellation fee should be agreed upon if a job is cancelled through no fault of the artist. Depending upon the stage at which the job is terminated, the fee paid should cover all work done, including research time, sketches, billable expenses and compensation for lost opportunities resulting from an artist's refusing other offers to make time available for a specific commission. In addition, clients who put commissions "on hold" or withhold approval for commissions for longer than 30 days should secure the assignment by paying a deposit.

8. A rejection fee should be agreed upon if the assignment is cancelled because the preliminary or finished work is found not to be reasonably satisfactory. The rejection fee for finished work should be upwards of 50 percent of the full price depending on the reason for rejection and complexity of the job. When the job is rejected at the sketch stage, a fee of one-third the original price is customary. This fee may be less for quick, rough sketches and more for highly rendered, time-consuming work.

9. Work done on speculation does not conform to industry trade practices and is contrary to the Joint Ethics Committee's Code of Fair Practice.

10. The Graphic Artists Guild is unalterably opposed to the use of work-for-hire contracts, in which authorship and all rights that go with it are transferred to the commissioning party and the artist is treated as an employee for copyright purposes only.

The artist receives no employee benefits and loses the right to claim authorship or profit from future use of the work forever. Additional information on work for hire can be found on page 15.

11. Expenses such as shipping fees, travel costs, consultation time and other unusual expenses should be billed to the client separately. An expense estimate should be included in the original written agreement or as an amendment to the agreement.

Pricing information in this section is based on a broad survey of medical illustrators in cooperation with the Graphic Artists Guild and the Association of Medical Illustrators. The ranges shown are meant as points of reference from which both buyer and seller are free to negotiate, taking into account usage, copyright, complexity, research and the artist's experience, skill and reputation.

The price ranges shown represent only the specific use for which the illustration is intended and do not necessarily reflect any of the above considerations. The buyer and seller are free to negotiate, taking into account all the factors involved.

Comparative fees for medical illustration in advertising

	Line	Tone	Color
Conceptual	$500 - 2,500	$1,000 - 3,500	$2,500 - 8,000
Anatomical/Surgical	500 - 2,500	1,000 - 3,500	2,000 - 8,000
Product	500 - 2,000	500 - 2,500	1,500 - 8,000
Poster	-	-	2,500 - 10,000
Spot*	300 - 750	500 - 1,200	500 - 1,500
Per diem rate for special consultation and/or research			250 - 1,000.

Notes:
1. The ranges in advertising rates reflect the difference between first use rights and all-rights transfers, as well as the size and complexity of the work.
2. Reuse fees ranging between 25 - 100% are based on when, where and how the art is to be reused and should be considered when the project is negotiated.
3. Sketches or comps are from 30% to 50% of the above rates.

*Because of the scientific complexity of the subject matter, reproduction size is often irrelevant in pricing. For the purpose of these charts, a spot is considered to be any illustration of a quarter page or less.

Comparative fees for medical illustration in editorial publications

Professional publications (medical journals)	Line	Tone	Color
Cover	-	$750 - 1,000	$750 - 1,500
Spread	-	750 - 1,000	1,000 - 2,000
Full page	200 - 600	450 - 850	750 - 1,500
Spot*	150 - 350	250 - 500	250 - 600

Comparative fees for medical illustration in editorial publications (continued)

Consumer health and science publications (magazines and books)	Line	Tone	Color
Cover	-	-	$1,500 - 3,500
Spread	-	-	1,500 - 2,000
Full page	800 - 1,200	800 - 1,500	800 - 2,000
Spot*	200 - 500	350 - 750	450 - 1,000

*Because of the scientific complexity of the subject matter, reproduction size is often irrelevant in pricing. For the purpose of these charts, a spot is considered to be any illustration of a quarter page or less.

Comparative fees for instructional illustration (college, medical, surgical textbooks; patient education publications)

	Line	Tone	Color
Simple	$100 - 150	$100 - 250	$200 - 375
Moderate	150 - 300	200 - 350	300 - 500
Complex	200 - 550	300 - 600	375 - 900

Note:
Rates shown are for limited noncommercial rights only. Reuse fees range from 25% to 30% of the original price and are based on the intended reuse.

Comparative fees for medical legal illustration

	Simple	Complex
Each image (per panel)*	$500	$1,500
Overlays	100	500
Rates for consultation, deposition or settlement brochure production	50 - 150 per hour	
Rates for testimony	500 - 1,000 per day	

Note:
An exhibit is comprised of one or more images on a single panel. An exhibit is usually 30" x 40". Related images for an inset or secondary part of the primary image may be less depending on complexity. Production costs and expenses are billed separately.

Comparative fees for model construction and 3-D illustration

	Simple	Complex	Hourly rate
Construction of model	$2,500 - 5,000	$5,000 - 20,000	$50 - 150

Note:
Unusual materials and expenses are billed extra.

Technical illustration

Technical illustrators are graphic artists who create highly accurate renderings of machinery, charts, instruments, scientific subjects (such as biological studies, geological formations and chemical reactions), space technology, cartography (maps) or virtually any subject that requires precision of interpretation in illustration. Technical illustrators often work directly with a scientist, engineer or technician to achieve the most explicit and accurate visualization of the subject and/or information.

Technical illustration is used in all areas of graphics communication in this age of high technology. Some of the areas most commonly requiring this specialized art are: annual reports, special interest magazines, industrial publications, package illustrations, advertising, corporate, editorial, computer graphics and audiovisuals.

These artists may work in a variety of media: ink, wash, airbrush, pencil, watercolor, gouache, computers, etc., and are often trained in mechanical drafting, mathematics, diagrams, blueprints and production.

In addition to intended usage and rights transferred, the factors affecting pricing in this field include: (1) research and consultation time; (2) travel; (3) reference materials; and (4) complexity of project.

All prices for illustration in the Guidelines are based on a nationwide survey that was reviewed by a special committee of experienced professionals through the Graphic Artists Guild. These figures, reflecting the responses of established professionals, are meant as a point of reference only and do not necessarily reflect such important factors as deadlines, job complexity, reputation and experience of a particular illustrator, research, technique or unique quality of expression and extraordinary or extensive use of the finished art. Please refer to related material in other chapters of this book, especially under *Business and Legal Practices For Commissioned Art Work* and *Standard Contracts*.

Trade practices

The following trade practices are accepted as standard:

1. The intended use of the art must be clearly stated in a contract, purchase order or letter of agreement stating the price and terms of sale.

2. Artists normally sell only first reproduction rights unless otherwise stated.

3. If artwork is to be used for other than its original purpose, the price should be negotiated as soon as possible. The secondary use of an illustration may be of greater value than the primary use. Although there is no set formula for reuse fees, a reuse fee ranging from 25 - 50 per cent of the fee that would have been charged had the illustration been originally commissioned for the anticipated usage is a fairly typical charge.

4. Illustrators should negotiate reuse arrangements with the original commissioning party with speed, efficiency and all due respect to the client's position.

5. Return of original artwork to the artist is automatic unless otherwise negotiated.

6. Fees for rush work will be higher than the figures listed here. Rush deadlines may increase the original fee by an additional 50 per cent.

7. A cancellation fee should be agreed upon if a job is cancelled through no fault of the artist. Depending upon the stage at which the job is terminated, the fee paid should cover all work done, including research time, sketches billable expenses and compensation for lost opportunities resulting from an artist's refusing other offers to make time available for a specific commission. In addition, clients who put commissions "on hold" or withhold approval for commissions for longer than 30 days should secure the assignment by paying a deposit.

8. A rejection fee should be agreed upon if the assignment is terminated because the preliminary or finished work is found not to be reasonably satisfactory. The rejection fee for finished work should be upwards of 50 per cent of the full price depending on the reason for rejection and complexity of the job. When the job is rejected at the sketch stage, a fee of one-third the original price is customary. This fee may be less for quick, rough sketches and more for highly rendered, time-consuming work.

9. Work done on speculation does not conform to industry trade practices and is contrary to the Joint Ethics Committee's Code of Fair Practice, because of its exploitive nature.

10. The Graphic Artists Guild is unalterably opposed to the use of work-for-hire contracts, in which authorship and all rights that go with it are transferred to the commissioning party and the independent artist is treated as an employee for copyright purposes only. The independent artist receives no employee benefits and loses the right to claim authorship or profit from future use of the work forever. Additional information on work for hire can be found on page 15.

11. Expenses such as shipping fees, travel costs, consultation time and other unusual expenses should be billed to the client separately. An expense estimate should be included in the original written agreement or as an amendment to the agreement.

The prices shown represent only the specific use for which the illustration is intended and do not necessarily reflect any of the above considerations. The buyer and seller are free to negotiate, taking into account all the factors involved.

Comparative fees for technical illustration for advertising

National magazine	B&W*	Color
Spread	$4,500	$6,000
Full page	3,000	4,500
Half page	2,000	3,500
Quarter page	1,500	2,500
Spot	1,000	1,500

Regional and mass trade magazine		
Spread	$2,700	$4,500
Full page	1,700	2,500
Half page	1,500	2,000
Quarter page	750	1,200
Spot	500	750

Specific trade and limited audience magazine		
Spread	$2,000	$3,000
Full page	1,500	2,000
Half page	750	1,000
Quarter page	500	750
Spot	250	500

National newspaper advertising campaign	B&W*
Spread	$4,000
Full page	2,500
Half page	1,500
Two column (quarter page)	750

Newspaper supplement	Color
Spread	$5,000
Full page	4,000
Half page	2,500
Two column (quarter page)	1,000

*Add 25% to black and white prices for each color overlay.

Comparative fees for technical illustration for editorial publications

In-house publication	B&W*	Color
Cover	$1,500	$2,000
Spread	1,250	2,000
Full page	1,000	1,500

Magazine		
Cover	$1,750	$3,000
Spread	2,000	3,000
Full page	1,500	2,000

Comparative fees for technical illustration for editorial publications (continued)

Brochures	B&W*	Color
Promotion and presentation	$1,500	$3,000
Packages		
"How to use"	$1,000	-
Books		
Full page, complex	$1,000	$2,000
Full page, simple	700	1,000
Spot	300	500
Presentations		
Flip charts (simple)		$500
Trade show material		2,500
Technical materials		
Product user and service manuals		$50 per hour
Data sheets		35 per hour
Consultation		
Per hour		$75 - 125
Per day		375 - 750

*Add 25% to black and white prices for each color overlay

Architectural/interior renderings

Architectural/interior renderers (also known as perspectivists), are hired to create accurate sketches and renderings to be used as part of the design presentation by an architect or designer to their client. The original rendering itself is often sold for design presentation purposes, but the reproduction rights are usually withheld by the artist.

Renderers are also commissioned by real estate project developers and/or their advertising agencies to create art for promotional purposes. Advertising and promotional reproduction rights are negotiated separately from the sale of the original art, and the intended uses for the work will affect the fee. (Please refer to "Advertising illustration" for more information).

The finished art is in the form of one or a combination of several media: airbrush, gouache, watercolor, pastel, colored pencil, marker and pen and ink. Computer - aided design programs are also becoming popular with renderers as they insure accuracy and allow the artist to quickly choose the views that serve the client's needs. However, the cost of hardware and the time required to use existing software hinders widespread use of computer generated final art. Technology is progressing at a rapid rate, so it is only a matter of time before renderers take better advantage of the computer.

Renderers are hired for their illustrative style and their accuracy in depicting the building, space, color and/or materials. They usually have a design background (in either architectural, interior or industrial design), and have moved into rendering as a career after being "in the business." As a result of these unique qualifications, they are often involved in a project before it is completely designed. Renderers do not need finished plans and elevations as reference to begin work on presentation drawings.

Factors involved in pricing include the complexity of the rendering project (which depend upon required views and the amount of detail required); the number of renderings; the media to be used and the amount of time required for travel and consultation for the project.

Expenses such as travel costs, production costs, consultation time and so on, are normally billed to the client separately. An expense estimate is usually included in the original written agreement or as an amendment to the agreement.

Trade practices

The following trade practices are accepted as standard:

1. The intended use of the art must be clearly stated in a contract, purchase order or letter of agreement stating the price and terms of sale.

2. Artists normally sell only first reproduction rights unless otherwise stated.

3. If artwork is to be used for other than its original purpose, the price should be negotiated as soon as possible. The secondary use may be of greater value than the primary use. Although there is no set formula for reuse fees, a reuse fee ranging from 25-50 per cent of the fee that would have been charged had the illustration been originally commissioned for the anticipated usage is a fairly typical charge.

4. Illustrators should negotiate reuse arrangements with the original commissioning party with speed, efficiency and all due respect to the client's position.

5. Return of original artwork to the artist is automatic unless otherwise negotiated.

6. Fees for rush work will be higher than the figures listed here. Rush deadlines may increase the original fee by an additional 50 percent.

7. A cancellation fee should be agreed upon if a job is cancelled through no fault of the artist. Depending upon the stage at which the job is terminated, the fee paid should cover all work done, including research time, sketches, billable expenses and compensation for lost opportunities resulting from an artist's refusing other offers to make time available for a specific commission. In addition, clients who put commissions "on hold" or withhold approval for commissions for longer than 30 days should secure the assignment by paying a deposit.

8. A rejection fee should be agreed upon if the assignment is cancelled because the preliminary or finished work is found not to be reasonably satisfactory. The rejection fee for finished work should be upwards of 50 percent of the full price depending on the reason for rejection and complexity of the job. When the job is rejected at the sketch stage, a fee of one-third the original price is custom-

ary. This fee may be less for quick, rough sketches and more for highly rendered, time-consuming work.

9. Work done on speculation does not conform to industry trade practices and is contrary to the Joint Ethics Committee's Code of Fair Practice.

10. The Graphic Artists Guild is unalterably opposed to the use of work-for-hire contracts, in which authorship and all rights that go with it are transferred to the commissioning party and the artist is treated as an employee for copyright purposes only. The artist receives no employee benefits and loses the right to claim authorship or profit from future use of the work forever. Additional information on work for hire can be found on page 15.

11. Expenses such as shipping fees, travel costs, consultation time and other unusual expenses should be billed to the client separately. An expense estimate should be included in the original written agreement or as an amendment to the agreement.

All prices for illustration in the *Guidelines* are based on a nationwide survey that was reviewed by a special committee of experienced professionals through the Graphic Artists Guild. These figures, reflecting the responses of established professionals, are meant as a point of reference only and do not necessarily reflect such important factors as deadlines, job complexity, reputation and experience of a particular illustrator, research, technique or unique quality of expression and extraordinary or extensive use of the finished art. Please refer to related material in other sections of this book, especially under *Business & Legal Practices for Commissioned Artwork* and *Standard Contracts.*

The price ranges shown represent only the specific use for which the illustration is intended and do not necessarily reflect any of the above considerations. The buyer and seller are free to negotiate, taking into account all the factors involved.

Comparative fees for architectural/interior renderings in design presentation

Simple rendering*	Small scale	Medium scale	Large scale
Marker	$325	$375	$500
Pencil	500	750	1,000
Watercolor	700	1,100	1,500
Pen and ink	500	750	1,000
Airbrush	2,500	2,500	3,000
Combined media	900	1,500	2,000

*Based on a two-point perspective of a single building or interior with no background or environmental context; simple exteriors, elevations, etc.

Complex rendering*	Small scale	Medium scale	Large scale
Marker	$575	$750	$900
Pencil	900	1,250	1,650
Watercolor	1,200	1,700	2,250
Pen and ink	750	1,200	1,500
Airbrush	3,500	4,000	4,750
Combined media	1,500	2,500	3,500

*Based on complex exteriors and perspectives of several buildings or interiors with environmental context; site plans; etc.

Highly complex rendering*	Small scale	Medium scale	Large scale
Marker	$1,000	$1,500	$1,750
Pencil	1,250	2,000	2,750
Watercolor	2,000	2,750	4,250
Pen and ink	1,500	2,000	2,500
Airbrush	4000	5,000	6,000
Combined media	2,500	3,500	4,500

*Based on elaborate architectural detailing with complex perspectives; cityscapes; aerial views; fully rendered exteriors or interiors; etc.

Marbling (marbled printing)

Marblers are artists who practice the centuries-old art of marbling by floating pigments with an oil content on a water sizing, manipulating the pigments into designs with the use of special combs and tools, and then transferring the designs to paper, fabric or other surfaces laid on top of the pigments.

Each sheet of marbled paper (or other surface) is unique, although the control of technical variables involved in the printing process make very close duplication possible. Traditionally, marbling was applied to the endpapers, covers and edges of books, and most people still associate marbling with book binding. With the popularity of this art on the rise, applications for it have extended into the graphic arts, enhancing all sorts of products with the reproduction of marbled patterns used to decorate them.

For example, marbled, or marbleized designs (both terms are correct), are now routinely reproduced as stationery, textile design, book jacket design, brochures, magazine and catalogue layouts, menu covers, package designs, backgrounds for television spots and many more.

With the recent renaissance of the long-neglected art of marbling, individual artists have been able to recreate historical patterns as well as create new ones. Each marbler's work has an individuality of style which can be readily identified by name, a result of years spent perfecting their technique and developing their style. Because the costs and expenses of operating a business are no different for marblers than for other graphic artists, and because the marbler's creations enhance the value of the client's product or service, fees are in line with industry standards. Most marblers today secure their copyrights by registering their patterns with the Library of Congress, and expect to be paid fees for reproduction rights.

Marbled papers are made available to art professionals and others through sale in art supply stores, paper stores or other specialty shops. The copyright notice is usually imprinted on the back along with the artist's name, address and telephone number. Because many papers are cut after purchase,

some artists stamp their work in several places so that even smaller cuttings can be identified. Even with these precautions, many users wrongfully assume that purchasing a marbled paper also licenses them to reproduce the design, so most artists working in this discipline must vigilantly protect their work against copyright infringement.

Many patterns are used for reproduction directly from the original purchased paper, making it a convenient, ready-to-use artwork. When a different, specific coloring is desired, the printing done to satisfy the requirements is considered a custom job and will be either included in the reproduction fee or charged separately. Factors affecting the pricing for custom work most often include: setup time to print; matching ink specifications; number of samples required by the client and printing time required; complexity of design; and cost of materials.

Usual and customary considerations in fees for reproduction rights may include: consultation time, intended use, extent of use (i.e. border, full page, spread, etc.), length of time for the specified use and the number of rights purchased.

Trade practices

The following trade practices are accepted as standard:

1. The intended use of the art must be clearly stated in a contract, purchase order or letter of agreement stating the price and terms of sale.

2. Artists normally sell only first reproduction rights unless otherwise stated.

3. If artwork is to be used for other than its original purpose, the price should be negotiated as soon as possible. The secondary use may be of greater value than the primary use. Although there is no set formula for reuse fees, a reuse fee ranging from 25-50 per cent of the fee that would have been charged had the illustration been originally commissioned for the anticipated usage is a fairly typical charge.

4. Marblers should negotiate reuse arrangements with the original commissioning party with speed, efficiency and all due respect to the client's position.

5. Return of original artwork to the artist should be automatic and immediate unless otherwise negotiated. Clients should make their selection of marbled papers for use within fourteen days.

6. Payment is expected upon delivery of the assignment, not upon its publication.

7. A cancellation fee should be agreed upon if a job is cancelled through no fault of the artist. If a custom job is canceled, a 100% of the fee is expected. Cancellation fees for reproduction rights after the contract is signed but prior to execution of finished art is normally 50% of the negotiated fee.

8. A rejection fee should be agreed upon if the assignment is terminated because the work is found not to be reasonably satisfactory. The rejection fee for finished work should be upwards of 50 per cent of the full price depending on the reason for rejection and complexity of the job.

9. Work done on speculation does not conform to industry trade practices and is contrary to the Joint Ethics Committee's Code of Fair Practice. However, the creation of work initiated by a marbler for presentation and sale is commonly accepted in the textile and greeting card industries. It is also standard practice to obtain a written guarantee of payment for creating any new work specifically requested by clients. The Guild opposes creating new work without such a guarantee accompanying the request.

10. The Graphic Artists Guild is unalterably opposed to the use of work-for-hire contracts, in which authorship and all rights that go with it are transferred to the commissioning party and the artist is treated as an employee for copyright purposes only. The artist receives no employee benefits and loses the right to claim authorship or profit from future use of the work forever. Additional information on work for hire can be found on page 15.

11. Fees for rush work will be higher than the figures listed here. Fees will also be greater for the requirement of unusually large number of custom samples. The client is responsible for making additional payments for changes or alterations requested by the client in the original assignment.

12. Fees for custom work are normally charged separately from any reproduction rights sold.

13. Fees for multiples of a marbled pattern(s) are often discounted below the per-pattern fee.

14. Samples of the finished product are always sent to the marbler upon completion, and this is usually specified in the contract.

All prices for illustration in the *Guidelines* are based on a nationwide survey that was reviewed by a special committee of experienced professionals through the Graphic Artists Guild. These figures, reflecting the responses of established professionals, are meant as a point of reference only and do not necessarily reflect such important factors as deadlines, job complexity, reputation and experience of a particular marbler, research, technique or unique quality of expression and extraordinary or extensive use of the finished art. Please refer to related material in other sections of this book, especially under *Business & Legal Practices for Commissioned Artwork* and *Standard Contracts*.

Comparative fees for marbling in editorial publications

Consumer magazines	National	Regional	Limited audience
Cover	$525	$500	$450
Spread background	500	475	400
Full page background	475	425	375
Full page border or frame	275	250	200
Spot border or frame	225	175	100

Newspapers		Major metro	Small city
Cover		$500	$425
Spread background		475	350
Full page background		400	350
Full page border or frame		200	150
Spot border or frame		125	100

Comparative fees for marbling for corporate and institutional uses

Corporate employee publications	Large company*	Medium company*	Small company*
Cover	$500	$450	$400
Spread background	550	500	425
Full page background	400	375	350
Full page border or frame	300	275	200
Spot border or frame	200	175	125

Annual reports	Large company*	Medium company*	Small company*
Cover	$500	$450	$400
Spread background	450	400	350
Full page background	425	400	375
Full page border or frame	325	300	275
Spot border or frame	250	225	200

Comparative fees for marbling in book publishing

Hardcover book jackets	Mass market	Major trade	Minor trade	Young adult	Textbook
Wraparound background	$750	$700	$650	$650	$600
Wraparound border or frame	625	600	550	550	475
Front cover background	600	600	500	500	475
Front cover border or frame	525	500	450	450	450

Paperback book covers	Mass market	Major trade	Minor trade	Young adult	Textbook
Wraparound background	$675	$625	$600	$600	$500
Wraparound border or frame	600	550	500	500	450
Front cover background	600	550	500	500	450
Front cover border or frame	525	500	475	450	450

Hardcover book interiors	Major publisher*	Minor publisher*
Spread	$750	$750
Full page background	500	500
Full page border or frame	350	350
Chapter heading	400	350

Young adult novels	Major publisher*	Minor publisher*
Spread	$750	$750
Full page background	500	500
Full page border or frame	350	350
Chapter headings	300	300

Juvenile workbooks	
Spread	$1000
Full page background	750
Full page border or frame	400
Chapter headings	350

Comparative fees for marbling in book publishing (continued)

Textbooks	College/ young adult	Juvenile
Spread	$750	$750
Full page background	500	500
Full page border or frame	350	300
Chapter headings	275	275

Comparative fees for marbling in advertising

Magazines	National consumer or mass trade*	Regional consumer or specific trade*
Cover	$850	$750
Spread background	650	650
Full page background	500	400
Full page border or frame	375	325
Spot border or frame	350	275

Newspapers	Major metro*	Small city*
Cover	$525	$500
Spread background	375	375
Full page background	300	300
Full page border or frame	300	300
Spot border or frame	300	300

Collateral and direct mail	Greater than 100,000 pieces	10,000- 100,000 pieces	Less than 100,000 pieces
Cover	$800	$650	$500
Spread background	750	600	350
Full page background	650	500	325
Full page border or frame	400	300	250
Spot border or frame	300	275	225

Advertorials (special advertising sections added to magazines & newspapers)	National consumer or mass trade*	Regional consumer or specific trade*
Cover	$850	$550
Spread background	750	500
Full page background	500	400
Full page border or frame	450	350
Spot border or frame	350	300

Comparative fees for marbling in packaging

Recording cover*

Major studio or distribution	$1200
Minor studio or distribution	$800

*Album covers include vinyl discs, compact laser discs and audiocassettes.

Software

Educational	300

Comparative fees for marbling for novelty, retail goods and surface design

Greeting cards

Flat fee only	$600

Calendars (cover and 12 backgrounds or borders)

Flat fee only	$1000 - 3,000

Surface design *(Flat fee only)*

Wallpaper	$650
Home decorative	950
Domestics	875
Apparel	750

SALARIES
AND TRADE CUSTOMS

Salaried Artists

For more detailed descriptions of positions mentioned in the pricing sections of this chapter, please refer to the appropriate freelance sections, which describe the role of each discipline. The positions included here refer to staff positions or do not appear in those sections.

A salaried graphic artist is usually employed solely by one company. Unless the artist or designer can negotiate a written agreement that states otherwise, all art created on company time is considered work for hire (please see the chapter on *Professional Issues* for more information on work for hire). Depending upon the responsibilities of the position and the employer, moonlighting for a competitor may be contractually or ethically prohibited. Generally, the income of the salaried graphic artist is limited to the artist's employing company.

Many of the disciplines listed below are not mutually exclusive. For instance, an art director may also produce illustrations, designs or built-up lettering. In fact, few salaried graphic artists are so rigidly specialized that they work only in one area. In most cases the needs of the position will dictate the talents required. Using the primary role to be filled, the salary guidelines on the following pages should give one an idea of what can be expected by professional artists being interviewed for staff positions.

These salary ranges are based on a standard 35-hour week with a benefits package including health insurance, vacation pay, holiday and sick pay. Bonuses, stock options and retirement plans are negotiable. The jobs described are creative positions and are not purely executive or supervisory functions.

Generally, larger companies hire full-time art staff (i.e., companies that produce a significant amount of graphic art in-house such as catalogs, surface designs, advertising, packaging, or corporate graphics). Freelance talent is often used to supplement an art staff. At times, independent agencies or design firms are put on retainer when there is no art staff or when the company chooses to subcontract large areas of a project (e.g., advertising, corporate identity programs, or annual and quarterly reports).

Over the last few years, the trend has been for agencies and corporations to dissolve their art departments in favor of using freelance talent. These companies will often hire back the same individuals as full-time freelancers to work on the same projects at a lower rate, without any fringe benefits. This cost-cutting method has serious implications for both the employer and the graphic artist involved. Please refer to the "Employment issues" section of the *Professional Issues Chapter* for further information.

Employment conditions

Artists should consider conditions of employment along with salary and type of work when applying for a salaried position. Among the conditions generally accepted as standard for full-time workers are:

Staff policy: Many employers have written staff policies that outline the way in which a company relates to its employees. In fact, New York State companies are required by law to notify employees "in writing or by publicly posting" of policy on sick leave, vacations, personal leave, holidays and hours. Other items that may be included in staff policies are: employee grievance procedures, cause for discipline (up to and including discharge), criteria for salary increases and promotions, maternity/paternity leave, etc. A written staff policy can reveal much about the working environment and a potential employer's attitude toward his or her staff. It is useful therefore to learn what is included (and excluded) from a staff policy before accepting a position.

Job benefits: Most companies offer some benefits packages to their employees that may include health, disability, life and dental insurance plans. Larger companies and corporations often offer pension, profit-sharing and stock option plans, day-care facilities or child-care subsidies.

Job descriptions: Just as a contract between a client and a freelance artist reflects their understanding of their relationship, a written job description can clearly indicate to artists what is expected of them during their term of employment. The Guild strongly recommends that all artists seeking a salaried position request a written job description, since it will help both employer and employee to avoid expectations and assumptions that are not shared by the other party. A written job description is also useful in the event a job changes significantly during the term of employment. Such changes may reflect greater responsibilities or functions, justifying a new title or greater compensation. If such changes are made, the job description should be rewritten to reflect those title changes and salary adjustments.

Job performance review: A periodic (semi-annual or annual) review of job performance is helpful to both employer and employee. A review allows employees to gauge how they're doing and raise questions about their job expectations. The review gives the employer the opportunity to discuss any evaluations on job performance and any changes in job description. Formal performance reviews also allow employer and employee to suggest ways to improve the "product" or the role being considered. When handled well, job performance reviews can anticipate any potential problems and help maintain good and productive relationships between employer and employee. Results of the job performance review should be kept on file and employees should be allowed to have access to them.

While many of the above conditions of employment are not mandatory, they are designed to help both employer and employee develop and maintain good relations during the term of employment.

Broadcast designers

The demands of the one-eyed television medium that sits in 98 percent of the living rooms in the United States present a unique challenge to broadcast designers. The challenge demands knowledge and creativity in every aspect of design.

For on-air duties, broadcast designers are required to be illustrators, cartoonists and type designers. It is necessary to know, prepare and sometimes shoot animation on both film and tape. Knowledge of stand and remote still photography is essential. For print media, broadcast designers devise everything from small-space program-listing ads to full-page newspaper ads, as well as trade publication ads, booklets, brochures, invitations and similar material.

Broadcast designers double as corporate designers who coordinate everything from the on-air look to the stationery, memo pads and sales promotion materials. Broadcast designers even design news vehicle markings and occasionally design helicopter markings.

In addition to the preceding fields, scenic design is another area of responsibility.

Here the understanding of construction techniques, materials and paints is important, along with an awareness of staging, furnishing, lighting spatial relationships and camera angles.

It is necessary for art directors in this field to be proficient in managerial skills such as organization, budgeting, purchasing, directing a staff and working with upper management.

Obviously, not all of these skills apply to every individual or situation, and each design staff is built around personal strengths; nevertheless, a broad spectrum of design possibilities does exist. The broadcast designer is called upon to meet these requirements and others.

This section on the broadcast designer was written by Gil Cowley, former chairman of the advisory board and president of the Broadcast Designer's Association.

Surface designers

The following trade practices are relevant to the salaried surface design artist.

1. Physical working conditions: Textile designers should survey prospective work space and evaluate such aspects as lighting, ventilation, cleanliness, equipment, supplies and other conditions necessary for effective work.

2. Freelance: Out-of-company freelance work is a common practice in the industry. If the converter, manufacturer or other hiring party requires the surface designer to sign a form stating that he or she will not work for other companies while employed by the converter, the surface designer may be considered a regular, if temporary, employee and may be entitled to all other employee benefits. (Please see the "Employee issues" section of the *Professional Issues* chapter.) Work should be competitively priced either by the project or by the hour, according to current market guidelines. It is to the converter's advantage to have surface designers on hand to complete work quickly and in the way wished; therefore, surface designers should not be penalized for helping the converter.

3. Work practices: According to the New York State Labor Board, at least one half-hour lunch in a 9 A.M. to 5 P.M. workday must be provided. Contact the board for other information on rest periods and working conditions. It is important for every surface designer to know his or her rights as an employee. The Guild discourages working extra hours consistently without overtime pay.

In mill work, for example, unsafe and abusive working conditions have existed for staff employees for years. Working through weekends, extended travel time, 24-hour shifts (with sleep deprivation) and enduring poor physical conditions at mills are common practices that are rarely compensated appropriately. These extra duties are expected for the usual salary and benefits without additional compensation.

However, some advances in these areas are being made through additional compensation, guaranteed days off, overtime pay and the hiring of additional personnel to limit shift hours. To achieve these goals, surface designers should negotiate firmly and/or organize for the purposes of collective bargaining. The Guild is prepared to assist any and all staff artists in improving their working conditions in this way.

4. Salary reviews: Most converters evaluate work quality and salary advancement on an annual basis, and staff artists should be acquainted with the policies of the company. Most converters do not offer raises very often, and when they do they are for only limited amounts. Each surface designer should know what to expect and negotiate or act accordingly.

6. Artists on per diem: Per diem rates are usually lower than prevailing freelance prices and consequently are not beneficial to surface designers. Furthermore, per diem surface designers do not receive fringe benefits such as medical, life insurance or pension benefits. However, hiring a per diem surface designer for even one day requires the company to pay taxes, social security and unemployment insurance to the government for that surface designer. Also, according to government regulations, those who work consistently on per diem may automatically be eligible for those fringe benefits. With respect to wages for per diem work, the Guild strongly recommends that surface designers review the ability level required and the work assigned to price the work accordingly.

7. Knock-offs: A textile/surface designer should not copy or "knock off" a design by another artist, unless that work is in the public domain. It is the special talent of the designer to be able to create a work that is original, yet satisfies the fashion dictates of the season or year. No designer should be forced to knock off or copy designs for an employer unless that converter is willing to indemnify the artist from any actions that may arise as a result of any potential infringement.

8. Changing jobs: Staff surface designers change jobs frequently in order to improve salaries, achieve promotions or better their working conditions. The Guild advises giving present employers a standard two-week notice when leaving a job. Anything less can jeopardize severance or vacation pay due.

Note: Some companies request test coloring samples as part of the interview process. The Guild recommends against this "work on speculation," unless the test colorings are paid for or remain the property of the artist.

9. Converters: Staff at converters in the textile field may include:

Stylist: Creative and managerial head of department, sometimes referred to as style director or art buyer.

Assistant stylist: Managerial and creative assistant to stylists; may or may not work at drawing board; may or may not buy art.

Studio head: Directly in charge of non-management studio personnel; answers to stylist; usually works at drawing board.

Designer: Executes original art work.

Colorist: Executes color combinations, usually painted but occasionally "chipped."

Repeat artist: Executes precise continuous repeat patterns, imitating original artist's "hand."

Mill worker: Can be any of the above employees trained to shade fabric at the mills.

10. Studios: Staff at studios may include:

Studio director: Creative and managerial head, in some cases the studio owner.

Rep: Sells original artwork or seeks clients who need colorings, repeats, etc. A few also solicit mill work.

Artists: Usually work at the studio; may execute original artwork, colorings, repeats.

Earnings gap still a problem: The surface design field has historically been composed of many more women designers than men. While this fact is well known in the industry, the corollary that men and women are not paid equally for the same job is less well publicized. According to 1990 U.S. Census Bureau statistics, women working in the design field earn only about 59 per cent of what men make. Where male designers made on average $597 per week, female designers made only $354.

The 1990 Graphic Artists Guild survey found that 68.5 per cent of those surveyed earned salaries ranging between $17,400 and $34,400, with an average of $26,000. Only 9 per cent of those responding reported earning salaries greater than $40,000.

The issue of equal pay for equal work has received a great deal of attention from women's groups and labor organizations. The Guild believes that equal pay standards should be promoted and supported. It encourages members with information on problems in this area to contact the Guild.

Comparative salaries of advertising agency staff*

	Small agency	Large agency
Creative director	$150,000+	$250,000+
Associate creative director or supervisor	-	125,000 - 150,000
Group head	-	150,000+
Senior art director	75,000 - 100,000	100,000 - 125,000
Art director	50,000 - 75,000	60,000 - 100,000
Junior art director	30,000 - 40,000	35,000 - 45,000
Senior promotional art director (direct mail and collateral)	60,000	60,000
Promotional art director	-	40,000 - 55,000

*A small agency has between $5 and $10 million in annual billings; a large agency has more than $100 million.

Note:
Agency size often has little or no bearing on salaries paid.

Comparative salaries of corporate art department staff*

	Medium	Large or Fortune 500
Manager, graphic design	$60,000 - 90,000	$75,000 - 150,000
Consultant art director	-	125,000 - 200,000
Senior art director/Design director	42,000 - 55,000	75,000 - 125,000
Graphic designer	30,000 - 38,000	36,000 - 47,000
Production artist	-	22,000 - 35,000

*A medium corporation has less than $300 million in annual sales revenues; a large corporation has $300 million or more.

Note:
In many instances relative size of company has little or no bearing on salaries paid.

Comparative salaries of book publishing art department staff

	Small publisher	*Large publisher*
Art director	$33,000 - 42,000	$70,000 - 90,000
Production manager	27,000 - 32,000	35,000 - 50,000
Production associate	18,000 - 22,000	20,000 - 28,000
Production asssistant	15,000 - 17,000	17,000 - 20,000

Comparative salaries of graphic design office or studio staff

Principal/partner	$55,000 - 150,000+
Design director	40,000 - 60,000
Senior graphic designer	35,000 - 55,000
Junior graphic designer	23,000 - 35,000
Entry-level graphic designer	21,000 - 24,000
Senior production supervisor	85,000 - 135,000
Senior production artist	30,000 - 40,000
Entry-level production artist	21,000 - 24,000

Notes:
All salaries are exclusive of additional job incentives such as bonuses, retirement packages, stock options and annual leave, etc.

Comparative salaries of broadcast station art department staff

	Smallest markets 51 - 100*	*Largest markets 1 - 10**
Art director or design manager	45,000 - 55,000	55,000
Graphic design engineer	30,000 - 40,000	50,000 - 52,000

*Market sizes are ranked according to population in the broadcast area. The most populous market (i.e., New York metropolitan area) is ranked number 1. Salaries do not reflect overtime and penalty pay, which can increase base pay by 33 to 50%.

157

PRICES AND TRADE CUSTOMS/SALARIED

Comparative salaries of animation staff artists*

	Hourly	*Weekly*
Director	$29.12	$1,165
Assistant director	23.74	949.76
Production boards	29.12	1,165
Layout	27.31	1,092.22
Animation artist	27.31	1,092.22
Staff comic strip artist	25.33	1,013.04
Assistant staff comic strip artist	21.53	861.52
Sheet timer	23.74	949.76
Story sketch	22.67	906.60
Scene planner	22.41	896.48
Animation checker	21.54	861.52
Breakdown	18.81	752.32
Blue sketch	18.43	737.20
Inbetweener	18.07	722.64

Ink and paint (inking, special effects, painters)	*Hourly*	*4-hour minimum call*
Assistant supervisor	$19.49	$779.44
Head special effects	19.06	762.44
Special effects	18.52	740.60
Color modelist	18.61	744.48
Ink checker	18.52	740.60
Key xerox processor	17.97	718.92
Xerox processor	17.74	709.48
Inker	17.87	714.96
Painter	17.74	709.48

*All figures were suppled by the Motion Picture Screen Cartoonists, Local 839 I.A.T.S.E., and represent the union-negotiated pay scales for journeymen for the contract effective August 1, 1992 through July 31, 1993.

Comparative salaries of textile/surface design staff

	Weekly	Annually
Entry-level colorist or designer	$325 - 450	$16,900 - 23,500
Colorist, junior designer	375 - 650	19,500 - 35,000
Repeat artist	475 - 815	25,000 - 42,500
Senior designer (with and without mill work)	600 - 1,035	31,200 - 53,820
Studio head	600 - 1,000	31,200 - 52,000
Assistant stylist	675 - 1,250	35,000 - 65,000
Stylist*	700 - 4,325	36,400 - 225,000
Student trainee	175 - 200	9,100 - 10,400

Note:
In most cases woven design personnel are not paid as much as print design personnel.

*In many cases, stylists also receive perks and bonuses based on the success of the line.

SURFACE DESIGN PRICES
AND TRADE CUSTOMS

Surface design

Surface designers are professionals skilled in visual communications and in endowing embellishment with a fine sense of aesthetics. As trained graphic artists, they use the elements of design to organize ideas to convey the appropriate visual impact and message.

Surface designers usually work within the constructs of prevailing fashion; or they create new styles, carrying fashion looks forward. Textile and surface designers create repeating and non-repeating patterns, illustrations, woven designs or patterns to be used in the apparel, home furnishings and giftware markets, among others. An understanding of markets and trends is essential to their advancement in their chosen field.

Many freelance textile/surface designers create individual designs or groups of designs that they sell or license to converters and manufacturers, often for a specific use or combination of uses. These artists are often commissioned to create an entire line of designs for use on sheets, pillowcases, comforters and other products for the home. Some work with and interpret existing pieces of "documentary" reference.

As "problem solvers," designers often conceptualize solutions to the specific need of a client and it is the accuracy of the solution, as well as his or her "track record," or known successes, that may help to determine the designer's fee. Other factors may also affect design fees such as: (1) complexity of the design relative to rendering technique and number of colors used; (2) transfer of copyright and/or usage rights; (3) time spent researching and rendering the design; and (4) advertising or selvage credit.

The Guild strongly recommends putting all agreements in writing. Designers should be sure to read any agreement carefully and try to restrict the sale of rights only to specific markets. This can be done by offering your own contract to the client, or by crossing out inappropriate sections on the client's contract or purchase order (see related material in the chapter on *Business and Legal Practices for Commissioned Artwork*). A word of caution: be especially sure to check any agreement for the words "work for hire," which may be a contract provision for which surface design is ineligible. See the chapter on *Professional Issues* for more information on work for hire.

Licensing

A license is an agreement whereby an artist or designer who owns the rights to the art permits another party, usually the client, to use the art for a limited specific purpose, for a specified time, in return for a fee or royalty. For example, designs for wallcoverings may be licensed to one party, and the same pattern licensed to another party for paper goods, dinnerware or barware. At the expiration of the license, the right to use the property reverts to the owner. An excellent book available on the subject of licensing is *Licensing Art And Design* by Caryn Leland (Allworth Press), available from the Graphic Artists Guild's national offices. A Model Short Form Licensing Agreement appears in the chapter on *Standard Contracts*. (See the chapter on *How Artwork Is Priced*).

In the textile and surface design industries, licensing agreements are normally negotiated for an entire line, collection or group of products for a particular market. For example, a licensing agreement for domestics would include designs for a number of entire "beds," (sheets, pillow slips, duvet and/or cover, ruffle, shams, etc.), or a license for bath products would include a shower curtain, mat and towels of various sizes. Although licenses are sometimes granted for a single product like a shower curtain or a beach towel, this is not the usual practice. Due to the perishable nature of fashion, licensing is virtually unknown in the apparel markets.

Royalties

A royalty is a percentage of the client's total sales paid to the designer and should be based on the *wholesale price* of the product. Actual percentages will vary by industry or by market. Current royalty percentages hover around 5 per cent, but those as low as a fraction of a per cent (on high volume items) exists. Virtually all royalties range between 2 and 10 per cent of the wholesale price. Royalty arrangements should always include a nonrefundable "up-front" payment to the designer as an advance against royalties. Advances are usually negotiated to cover the designer's labor and expenses at a minimum, and are often equal to the cost of the artwork if it were sold outright.

When a designer works on a royalty basis, he or she assumes some of the risks in the success or failure of a product. Working without an advance against royalties is strongly discouraged by the Guild. With no financial commitment from the licensee, there is no guarantee of income, and this amounts to the artist working on speculation. Extreme caution should be exercised before entering into any speculative venture.

Representatives

Representatives or agents have the legal right to act on behalf of the artists they represent only in the ways agreed to by both parties. A Guild-recommended "Surface Designer/Agent Agreement" can be found in the *Standard Contracts* chapter of this book. An attorney should always be retained to review any contracts, and the terms should be clearly understood by the designer before signing a contract.

Exclusivity or nonexclusivity is a crucial issue in any contract, as it is imperative to the success of the designer that his work is properly marketed. Agents asking for the right to represent an artist exclusively should be willing to identify the other artists they represent, and should not be free to represent unlisted artists unless mutually agreed upon.

The Guild strongly recommends that a designer allow an agent to represent him or her only on a commission agreed to *in writing* by both parties. Currently, standard commission for agents is between 25 and 50 per cent, often depending on whether the agent negotiates licensing agreements or makes direct sales for flat fees. Work left with an agent should be acknowledged by a written receipt. In addition, in cases where the client is not billed for shipping costs, the agent usually absorbs that expense.

Trade Practices

The following trade practices are accepted as standard and are particularly relevant to freelance textile and surface designers (see the surface design business and legal forms in the *Standard Contracts* chapter of this book).

Appropriate speculation: The creation of artwork for presentation and sale is accepted as standard in the industry only if the work is created completely of the artist's own volition, and not at the specific request of potential clients. It is standard for the artist to expect payment for any work created at the request of a client. (See the "Confirmation of engagement" form in the *Standard Contracts*

chapter).

Billing for a sale: When a sale is made, an invoice should be written and given to the client. The terms of payment should be negotiated prior to the sale and these terms should be stated on the invoice, with a penalty indicated for late payment. As they largely reflect the designer's labor, invoices for design should be made payable upon receipt. Surface designers should be paid promptly; however, it is understood that it often takes companies 30 days to pay invoices. Interest should accrue on all amounts unpaid after 30 days, and this condition should appear in writing on the invoice.

Cancellation (kill) fees: A cancellation or kill fee is normally due if an assignment is cancelled through no fault of the artist. Depending upon the stage at which the job is terminated, the fee paid should cover all work done, including research time, sketches, billable expenses and compensation for lost opportunities resulting from a surface designer's refusing other offers to make time available for a specific commission. Ownership of all copyright and artwork is retained by the artist. If a job based on "documentary" work or other original art belonging to a client is cancelled, payment of a time and/or labor charge is a widely accepted practice.

Client responsibilities: Additional payment is due to an artist when: (1) the client requests artwork changes that were not part of the original agreement; (2) ordered corners are not developed into purchased sketches (a cancellation fee will be charged and ownership of all copyright and artwork is retained by the designer); and (3) all sales taxes due must be collected on all artwork, except when original work is returned to the designer.

Credit to artist: For the creative work they provide, many designers receive credit and their copyright notice on the selvage of the fabric, or on the product if other than fabric.

Expenses: Expenses such as travel costs, consultation time, shipping and mailing charges and other out-of-pocket expenses should be billed to the client separately. Estimated expenses should be included in the original agreement or billed separately as they occur.

Holding work (pertinent to non-commissioned, speculative work only): Although previous work experience with a client who wishes to hold work prior to committing to its purchase should be your guide to allowing this practice, the Guild discourages consenting to an extended holding time as the work may be damaged or lost. Most stylists and design directors have the authority to purchase artwork on the spot, and they should be encouraged to do so. When this is impossible, a maximum holding period of three days is tolerated by some artists, but most limit this period to several hours or one day, pending completion of a written holding form. Longer periods are impractical due to the perishable nature of fashion items. which are valid for only limited periods of time. However, on more standard or classic designs, some artists consider allowing clients to hold them for several weeks for consideration of a "leasing fee."

Knock offs: A textile/surface designer should not copy or "knock off" a design by another artist, unless that work is in the public domain. It is the special talent of the designer to be able to create a work that is original, yet satisfies the fashion dictates of the season or year.

Quantity orders: The Guild discourages reduced fees for large orders. Each surface design is individual in nature, and its creation is labor intensive.

Return of original artwork: Return of original artwork to the artist or designer should be automatic unless otherwise negotiated. Surface designers particularly need their artwork returned in order to obtain additional exposure (such as by display of designs as artwork).

Rush work: Fees for rush work will be higher than the figures listed here. Rush deadlines may increase the original fee by an additional 50 per cent.

Uses and limitations: For commissioned or licensed work, the intended use of the art must be clearly stated in a contract, purchase order or letter of agreement stating the price and terms of sale. For example, if the design is sold for sheets and pillowcases only, the surface designer can sell the same design in other markets (e.g., for bath items, toweling, etc.).

If the client wishes to make additional use of the work for other than its original purpose, the artist is due additional compensation, which should be negotiated with speed, efficiency and all due respect to the artist's and client's positions. Since the secondary use of the art or design may be of greater value than the primary use, there is no set formula for reuse fees.

All prices for surface design in the *Guidelines* are based on a nationwide survey that was reviewed by a special committee of experienced professionals through the Graphic Artists Guild. These figures, reflecting the responses of established professionals, are meant as a point of reference only and do not necessarily reflect such important factors as deadlines, job complexity, reputation and experience of a particular surface designer, research, technique or unique quality of expression, ork extraordinary or extensive use of the finished art. Please refer to related material in other sections of this book, especially under *Business & Legal Practices for Commissioned Artwork* and *Standard Contracts*.

The prices shown represent only the specific use for which the surface or textile design is intended and do not necessarily reflect any of the above considerations. The buyer and seller are free to negotiate, taking into account all the factors involved.

Comparative flat fees for surface design of apparel*

Textiles

Corner	$100-350
Concept	100-350
Croquis	275-600
Design in repeat	475-1,200
Tracing repeat layout	175-450
Colorways	60-250
Repeats	200-900

Painted wovens

Stripe	$40-200
Design in repeat	100-400
Colorways	75-200

*Fees indicated are for each design; ranges reflect design complexity.

Comparative flat fees for surface design of domestics*

	Concept/ croquis	Design in repeat
Sheets	$700-1,000	$900-1,500
Pillow slips	-	300-700
Duvet/covers	-	900-1,500

Repeats for domestics

9 inches	$650-900
18 inches	800-1,300
36 inches	1,000-1,800

*Fees indicated are for each design; ranges reflect design complexity.

Comparative flat fees for surface design of home decorative items*

	Wallcovering/ curtains	Drapery/ upholstery	Rug/carpet
Corner	$150-550	$375	-
Croquis (sketch)	700-1,800	800	-
Design in repeat	1,000-2,000	1,400-2,500	2,000
Tracing repeat layout	200-500	250-500	-
Colorways	175-500	250-500	250-750

Repeats for home decorative products

9 inches	$750-1,000
18 inches	1,000-1,300
36 inches	1,200-1,800

*Fees indicated are for each design; ranges reflect design complexity and number of colors.

Comparative flat fees for surface design of scarves and handkerchiefs*

Concept	$175 - 1,000
Design	500 - 2,400

*Fees indicated are for each design; ranges reflect design complexity, size and number of colors.

Comparative flat fees for surface design of tabletop products*

Tablecloths	$600 - 2,000
Napkins	250 - 350
Placemats	275 - 600
Chinaware	825 - 650
Giftware	325 - 900

*Fees indicated are for each design; ranges reflect design complexity.

Comparative flat fees for surface design of bath products*

	Concept/croquis	Design, engineered or in repeat	Colorway
Shower curtain	$500 - 1,200	$900 - 2,000	$175 - 250
Towels *(guest, wash and hand)*	200 - 350	450 - 500	-
Towels *(bath)*	300 - 350	750 - 900	-
Towels *(beach)*	400 - 500	750 - 1,000	-

*Fees indicated are for each design; ranges reflect design complexity, size and number of colors.

Comparative flat fees for surface design of kitchen products*

	Design, engineered or in repeat
Potholders	$250 - 350
Oven mitts	500 - 1,000
Towels	275 - 500

*Fees indicated are for each design; ranges reflect design complexity, size and number of colors.

Comparative flat fees for surface design of retail and novelty products*

	Concept	Design	Complete design
T-shirts (engineered)	$300 - 600	$450 - 750	-
Greeting cards	125 - 250	400 - 500	-
Giftwrap (in repeat)	225 - 350	400 - 500	400 - 1,200

*Fees indicated are for each design; ranges reflect design complexity, size and number of colors.

Comparative advances and royalties for surface design*

	Advance	Royalty
Domestics *(per bed)*	$5,000	5%
Home decorative *(per program)*	5,000	5%
Tabletop products *(per program)*	5,000	5%
Tabletop *(paper goods)*	-	5%
Tableware	1,500	5%
Bath products	5,000 - 10,000	5%
Kitchen products	5,000	5%
Novelty/retail	-	5%

*Royalty percentages reflect arrangements with department stores and are based on wholesale price. For mass market distribution (i.e., chains and discount stores), percentages may be 2 points less.

Comparative fees and rates for miscellaneous surface design*

Hourly fee	$35 - 75
Day rate	250 - 400

*Includes color separations, mill work, hand and machine knits and hand-painted fabrics for the apparel and home decorative markets.

Business Management

As creators, graphic artists have the right to share in the economic benefits generated by their creative product. As business people, securing these economic interests and rights is their responsibility. Developing the ability to market and protect their art successfully is *the* basic survival skill for graphic artists.

Artists must be able to pinpoint and evaluate the critical terms of a job offer. Understanding contract terms, copyright basics and usual business practices is crucial. Since negotiation is often the key to a profitable and satisfying commission or job, learning negotiation skills is important. The fine art of negotiation can often make the difference in an artist's ability to reach his or her business and personal goals.

Graphic artists must know how to retain and exercise economic control of their artwork. Awareness of legal rights and resources to protect themselves against potential problems, therefore, is fundamental.

Graphic artists, like all businesses, must maintain appropriate job records, send invoices and track outstanding fees. Record keeping is important both for assessing how one's business is doing and for providing accurate documentation should problems occur.

In short, the viability of the artist's professional life is dependent to a great degree on acquiring relevant business and legal knowledge. This chapter of the *Guidelines* discusses the fundamental business management issues common to all professionals in the graphic arts.

Negotiation

In the graphic arts industry a great deal depends on repeat business and a professional and honorable reputation. In negotiations, a "winner-take-all" attitude can do more harm than good. Whenever possible, an atmosphere of mutual trust and collaboration should be established and encouraged by the parties involved. From that point, both sides can create an agreement that will satisfy their respective needs.

This cooperation is attained not merely by the exchange of concessions but through the attitudes and professional manner of the persons negotiating. Since the terms of a final agreement may not be those initially stated by either party, the participants must use their creative energies to manufacture solutions that meet the needs of all concerned.

It is important for artists to remember that art buyers are not "the enemy." During the years the Guild has handled grievance procedures between artists and clients, a common source of complaints has been a failure on the part of *both* sides to communicate effectively prior to the commencement of work. Artists and their clients must take responsibility for knowing their own needs, articulating them and taking the other party's needs into account. Even if only one of the negotiators is making a conscientious effort to understand the other party's point of view as well as their own, chances of a misunderstanding and/or conflict are greatly reduced.

Many artists are reluctant to ask questions or raise objections to clients' demands for fear of appearing difficult to work with. In the Guild's experience, however, as long as the discussion is carried out in an appropriately professional manner, clients appreciate artists who can be specific in their dealings, since it prevents future misunderstandings.

Attitude

Relaxation is very important in negotiation. By preparing properly and making the situation as comfortable as possible, it is possible to relax. Focusing on breathing and concentrating on relaxing muscles in the head, neck and shoulders can be surprisingly useful in a stressful situation. At the moment the deal at hand may seem like a "make it or break it" proposition, but that is usually not the case. In fact, most careers in the graphic arts are built upon hundreds of projects, not one. It is important to create a mental distance from the anxiety that can come into play in a negotiation. Being objective can also help one respond with agility so that the opportunity to get the right job at the right price won't slip away.

When faced with a negotiation, both sides begin by implying or stating a set of demands based on their needs. These demands should not be confused with underlying needs. It is these needs that a skilled negotiator attempts to discern.

When the problem stated is, "My company is looking for a first-class brochure that we can produce for under $10,000," there may be several underlying needs that are not articulated directly. The art buyer may be asking, "Do you want this project?;" "Are you excited about it?" and "Are you going to mess up and cost me my job?" In attempting to determine what kind of brochure is required, what degree of work is involved and the amount of money the client will have to pay for it, a skilled negotiator is communicating other messages as well, i.e., "I'm just the right person for this job;" "I know what I'm doing" and "I'm going to make you look good."

It is important to convey positive expectations about the job. Instead of "What is the deadline?," use a phrase like, "When would you want me to deliver the art?" From the outset, contact with a client can show a personal interest and attachment to the project that is contagious.

The answer to a stated problem will not always be obvious. It is critical to be able to relax and perceive the other person's position. By understanding that, there can be a positive response to the subtext of what is being said, and the negotiation can proceed with harmony.

Know when to quit. Getting greedy when things start to go well or pushing too far can lead the other party to abandon the whole deal out of spite. A show of generosity may pay off in future negotiations.

Preparation and research

Adequate preparation is a key ingredient to successful negotiation. Artists should attempt to know everything possible about a client prior to a meeting. Business libraries contain valuable information about the marketplace: directories for corporations and advertising agencies, such as the Standard Rate and Data series, show amounts of billing, circulation, officers, media bought, etc.

In addition, publication directories list magazines with circulation, advertising rates, names of staff, etc. A business librarian can help locate the appropriate publications.

Subscriptions to all appropriate major trade magazines should be maintained.

Active membership in the Guild helps to give artists the extra "edge" they need in a job situation. Magazine stands, mass transit posters, billboards, retail stories, supermarkets, and bookstores all contain valuable information about clients that artists may use with a new client.

Agendas and contracts

When a negotiation begins, it is important to ask the right questions and formulate an agenda for meetings or phone calls that outlines the topics to be covered. Additionally, artists should establish a "position paper" that will help answer the most important question of all, "What do I want from this job?" and "What will I do *instead* if I turn it down or am not right for it?"

Whether a project is interesting purely for the money, because it is a valuable showcase or because it will help establish a working relationship with a new client, an agenda will affect what the artist will agree to in negotiations.

Before starting work, agreements should be put in writing whenever possible. This protects the client as well as the artist by confirming terms before a misunderstanding can arise. The document can be as simple or complicated as the situation requires, from an informal letter of agreement to a complicated contract requiring the signatures of all parties. Formulating such letters and contracts or analyzing contracts offered by clients requires a thorough working knowledge of copyright law and its common terms. By reviewing the model contracts and supplementary sections of this book and other publications carefully (see *Resources*), artists will be able to rephrase contractual terms on the spur of the moment.

The majority of art directors and creative services personnel who commission art have little or no expertise in the area of copyright and contracts. Like artists, most of them would prefer not to have to deal with the subject. They are too busy conducting business in what are usually hectic, high-pressure surroundings. Having a clear understanding of how to suggest contract amendments and put them into writing can help avoid problems.

When clients use work-for-hire clauses in contracts or demand all rights to artwork, every effort should be made to determine what the client really needs. Often such terms in a contract were put in by a lawyer trying to cover all bases. But such terms are usually excessive, and, if priced accordingly, make work too expensive to afford.

Keep thoroughly written records of a job's progress, including the initial checklist containing job description, deadlines, fees and expenses; notes on the person representing the client; records of follow-up meetings and phone calls; hours on the job; layouts; memos; sketches; contracts; invoices and business letters. This will form a "job packet" that is a paper trail in the event that a disagreement or misunderstanding gets in the way of completing a project and payment.

The meeting

As much as possible, create an environment for meeting that will allow as comfortable a situation as possible. If negotiating "on your own turf" is impossible, bring your own turf with you. Clothing should always be professional and neat, but make sure it is also *comfortable.* Any presentation or portfolio should show the very best work. An unusual, thoughtful and creative presentation that is well designed goes a long way in establishing the expertise of an artist—and making a sale.

Negotiations should be avoided if the artist lacks sleep, is overtired, taking medication, under the influence of alcohol or has recently eaten a heavy meal. Very expensive errors can occur when artists are not as sharp as they should be. If the situation is uncomfortable or potentially disruptive, arrange to conduct the negotiation another time. There is a right and wrong time for negotiation. Recognize an opportunity and make use of it, but recognize also when there is *no* opportunity and wait for another day.

The golden rules during a meeting are: Stop, look and listen. *Stop*: Quiet down, breathe, relax and get centered. Refrain from lots of small talk, unless what's being said has a purpose for the business at hand. A well-placed word here and there does

more to establish credibility; giving information not asked for can inadvertently give clues about the artist's situation and weakness. Conducting presentations can also distract clients from carefully reviewing the work.

Look: A great deal can be learned by close attention to physical clues and the behavior of others. Office environments (wallpaper, furniture, desktops, artwork and photographs) can give clues about the client's personality. Notice if a seat is offered, if the client constantly consults a watch or is not focused on the discussion. Understanding behavioral clues and "body language" can be a substantial negotiating advantage.

Listen: People appreciate someone who is alert, attentive and indicates that he or she understands what is being said. It is important to indicate that understanding even if the listener doesn't agree with the point made. Listen *actively,* with nods of agreement, encouraging the other party to express themselves. It is very useful to repeat what was heard, such as, "Let me see if I understand correctly; you're saying that..." This indicates a good listener who is eager to understand. Listening effectively helps to determine and address the other party's needs and expectations.

Power

Negotiation itself cannot turn every situation into a golden opportunity. There are some relationships where the balance of power is so out of alignment that one party must either yield to unfavorable conditions or give up the negotiation. However, it is possible to maximize assets and protect yourself from an agreement that may be detrimental.

Remember that not every negotiation is destined to end in a deal. Two parties can "agree to disagree" most amicably and part ways hoping for another try at a later date. It is this ability to regard a negotiation with a level-headed objectivity, keeping it in perspective, that provides a skilled negotiator with the relaxation and attitude necessary to obtain the most favorable agreement.

Both parties should bear in mind what their course of action will be if the negotiation ends without agreement. "What other jobs do I have? What else will I do with my professional time if I don't take this assignment?" are questions that artists should ask themselves, just as the client is asking, "What else can I do, or who else can I hire to make this project work?" These questions provide both parties with a realistic assessment of how much leverage they actually have in a negotiation. Power can be regarded as the ability to say no; assessing alternatives, therefore, clarifies a position.

Often parties will establish an arbitrary limit from which they will not bend, such as "I won't pay more than $25,000," or "I won't accept less than $3,000." Since the figures or conditions are often arbitrarily selected in the first place, it is important to be able to ignore such a limit if necessary. A bottom line can become a focal point that inhibits the imagination necessary to establish terms that meet both parties' needs.

When entering into negotiations, it is important to decide what to do if negotiations break off. It's much easier to say no when there is a favorable alternative to pursue. As the saying goes, a bank will lend you money if you can prove don't need it. In the same way, it's much easier to get a job if you already have one. If an artist is not busy with other jobs, the best alternative is to create a mental priority list of important and valuable projects to pursue. This helps alleviate the often ill-founded notion that the deal must be made at any cost.

Tactics

Tactics are used throughout every negotiation, whether intentional or not. By separating emotional responses from calm, detached observations of tactics, the effectiveness of the tactic is defused. It is important not to take things personally during any phase of negotiation. Performance and ability to maneuver are seriously hampered when egos take charge.

Consider a few examples: (1) Limited authority: A person claims to have no final say on the terms of a deal. This enables one negotiator to make rigid demands, leaving the other to offer concessions in order that some headway is made. One possible solution is to treat the project under discussion as a joint venture, recruiting the other person as your new-found "partner." By emphasizing terms that create partnership and sharing a stake in decisions, that person is encouraged to go to bat with the higher-ups to defend the artist's needs and goals. (2) Phony legitimacy: It is stated that a contract is a "standard contract" and cannot be changed. Contracts are working documents that serve to protect two or more parties in an agreement. Don't agree to sign standardized contracts if they don't protect you. Don't be reluctant to strike out unfavorable sections or terms. If necessary, the defense "my attorney has instructed me not to sign contracts with these conditions" may be used to suggest alterations (see the Guild's sample contracts for guidelines). (3) Emotions: Anger, threats, derisive laughter, tears or insults may be convincing and may, in fact, be genuine, but should be regarded as tactical maneuvers. Listen carefully to the *point* of the message and separate it from the style of delivery. Never escalate an emotional situation. Any attempt to "roll up your sleeves and jump in" is very risky.

Phone

Telephones seem to be very easy for some people to work with and much harder for others. Like personal contact, negotiating by phone has its good and bad parts. Phone calls have distinct advantages over in-person meetings. They provide ample opportunity to refer to written materials for reference and support. Often, when calling from the office or home, being surrounded by one's own environment can bolster confidence.

Telephone skills are very important to a good negotiator: some individuals go as far as to write "scripts" for particularly difficult situations, where performing under pressure can cause confusion. A simpler negotiation agenda or checklist can be used to outline all the points that need to be covered. This prevents the problem of forgetting important details and helps keep the conversation centered on the important matters at hand. Taking notes during phone conversations is highly recommended. Artists must simultaneously understand the esthetic requirements of a project, agree on the business arrangements and establish rapport with the individual on the phone. These are complicated details and should be written down. Such notes can also be valuable references should a misunderstanding occur during the project.

Negotiating by phone has disadvantages as well. It is easier to refuse someone over the phone. If a difficult demand has to be made, it might be preferable to arrange a meeting. It is also difficult to judge reactions to what is being said when it is impossible to see the other person's face. A person's attention to what is being said may not be focused, and this can make it more difficult to establish the rapport and partnership that is so important to any successful negotiation.

If a discussion becomes difficult, put the caller on hold or get off the telephone and call back when it is more advantageous. This allows time to consult research materials or make phone calls for more information, to cool off if emotions are in play, or just time to make a difficult decision.

Money

Money should be the *last* item in a discussion, for several reasons. It is the one area where the majority of disagreements can occur, and it is important in the earliest stages of a negotiation to focus on areas where there is accord. In this way the partnership stressed earlier is given time to bloom. Also, money should only be a reflection of all the factors that lead up to it.

The job description, usage and reproduction rights, deadline, expenses, difficulty of execution, etc., all tell the story of how much value a particular job holds for the client. So negotiating about money before reaching agreement on these other items is premature and can be a costly error.

When discussing money, whenever possible outline your expectations, then try to get the other party to make the first offer. The old game of "I say 10, you say 6, I say 9, you say 7, we agree on 8," is still played out but is not always necessary. Depending on how it is stated, though, a first offer is rarely a final offer and should almost always be tested. Once again, one must weigh the risk of losing a possible working relationship by refusing to budge past a certain price. It always depends on the situation.

Don't feel obligated to respond right away if someone starts out a negotiation with "I only have $500, but I think you'd be great for the job." One can acknowledge the figure and still bring it up *later* when there is a foundation of a working relationship on which to base requests for more money.

Often, artists are asked to bid on jobs. It is important to clarify the nature of the bid. Is the client looking for a sealed bid that will be used to compete against other artists? Is this bid an attempt to help structure a budget? Is it only a ballpark estimate? Do they wish to negotiate directly? Since a sealed bid encourages negotiation against yourself, it should be clarified whether the bid is final and binding. It is unfair to ask an artist to develop a competitive sealed bid and then seek further concessions in later negotiations. In a ballpark estimate, the client will often hear only the low figure, so use care to offer a set of figures that brackets your price in the middle. When asked in person for a bid, artists should not hesitate to withdraw and say, "I'll call you later today with a quote." This gives artists time to consider their agenda and their needs.

It is not only practical, it's actually good business to ask for a price slightly higher than what you would expect. Like it or not, people in business often like to feel that they've gotten you to bend somewhat, and in that sense it is an obligation to manufacture a few concessions without harming your own interests.

Hourly rate formula

Whether pricing on a fee-for-use basis or by the hour, graphic artists must know what it costs to conduct business in order to know whether the client's fee for each project will mean profit, break-even or loss. Establishing an hourly rate is a businesslike way of doing this.

One simple way to establish an hourly rate is to first total all annual business "overhead" expenses such as rent, utilities, insurance, employees' salaries and benefits, promotion, outside professional services, equipment, transportation, office and art supplies, business taxes and entertainment. Using the figures in Schedule C of IRS Form 1040 makes this task easier. Add in a reasonable salary for yourself that reflects current market conditions (see the chapter on *Salaried Prices and Trade Customs*). Divide the total by 1680, which is the number of hours worked in an average year (52 weeks less four weeks' vacation, holiday and sick time). Add to this figure a reasonable profit margin of 10 to 15 per cent. The resulting figure is an hourly rate based on a 35-hour week that can be expected to cover all costs of doing business including the artist's own salary.

However, most artists, especially those who are self-employed, should divide the annual overhead figure by a much smaller number of working hours to allow for time spent on non-billable work such as writing proposals, billing and self-promotion. A figure from 20 to 45 per cent less, or roughly 900 to 1350 hours, is probably more practical and accurate. A profit margin should still be added.

When a project is being considered, it is important to closely estimate the required hours of work. This estimate multiplied by the hourly rate will demonstrate whether the client's fee for the project will cover costs. If it will not, the artist may negotiate with the client for more money, propose a solution to the project that will take less time or search with the client for another mutually agreeable alternative.

Many large jobs, such as corporate design projects, require that the hours involved be used as a gauge to see if the project is on budget.

Copyright registration

Although current copyright law automatically protects original artwork from the moment it is created even without inscribing a copyright notice, there are advantages in formally registering the art with the Copyright Office. Registration establishes a public record of the artist's copyright claim to the artwork. Then if someone infringes or copies the art to the artist's detriment, the artist possesses presumptive evidence of ownership, leaving the burden to prove differently on the other party. With registration, the artist also gains a broader range of legal remedies in the event of in-

---

FORM VA
UNITED STATES COPYRIGHT OFFICE

REGISTRATION NUMBER

VA   VAU

EFFECTIVE DATE OF REGISTRATION

Month   Day   Year

DO NOT WRITE ABOVE THIS LINE. IF YOU NEED MORE SPACE, USE A SEPARATE CONTINUATION SHEET.

1 TITLE OF THIS WORK ▼   NATURE OF THIS WORK ▼ See instructions

BUSINESSWOMEN AT DESKS   *PEN AND INK AND WATERCOLO*

PREVIOUS OR ALTERNATIVE TITLES ▼

PUBLICATION AS A CONTRIBUTION   If this work was published as a contribution to a periodical, serial, or collection, give information about the collective work in which the contribution appeared.   **Title of Collective Work ▼**

EXECUTIVE TABLETOPS

If published in a periodical or serial give: **Volume ▼** *1*   **Number ▼** *3*   **Issue Date ▼** *9/15/90*   **On Pages ▼** *55-56*

2 NAME OF AUTHOR ▼   DATES OF BIRTH AND DEATH
Year Born ▼   Year Died ▼

a   *VANESSA VANGO*   *1963*   —

Was this contribution to the work a "work made for hire"? ☐ Yes ☑ No

AUTHOR'S NATIONALITY OR DOMICILE
Name of Country
OR { Citizen of ▶ _____
Domiciled in ▶ *USA*

WAS THIS AUTHOR'S CONTRIBUTION TO THE WORK
Anonymous? ☐ Yes ☑ No
Pseudonymous? ☐ Yes ☑ No
If the answer to either of these questions is "Yes," see detailed instructions

NOTE
Under the law, the "author" of a "work made for hire" is generally the employer, not the employee (see instructions). For any part of this work that was "made for hire" check "Yes" in the space provided, give the employer (or other person for whom the work was prepared) as "Author" of that part, and leave the space for dates of birth and death blank.

NATURE OF AUTHORSHIP   Briefly describe nature of the material created by this author in which copyright is claimed. ▼
ARTWORK

b   NAME OF AUTHOR ▼   DATES OF BIRTH AND DEATH
Year Born ▼   Year Died ▼

Was this contribution to the work a "work made for hire"? ☐ Yes ☐ No

AUTHOR'S NATIONALITY OR DOMICILE
Name of country
OR { Citizen of ▶ _____
Domiciled in ▶ _____

WAS THIS AUTHOR'S CONTRIBUTION TO THE WORK
Anonymous? ☐ Yes ☐ No
Pseudonymous? ☐ Yes ☐ No
If the answer to either of these questions is "Yes," see detailed instructions.

NATURE OF AUTHORSHIP   Briefly describe nature of the material created by this author in which copyright is claimed. ▼

c   NAME OF AUTHOR ▼   DATES OF BIRTH AND DEATH
Year Born ▼   Year Died ▼

Was this contribution to the work a "work made for hire"? ☐ Yes ☐ No

AUTHOR'S NATIONALITY OR DOMICILE
Name of Country
OR { Citizen of ▶ _____
Domiciled in ▶ _____

WAS THIS AUTHOR'S CONTRIBUTION TO THE WORK
Anonymous? ☐ Yes ☐ No
Pseudonymous? ☐ Yes ☐ No
If the answer to either of these questions is "Yes," see detailed instructions.

NATURE OF AUTHORSHIP   Briefly describe nature of the material created by this author in which copyright is claimed. ▼

3 YEAR IN WHICH CREATION OF THIS WORK WAS COMPLETED This information must be given in all cases. *1990* ◀ Year

DATE AND NATION OF FIRST PUBLICATION OF THIS PARTICULAR WORK Complete this information ONLY if this work has been published. Month ▶ *SEPT* Day ▶ *10* Year ▶ *1990* Nation *USA* ◀ Nation

4 COPYRIGHT CLAIMANT(S) Name and address must be given even if the claimant is the same as the author given in space 2.▼

See instructions before completing this space.

TRANSFER If the claimant(s) named here in space 4 are different from the author(s) named in space 2, give a brief statement of how the claimant(s) obtained ownership of the copyright.▼

DO NOT WRITE HERE OFFICE USE ONLY
APPLICATION RECEIVED
ONE DEPOSIT RECEIVED
TWO DEPOSITS RECEIVED
REMITTANCE NUMBER AND DATE

MORE ON BACK ▶ • Complete all applicable spaces (numbers 5-9) on the reverse side of this page • See detailed instructions • Sign the form at line 8.

DO NOT WRITE HERE
Page 1 of _____ pages

fringement.

The registration procedure is not at all complex or lengthy. Form VA is generally used by graphic artists to register pictorial, graphic or sculptural artwork. Along with the properly completed form, one or two copies of the entire artwork must be enclosed (depending on whether the art is unpublished or published) with a $20 fee. The accompanying example of a completed VA form is for a published illustration appearing in a book.

At times other registration forms may be needed by graphic artists. If audiovisual work is created, including motion pictures, then Form PA is the appropriate registration form. When an artist is creator of both art and text in a work and the text predominates, Form TX should be used to register the work and the description should indicate "text with accompanying art.". For computer software, Form TX is used and for computer graphics, Form VA. All forms are accompanied by line-by-line instructions *if* the instructions are specifically requested from the Copyright Office.

It is best if the artist's copyright notice accompanies a public distribution or publication of any art. The elements that make up a copyright notice are Copyright,

---

EXAMINED BY

CHECKED BY

FORM VA

☐ CORRESPONDENCE
Yes

☐ DEPOSIT ACCOUNT
FUNDS USED

FOR
COPYRIGHT
OFFICE
USE
ONLY

DO NOT WRITE ABOVE THIS LINE. IF YOU NEED MORE SPACE, USE A SEPARATE CONTINUATION SHEET.

PREVIOUS REGISTRATION Has registration for this work, or for an earlier version of this work, already been made in the Copyright Office?
☐ Yes ☑ No If your answer is "Yes," why is another registration being sought? (Check appropriate box) ▼
☐ This is the first published edition of a work previously registered in unpublished form.
☐ This is the first application submitted by this author as copyright claimant.
☐ This is a changed version of the work, as shown by space 6 on this application.
If your answer is "Yes," give: **Previous Registration Number** ▼   **Year of Registration** ▼

5

DERIVATIVE WORK OR COMPILATION Complete both space 6a & 6b for a derivative work; complete only 6b for a compilation.
a. **Preexisting Material** Identify any preexisting work or works that this work is based on or incorporates. ▼

b. **Material Added to This Work** Give a brief, general statement of the material that has been added to this work and in which copyright is claimed. ▼

6

See instructions before completing this space.

DEPOSIT ACCOUNT If the registration fee is to be charged to a Deposit Account established in the Copyright Office, give name and number of Account.
Name ▼   **Account Number** ▼

7

CORRESPONDENCE Give name and address to which correspondence about this application should be sent. Name/Address/Apt/City/State/Zip ▼
VANESSA VANGO
64 PIGMENT DRIVE
GIVERNY, GA 30349

Area Code & Telephone Number ▶ 404/976-0001

Be sure to give your daytime phone number

CERTIFICATION* I, the undersigned, hereby certify that I am the
Check only one ▼
☑ author
☐ other copyright claimant
☐ owner of exclusive right(s)
☐ authorized agent of _____
Name of author or other copyright claimant, or owner of exclusive right(s) ▲

8

of the work identified in this application and that the statements made by me in this application are correct to the best of my knowledge.

Typed or printed name and date ▼ If this is a published work, this date must be the same as or later than the date of publication given in space 3.
VANESSA VANGO   date ▶ 9/15/90

Handwritten signature (X) ▼
Vanessa Vango

MAIL CERTIFICATE TO

Certificate will be mailed in window envelope

Name ▼
VANESSA VANGO

Number/Street/Apartment Number ▼
64 PIGMENT DRIVE

City/State/ZIP ▼
GIVERNY, GA 30349

9

Have you:
• Completed all necessary spaces?
• Signed your application in space 8?
• Enclosed check or money order for $20 payable to Register of Copyrights?
• Enclosed your deposit material with the application and fee?
MAIL TO: Register of Copyrights, Library of Congress, Washington, D.C. 20559

* 17 U.S.C. § 506(e): Any person who knowingly makes a false representation of a material fact in the application for copyright registration provided for by section 409, or in any written statement filed in connection with the application, shall be fined not more than $2,500.
☆U.S. GOVERNMENT PRINTING OFFICE: 1988 202-133/80,001

June 1988 100,000

Copr. or ©, the artist's name, and the year date of publication; for example, ©Jane Artist1991. (See p. 35 for more information.). The form and placement of the notice should be covered in the written agreement with the client. When use of the art has been temporarily granted to a client, the name in the notice should preferably be the artist's, but may be the client's for the duration of the usage.

Unpublished artworks may be grouped under a single title and registered together for a $20 fee. For example, an artist may collect 75 drawings, put them into an orderly unit and register them under a single identifying title. Inexpensive, group registration is also available for published artwork which appeared in periodicals. Such contributions to periodicals must have been made within a one-year period and must include the individual artist's copyright notice. In this latter instance, Form GR/CP must be completed in addition to the other appropriate forms.

In submitting copies of the artwork along with the registration form, original art need not be submitted. The artist can submit tearsheets, photocopies or transparencies. The Copyright Office prefers the best edition of published work.

Whatever type of copies are submitted, they should show all copyrightable contents of the artwork.

Free registration forms and information on the copyright law and registration procedures are available by calling or writing the Copyright Office. The address is Copyright Office, Information and Publications Section, Library of Congress, Washington, D.C. 20559; (202) 479-0700 (during business hours only). To leave a recorded request for forms at any time, call (202) 707-9100. Please refer also to "Copyright" in the chapter on *Business and Legal Practices For Commissioned Art Work* and other related topics in the index.

Artists' legal risks of invasion and infringement

Any illustration or design could involve problems of invasion of privacy and copyright infringement. For example, the "advertising or trade" use of a living person's name or likeness without permission is an invasion of privacy. In this field claims may be in the hundreds of thousands of dollars for an infringement. "Advertising or trade" means virtually all uses outside of factual editorial content of magazines, newspapers, books, television programs, etc.; it includes print and TV ads, company brochures, packaging and other commercial uses. Public and private figures are protected equally.

The test of "likeness" is whether an ordinary person would recognize the complainant as the person in the illustration in question. It needn't be a perfect likeness. The best protection in these cases is a signed release from the person whose likeness is used ("model release"), and any contract should provide for this if a problem is likely to arise.

If the artist copied another work (say a photograph) in making the illustration, the photographer or copyright holder might sue for copyright infringement. The test of an infringement is whether an ordinary person would say that one work is copied from the other; the copying need not be exact.

Given the substantial amount of photography used in reference files for illustration as well as the frequent incorporation of photographs into designs, it is likely that everyone should be exercising extreme caution in this area. Of course, common themes and images (such as squares or triangles) are in the public domain and may be used freely. Infringement requires the copying of a substantial portion of a work, so a mere similarity of style or concept will not be an infringement.

Because of the privacy and infringement risks, many firms carry advertisers' (or publishers') liability insurance to cover claims pertaining to these subjects. That however, may not provide complete protection, particularly for the freelance artist, who may be sued as well as the client. Or clients might require that artists incorporate images which might infringe someone's right of privacy or copyright. Claims and lawsuits mean increased insurance premiums or loss of coverage altogether. For these reasons, caution in the use of artwork is always necessary. Freelance artists should make sure that their contracts contain *indemnification* protecting them from lawsuits that might arise from using images required by the client.

Checks with conditions

It is not uncommon for artists to receive payment in the form of a check with several conditions stated on the back. Usually these will be conditions to the effect that endorsement of the check constitutes a transfer of all reproduction rights and/or ownership of the original art to the payer. Although legal opinion is divided on the matter, it is doubtful that endorsement of such a check would constitute a legal contract, especially if it conflicts with a previous contract. An artist has at least three options to consider when handling checks with conditions.

First, simply return the check and request that a new check be issued without conditions. If the conditions on the check violate a prior contract, a refusal to issue a check without conditions will be a breach of contract.

Second, if an artist has signed a contract or sent an invoice that restricts the client's rights of use, the artist should strike out the conditions on the check and deposit it if the artwork has already been used. In making the deposit, the artist should probably not *sign* the back of the check, but instead use an endorsement stamp after striking out all the conditions. If the artwork has not been used, the artist should notify the client in writing that he or she is striking out the conditions on the check. If the artist does not hear from the client within two weeks, the check can be deposited safely.

Finally, if the artist has neither signed a contract with the client nor sent any prior invoice restrictions on the rights of use, that check should be returned in order to protect all rights. Along with the check the artist should include an appropriate invoice restricting the rights of use. Of course, the best procedure is to specify in writing which rights will be transferred before beginning an assignment.

Records, billing and bill tracking

Getting paid on time and in full is the just entitlement of any business, including artists. Proper planning and preparation at the right time, in writing, can do much towards having this expectation met. These preparations may, at times, require an extra effort on the artist's part,

but they will certainly pay off in the long run.

At the start of each job, artists should have a complete understanding of the negotiated terms and obtain a final agreement in writing to help insure timely and proper payment of fees.

To encourage timely payment, artists may include additional terms providing penalties for accounts that are past due and retaining rights until full payment is received. Since job changes often alter the original terms, it is particularly important to confirm in writing any additional fees due to the artist as a result of such changes.

The Guild's model business forms incorporate a number of these measures and can aid Guild members in securing their agreement and rights.

To facilitate accurate billing, artists should maintain proper records through job files, job ledgers or a similar system. Tracking invoices provides the means to remind buyers of outstanding obligations and to take such follow-up steps as are necessary to obtain payment.

When a buyer refuses to make payment, written agreements and invoices can serve as a basis to protect the artist's rights, either through negotiation, arbitration or a lawsuit.

Keeping records

All artists should have a system for recordkeeping. Such a system facilitates billing, bill tracking and fee collection and provides a basis for claiming and verifying tax deductions.

Job file: One common method of recordkeeping is the use of a folder or envelope labeled for each assignment. All information and documents such as agreements, messenger and expense receipts, letters, phone memos, invoices and so on are put into this job file as they are received. The file then provides a single and complete record of all decisions and documents.

Identifying information is usually placed on the folder cover. This may include the job number, the title of the project, the buyer's name and the delivery date. If the job is complex, the job file should be subdivided into sections to permit easy access to information. All sketches and drawings should be retained as well, at least until payment is received.

Job ledger: A job ledger contains standard columns for information such as the *job description* (Job Number, Client,

Description of Artwork, Delivery Date), *rights granted* (Usage Rights Granted, Status of Original Artwork), *fees and expenses* (Fee or Advance, Reimbursable Expenses, Sales Tax, etc.), and *billing information* (Invoice Date, Invoice Amount, Payment Due Date, Amount Received, Date Received, Late Penalties, Balance Due, Artwork Returned Date.)

With a job ledger, an artist can at a glance determine the status of each aspect of a job. The ledger's format can vary from a form specifically created by the artist to a printed journal readily available in stationery stores.

Billing procedure

Most art assignments, whether written or verbal, are contractual arrangements. Essentially, the buyer promises to make a specific payment in return for the artist's grant of usage rights. Invoices serve as formal communications to the buyer of monies that have or will become due.

The manner and time of payment are normally established in the written agreement. If the parties have not specified a payment due date, the generally accepted practice is payment within 30 days of delivery of the art.

An invoice should be presented whenever a payment becomes due. In many instances, invoices should accompany delivery of the finished art. When a partial payment is due or costs are to be billed during the job, the invoice or statement should be delivered accordingly. If cancellation or rejection occurs, the buyer should be billed immediately according to the agreement, or, if such a provision is absent, according to the standards discussed in the chapter on *Professional Issues*.

Verbal requests for payment are not substitutes for invoices but are additional means to use in the collection process. In many businesses an invoice is mandatory for the buyer or others to authorize and issue a check. A copy of the invoice should also be sent to the accounting department, if the business is large enough to have one, to facilitate prompt processing.

The wording of invoices should be accurate and complete to avoid payment delays. The artist's Social Security number or federal identification number should be included. Billing may be expedited by including the instructions, "Make check payable to Jane Artist or J. Artist Associates,"

whichever is applicable.

Copies of receipts for reimbursable costs are usually attached to document expenditures. At least one copy of the invoice should be retained by the artist.

Tracking outstanding payments

Once the invoice has been given to the buyer, the artist will want to monitor the outstanding debt until it is paid. A tracking system should be set up that ties into the artist's recordkeeping.

One simple method is to label a folder "Accounts Receivable." Copies of all invoices forwarded to buyers in order of payment due date, the artist's job number or the billing date should be kept in this folder.

To track fees, these invoices should be reviewed periodically. When payment is received, the invoice is moved to the individual job file.

Artists using a job ledger can determine at a glance which payments remain outstanding by referring to the "Payment Due Date" column. When payment is received, the date is entered under "Payment Received Date."

Continual tracking of outstanding payments also keeps information on cash flow current and allows for timely follow-up steps to collect past-due fees or other outstanding obligations

Collecting

Having completed and delivered artwork that meets the buyer's specifications, it's natural to expect that payment will be made as agreed. Graphic artists who are not paid in a reasonable time will need to undertake additional efforts to collect outstanding fees if they are not to absorb personal losses of income and productive time.

Artists can often prevent payment problems by taking certain precautions beforehand. The principal safeguard for artists is to outline payment and related terms clearly in a written and signed agreement right at the start of a job. Once the job has begun, the artist's use of certain protective practices to deal with job changes and to provide proper billing will further encourage timely and full payment. This advance preparation gives artists something to fall back on and facilitates the collection of fees should nonpayment occur.

Whether or not these preparatory steps have been taken, artists who do not receive timely payment for their work will want to implement appropriate and efficient collection strategies. This section looks at some of the collection resources available, how they work, what they entail and when they may be used.

Formulating a collection strategy

If payment is not received in full by the date due, the artist should put into effect a previously planned collection strategy. Invoices tend to get more difficult to collect as they get older, so prompt action is important. Artists and buyers can lose or misplace important documents or experience memory lapses, or new events may complicate matters.

The first step in a collection strategy is direct communication between artist and buyer. Subsequent steps depend on the nature of the problem and the buyer's response.

If a misunderstanding or error is involved, a direct discussion between artist and buyer may solve the problem. If discussion is not sufficient, artist and buyer can take advantage of the support services of a local Guild Grievance Committee, mediation or arbitration.

If the artist encounters an unreasonable or evasive buyer, more forceful measures may be required to collect outstanding fees. Artists may have to sue in small claims court or engage a collection agency or lawyer.

Direct negotiation

The first step in the collection process is direct communication with the buyer to determine why payment has not been made. Unless complex legal matters or large amounts of money are at issue, direct negotiation is usually the most appropriate approach. The other steps discussed below should be used only when direct negotiation is unsuccessful.

A phone call or a personal visit may be most effective in resolving a payment problem. Alternately, the artist might send a brief, businesslike letter with a copy of the original invoice attached and marked "Second Notice." The buyer should be reminded of and requested to provide the overdue payment immediately.

At this stage the artist usually can presume that human error or "red tape" was involved and that the call or letter will clear things up. These reminders often prove sufficient. There is, therefore, no need to alienate anyone, at least until it is clear that the nonpayment is deliberate.

It is in the artist's best interest to act professionally at all times in dealing with the buyer or anyone else who may be contacted. Artists should be objective and realistic while conducting collection efforts.

When payment problems occur or are anticipated, letters and invoices should be sent by certified mail, return receipt requested. Artists should keep copies of correspondence and memos of discussions between the parties. Establishing a "paper trail" of the proper documentation may prove to be crucial at a later stage.

Causes of nonpayment

Artists usually learn why the payment has not been made from the first contacts with the buyer. Following is a look at some of the more common causes of nonpayment and suggested strategies for responding to them. These basic negotiation concepts can be applied to other nonpayment situations as well.

Buyer's error: Once the artwork is delivered, it's on to the next project for the buyer. Buyers may forget to process the check. One purpose of an invoice is to serve as a physical reminder; the buyer should not be expected to send the check automatically, nor are verbal requests for payment sufficient.

If the cause of nonpayment is oversight, a new due date should be established and the buyer requested to follow up personally. The artist should send a letter confirming when payment will be made.

Artist's error: The artist may be the cause of the delay in payment. Perhaps an invoice was not provided, was sent to the attention of the wrong person, was incomplete or illegible or did not document reimbursable expenses. In this situation the artist must correct the error in order to expedite the payment process.

Disputes over the agreement or professional standards

Not all disputes are the result of deliberate abuse. Some are unintentional or caused by lack of knowledge of professional standards. For example, buyers may have made a wrong assumption or may not have been aware of appropriate professional conduct in a particular situation.

If the reason why payment has not been made or other rights not respected is contrary to the agreement or to professional standards, then inform the buyer of the correct position. When contacting the buyer, refer to the written (or verbal) agreement. Well-negotiated agreements will usually address the disputed issue and therefore specify either the obligations of the buyer or the rights of the artist. If necessary bring provisions in the agreement providing alternatives or penalties to the buyer's attention. These provisions can provide additional negotiating leverage.

The buyer's attention may also be directed to appropriate professional standards such as the industry's "Code of Fair Practice" and the Guild's *Pricing & Ethical Guidelines.*

The buyer should be asked to comply with the artist's request or to respond to the issue if further discussion appears appropriate.

Extension of payment time

A buyer may claim to be experiencing a cash-flow problem, that is, not having sufficient funds on hand to pay. It is difficult to verify whether this is a legitimate reason or an evasive maneuver.

Nor is it unusual for the buyer to blame the late payment on the company's computer. Long intervals between programmed payments, however, are unreasonable. Exceptions to automatic payments can be, and are, made all the time. In this case, insist that a handwritten check be authorized within a specified number of days.

If the cause of the delay appears legitimate and future payment clearly will be made, the artist may wish to accommodate the buyer and grant a reasonable extension. If an extension is granted, the new payment deadline should be put in writing.

Granting extensions should be viewed as a professional courtesy on the part of the artist, not the buyer's right. To compensate the artist fairly for the delay, the buyer should be willing to pay an additional stated percentage of the balance due as a service fee. This practice should be used particularly when longer extensions are granted.

Refusal to negotiate

After attempting direct negotiation, a buyer may still refuse to make payment. The buyer may not respond to the artist's letters and calls, may make unreasonable explanations, not address the issue at hand or not make payment as promised according to the newly negotiated terms.

Faced with this situation, and as a last effort before turning to other alternatives, the artist should send a demand letter. This can be done either directly or through a lawyer. The basis of the artist's claim should be briefly restated with a demand for immediate payment of any outstanding balance.

The demand letter should also state that legal action will be taken unless payment is received. In view of the artist's determination to pursue his or her legal rights, the buyer will have to reconsider.

Planning ahead

Up to this point, a number of reasonable efforts have been made and sufficient time has elapsed to allow the buyer to respond or pay the debt. The artist has also established a "paper trail" of proper documentation verifying the continued indebtedness and the artist's attempts to collect.

If the buyer still fails to respond or pay, or acts evasively, the artist may reasonably assume that the buyer is intentionally avoiding payment. The artist must now select the next course of action from among the alternatives discussed in the following sections.

The Guild's Grievance Committee

The Guild's Grievance Committee provides guidance and assistance to members in good standing to resolve differences with their clients. Guild members requiring this service may contact the Grievance Committee of their local Guild chapter.

The following information should be included when submitting a grievance:

1. The member's personal and business names, addresses and phone numbers;

2. The name of the client, the name and title of the art buyer and the relevant addresses and phone numbers;

3. The exact job description;

4. The nature of the grievance, including a chronological narration of facts and the respective positions of the parties;

5. The names of other agencies and persons (e.g., collection agencies or lawyers) contacted in regard to the grievance and the result of such contacts;

6. Copies, *not originals*, of relevant documents substantiating the grievance; i.e., agreement forms or purchase orders, invoices, correspondence, receipts and so on.

7. A statement of what the member would consider an appropriate solution of the grievance.

Members may not claim the support of the Grievance Committee until the Committee has reviewed the case and has notified the member that the case has been accepted. The Grievance Committee may not take a case if the member has already begun formal litigation.

The Committee reviews grievances at its earliest opportunity. If it is determined that the grievance is justified, the Committee contacts the member. A plan of action is recommended and appropriate support provided, ranging from direct communication with the client to written testimony to the court supporting the member in any follow-up litigation. It is crucial that the member participate fully and keep the Committee advised of subsequent developments.

The Grievance Committee will not offer assistance in a dispute involving questionable professional conduct on a member's part, such as misrepresentation of talent, accepting work on speculation, plagiarism or any violation of the Code of Fair Practice.

Mediation and Arbitration

Mediation and arbitration are long-established processes for settling disputes privately and professionally. They use the services of an impartial outsider to bring about a resolution.

A mediator, acting as an umpire, will do everything possible to bring the parties to agreement, but cannot impose a decision upon them. If the parties cannot reach an agreement, they must proceed to either arbitration or court to resolve the dispute. In arbitration, the arbitrator acts as a judge, reviewing the facts presented by both sides and then making a legally binding decision.

Submitting to mediation or arbitration is voluntary and both parties must agree

in order to use these services. An arbitration provision in an artist's contract establishes the buyer's consent once the contract is signed. Should the buyer not appear for arbitration, a binding decision may be reached in the buyer's absence.

Mediation and arbitration are speedier and far less expensive than suing in formal court. Their conciliatory and private atmosphere may be more conducive to parties who have had or who anticipate a long business relationship. These services may also be relevant if the artist's monetary claim exceeds the limit of small claims court. Arbitrators' fees, which are split between the parties, are usually moderate and normally consist of a flat fee plus expenses.

The Joint Ethics Committee, comprised of organizations representing artists, art buyers and agents, including the Guild, has provided these services to the metropolitan New York City area for over 20 years. The JEC is not a collection agency; it deals with ethical issues only. This independent organization is unique to the industry, as most of its arbitrators and mediators are graphic art practitioners. A full discussion of the JEC appears in the chapter on *Ethical Standards*.

The American Arbitration Association is available in 24 cities around the country and its services may be requested in other localities. Arbitration and mediation may also be sponsored by some of the volunteer arts-lawyer groups including Volunteer Lawyers for the Arts in New York City and Bay Area Lawyers for the Arts in San Francisco.

Small claims court

Small claims courts give access to the legal system while avoiding the usual encumbrance, costs and lengthy duration of formal courts. The small claims procedure is streamlined, speedy and available for a minimal fee.

Artists can handle their own cases with a little preparation. Information can be obtained from flyers prepared by the court, "how-to" publications and, perhaps best, from local rules books. The court clerk or, in some localities, a legal advisor is often available to help with preparation. The small claims procedure forms are also known as "trespass and assumpsit" claims forms.

Artists may bring claims seeking a monetary judgment to small claims court. Such claims may include nonpayment for completed or cancelled artwork as well as nonpayment for purchase of the original art, unauthorized reuses or unreturned or damaged art.

Each court has a dollar limit for what it considers a small claim. Amounts in excess of the limit would normally have to be brought to a formal court. Considering the higher costs of pursuing a claim through formal court, it may be economical to reduce the claim to an amount that qualifies as a "small claim," especially if the amount in dispute is only slightly higher than the court's limit. However, this claim must be made with the understanding that the balance above the court's limit is permanently forfeited. It may be possible to split up a larger amount of owed monies into several smaller claims to be sued for individually; for example, if a client owes a large sum made up of payments due from several assignments.

Many small claims court cases are heard by arbitrators rather than judges. This does not prejudice one's case and can even expedite a decision.

Collecting after a judgment

Should a buyer fail to pay after the court has rendered its decision or affirmed an arbitration award, the law authorizes a number of collection remedies for the artist. The artist gains the right, within limitations, to place a lien on the buyer's funds and assets. Available funds, such as bank accounts or a portion of an individual's salary, may be seized by a sheriff or marshal and turned over to the artist. Similarly, the proceeds of property or cars sold at a public auction may be used to settle the debt.

Collection services

Commercial collection agencies are available to seek payment on the artist's behalf before an arbitration decision or court judgment is sought. Their efforts involve escalated demands on the buyer through letters, phone calls or visits or by using a lawyer.

Collection agencies' fees, in addition to their routine expenses, range from 20 per cent to 50 per cent of the monies actually recovered. If the agency engages a lawyer, an additional fee is usually required.

A signed agreement between the artist and the agency should be reviewed carefully for actions the agency will take and what it will charge. Particular care should be taken in dealing with a commercial agency that may use practices that could be deemed unprofessional since they may reflect unfavorably on the artist.

Consulting or hiring a lawyer

The services of a lawyer can assist in a number of ways and at different stages in a collection strategy. Consulting with a lawyer about a problem at hand may provide sufficient information to continue individual collection efforts. Whether a problem relates to rights or to payment due, the artist may desire an initial consultation with an attorney, whether in person or by phone, to confirm what the relevant law is and whether the artist's position is supportable under the law. The lawyer may be able to advise about available resources, chances for successful resolution and other legal matters to consider.

For simple payment-due problems a general practitioner or collection lawyer can be engaged. The lawyer's efforts would be similar to that of a collection agency. The psychological effect of receiving a lawyer's letter or call often produces quick resolutions or conclusions to disputes.

If the nature of the dispute involves the artist's legal rights in and economic control over artwork, a lawyer specializing in art matters should be selected. It is important that the lawyer be familiar with the applicable laws as well as the business aspects of the artist's profession.

When a dispute must be cleared up before payment can be made, engaging a lawyer to negotiate with the buyer might be helpful. The lawyer may be able to take a more forceful role on the artist's behalf and may bring about a fairer and quicker settlement. A lawyer's presence and negotiation skills may also result in avoiding a lawsuit. When the problem is resolved, and if it proves advisable, a lawyer can provide a written agreement to bring complex issues to a final and binding close.

The Guild offers its members access to a Legal Referral Service. Members who needs a lawyer's services should contact their local chapters for the names of attorneys with expertise in a particular area. Attorneys participating in the Legal Referral Service will often offer reduced rates to Guild members, although any fees and expenses are negotiated directly between the member and the attorney. In addition, legal services for personal and business matters are available through the Guild for a reasonable annual retainer fee. Contact the Guild's national office for more information.

Lawyer's fees and structures vary. Some charge flat fees, some a percentage of the monies recovered. Initial one-time consultation fees are often lower. Artists should discuss fees with the attorney *before* accepting their advice or assistance. Artists with limited incomes may be able to take advantage of volunteer arts-lawyer groups for collection and other legal needs. Some of these groups around the country are:

San Diego Lawyers for the Arts
1205 Prospect Street, Suite 400
La Jolla, CA 92037
619-454-9696

California Lawyers for the Arts
Building C, Room 255
San Francisco, CA 94123
415-775-7200

Colorado Lawyers for the Arts
P.O. Box 300428
Denver, CO 80203
303-892-7122

Volunteer Lawyers for the Arts, D.C.
918 Sixteenth Street, N.W., Suite 503
Washington, D.C. 20006
202-429-0229

Business Volunteers for the Arts
150 West Flagler Street, Suite 2500
Miami, FL 33130
305-789-3590

Georgia Volunteer Lawyers for the Arts
34 Peachtree Street, N.W.
Atlanta, GA 30303
404-525-6046

Lawyers for the Creative Arts
213 West Institute Place, Suite 411
Chicago, IL 60610
312-944-2787

Louisiana Volunteer Lawyers for the Arts
c/o Arts Council of New Orleans
821 Gravier Street, Suite 600
New Orleans, LA 70112
504-523-1465

Maryland Lawyers for the Arts
Belvedere Hotel
1 East Chase Street, Suite 1118
Baltimore, MD 21202
301-752-1633

The Artists Foundation, Inc.
8 Park Plaza
Boston, MA 02116
617-227-2787

St. Louis Volunteer Lawyers & Accountants for the Arts
3540 Washington
St. Louis, MO 63103
314-652-2410

Volunteer Lawyers for the Arts Program
Albany League of Arts
19 Clinton Avenue
Albany, NY 12207
518-449-5380

Volunteer Lawyers for the Arts
1285 Avenue of the Americas, 3rd Floor
New York, NY 10019
212-977-9270

North Carolina Volunteer Lawyers for the Arts
P.O. Box 26484
Raleigh, NC 27611
919-741-7508

Philadelphia Volunteer Lawyers for the Arts
251 South 18th Street
Philadelphia, PA 19103
215-545-3385

Texas Accountants & Lawyers for the Arts
5151 Belt Line Road, #1005
Dallas, TX 75240
214-701-8275

Texas Accountants & Lawyers for the Arts
1540 Sul Ross
Houston, TX 77006
713-526-4876

Washington Lawyers for the Arts
1331 Third Avenue, #512
Seattle, WA 98101
206-223-0502

Suing in formal court

Bringing a suit in formal court is not normally necessary to resolve a payment or other dispute. Various alternatives already noted are available to the artist and buyer for resolving most disputes.

Formal court should only be considered as a last resort when the buyer refuses to negotiate or does so unrealistically, leaving the artist with no other choice.

Monetary claims in excess of the small claims court limit must be brought to formal court. Non-monetary issues, such as copyright disputes or action required of the buyer, must also be taken to formal court.

The artist does not necessarily have to hire a lawyer in order to sue in formal court. The law allows a person to appear as his or her own lawyer. In disputes where the issue is clear, artists will usually not be prejudiced by representing themselves in court. In disputes not involving large sums of money, a lawyer may be hired to advise the artist on how to prepare the case, keeping legal costs down.

Of course, when a great deal of money or complex legal issues are involved, it is prudent to hire a lawyer to handle the entire matter. In such an event, the fees and expenses should be discussed with the lawyer at the outset.

Putting it into perspective

Preparation for the possibility of nonpayment of fees is best made right at the beginning of the job. Written agreements should clearly establish the buyer's payment obligations as well as any conditions that would go into effect when payment is not made as agreed.

The first step in fee collection is direct contact with the buyer to ascertain the nature of the problem. Once that is known, the artist must determine which alternative to pursue.

The services of an outside party such as an arbitrator (which should be provided for in the original agreement), mediator, or the Guild's Grievance Committee may assist the parties in achieving a resolution.

Should arbitration not be available or the buyer prove uncooperative, the artist may be required to use more forceful alternatives.

Small claims court can provide an inexpensive and speedy legal determination of claims within its jurisdiction.

When payment is refused despite a favorable arbitration decision or court judgment, the artist can use the services of a sheriff or marshal.

Lawyers may be engaged at any stage of the collection process, depending upon the issues involved, to provide advice or full representation.

Commercial collection agencies may also be used to seek payment of fees in the artist's behalf.

Establishing written safeguards early can prevent payment problems as well as provide the artist with practical alternatives.

These alternatives protect the artist's rights and facilitate the collection of outstanding fees. And, *getting paid,* is, of course, the just entitlement of graphic artists.

Standard Contracts

The Guild has created a number of standard contracts for use by its members and other professionals. The Guild's contracts conform to the Code of Fair Practice and provide a basis for fair dealing between the parties. The purpose of these standard forms is to aid both creators and art buyers in reaching a thorough understanding of their rights and obligations.

A contract is a binding agreement between two or more parties. Normally each party gains certain benefits and must fulfill certain obligations. To be valid a contract must include the important terms of an assignment such as the fee and the job description. Other terms, such as a time when payment must be made, will be presumed to be reasonable (such as within thirty days of submitting an invoice or completing the assignment), if the parties have not actually specified them in writing. Although it is wise to have written contracts, oral contracts are also binding in many cases and can be the basis of legal suit. Thus contracts can take many forms: oral, purchase orders, confirmation forms, letters, an exchange of letters or more formal documents.

Both parties need not sign a contract to make it binding, although it is wise to do so. For example, if a buyer receives a confirmation form from an artist and does not object to the terms of the form, the artist is justified in starting work with the uncontested form as a binding contract. Even purchase orders or invoices can be used as evidence to prove the terms of the unwritten contract on which the artist relied to start his or her work.

A common way of entering into a contract is to have one party send a letter to the other party. If the party receiving the letter agrees with the terms set forth in the letter, he or she signs at the bottom of the letter beneath the words "Agreed to" and returns a signed copy of the letter to the party who sent it. While informal, such a letter of agreement is binding. In the event that one party is signing a contract on behalf of a corporation, that person should give the corporate name, their own name, and their title that authorizes them to sign for the corporation, such as "XYZ Corp. By Alice Buyer, Art Director."

In creating a contract, there must be an offer and an acceptance. If one party makes an offer and the other party makes a counteroffer, the original offer is automatically terminated. For a contract to be binding, each party must give something of value to the other party, called consideration. The most common form of consideration is a promise to do something or refrain from doing something. A promise to work or a promise to pay could be consideration, although doing the work or making the payment would also be consideration. For a contract to be enforceable, its purpose must be both legal and not against public policy, as might occur if, for example, a contract provided that the public be misinformed as to some aspect of a product.

One common problem that arises in contracts is the battle of the forms. Each party sends its own forms to the other, but the terms are rarely the same. The question then arises: whose form will govern if a dispute arises? If work is begun on the basis of one form, that form should take precedence over forms sent after completion of the work (such as invoices or a check with a condition on its back). However, the best way to resolve this problem is to deal with it directly. As soon as either party realizes that agreement has not been reached, the other should be notified. The points of disagreement should then be discussed and worked out to the satisfaction of both parties. Only in this way can the ambiguities that cause contractual problems be avoided.

Each of the Guild's contacts is a

model that can be used directly or that can be modified to suit individual needs and circumstances. By word processing the contracts and saving them to disk, they can then be tailored and personalized for each assignment.

Purchase orders and holding forms

Purchase orders often are used by clients at the beginning of an assignment. If the purchase order is merely an assignment description, artists will want to use a confirmation form, or order-acknowledgement form, detailing rights, payments, and other terms. An estimate is normally given before a purchase order is used.

Holding forms are used by artists when they leave work for consideration by a client. These forms detail the work that is being left by the artist, the date and time the client received the work, and the projected response date. An invoice is normally presented to a client with the finished work.

Most of the forms have been discussed in detail in various parts of the text (the Surface Designer-Agent Agreement is accompanied by its own introduction). All contracts and forms in this book are based on U.S. Copyright Law, which provides for the sale of individual reproduction rights by artists based on the needs expressed by their clients. Each right of usage should be clearly specified, as are all terms for usage.

Usage limitations take the following format:

Title of publication or name of product.

Category of use: Limits specific uses to advertising, promotion, editorial, corporate, or other uses, so that artwork purchased for one market (e.g., editorial art) may not be used in another market (e.g., advertising) without further agreement or consideration.

Medium of use: Specifies the form in which the art will reach the public, such as trade magazine, brochure, annual report, album cover, etc.

Edition: Limits usage to a given edition, such as a hardcover, quality paperback, or other edition.

Geographic area: Limits the territory in which the art can be distributed.

Time period: Limits the length of time during which the art can be used.

All of these concepts can be refined to fit the exact needs of artist and client.

Clients establish the usage needed, and the artists suggest the appropriate fees. If further uses are necessary after the contract is negotiated, an appropriate reuse fee can be established in most cases.

Writing a proposal

Graphic designers often provide clients with full service design projects from concept through production and final delivery. In providing this service, they often coordinate their own art direction and design services with copywriters, illustrators, photographers, retouchers and printers, and bill the client for the entire package.

Standard contracts, like those appearing in this book, do not provide the detail and explanatory material required by this kind of complex, multi-phased project. In such cases a design proposal can provide greater scope and, when bidding on a major commission, a more comprehensive structure.

At their initial meeting, it is important for both client and artist to discuss *specific* directions about what is being bid upon. Being specific serves two purposes: it will ensure that the proposal will cover the same project and items as other proposals submitted, and both parties will be able to avoid surprises in the scope and estimates of the project after the proposal is accepted.

The information supplied in the proposal is only for the design directions already discussed, specified and agreed upon by client and artist at their initial meetings. Since clients often compare a number of proposals before choosing an artist for the job, a proposal should be clear and thorough enough to be reviewed without the artist present. It is customary for design proposals to be submitted to clients as a complimentary service, although any fees and expenses incurred thereafter on a client's behalf and with the client's consent are billable. If the client accepts the proposal, the terms and conditions expressed in writing are signed by the client and the designer. Always make at least two copies of the proposal for both client and artist to retain as original signed copies if the commission is accepted. When signed by both client and designer, a proposal is legally binding as a contract.

The organization and appearance of a design proposal can be crucial in winning a job, especially if a design firm is competing against others. A proposal's appearance reflects a designer's ability and polish as much as the information contained within it. Consequently, proposals should be logically organized, well written, well designed and professionally presented.

When preparing a proposal for a new client, it helps to include collateral material such as biographies of those involved in the project, promotion pieces, reprints of published work, examples of similar projects produced by the designer, etc.

What to include

The proposal will reflect many of the following factors: (1) objectives and requirements of the project; (2) research; (3) art and/or copy that will be developed by the designer; (4) typography and other production services; (5) printing requirements; (6) intended use of the printed piece; and (7) schedule. Additionally, designers frequently prepare documents explaining subcontractor (such as illustrator or photographer) relationships, billing procedures and contract terms.

A proposal should begin with an overview, a clear and concise description of the project. All proposals should also include a disclaimer that prices and fees quoted are based on rough verbal specifications of the items listed; if the items change, fees will change accordingly.

Proposals, like the projects they reflect, are divided into parts. These parts include: *(1)* a description of design and production; *(2)* a description of fees; *(3)* a payment schedule for the phases of work involved; *(4)* rights, usages, terms and conditions, and *(5)* collateral material to help sell the designer's abilities to the client.

Defining and describing the phases for a project helps facilitate the billing process and ensures the work will not proceed to the next phase until payment is received according to agreed upon schedules. These check points also give clients very clear and tangible input at appropriate times as the project develops.

Parts and phases of a proposal

Part 1: Design and production: Phase 1, design: Describing the design phase of the project fully, including what form the design presentation will take, how many versions will be presented, the client approval process and the time schedule for this phase.

Phase 2, mechanical preparation: After client approval of the design phase, explaining the production process including: assigning of illustration and/or photography, copywriting, typesetting, proofreading, supervision of those components, exact print/production time estimates, client approval schedules and time required.

Phase 3, final production: After client approval of the previous phases, final production begins. Depending on the end product(s) a design firm has been commissioned to produce, this phase may be a matter of going on press and/or supervising the fabrication or manufacturing of products within a prescribed schedule. After the end product is approved, the project is considered billable.

Part 2: Fees: Fees and expenses may be handled in a number of ways. During the first phase, the studio may arrange to bill on an hourly or project basis. If clients prefer to be billed on a project basis, they will usually establish an acceptable "cap" on the total amount billed. Again, outline the project in briefer form than Part 1 and outline the fees required for design, copywriting, photography, illustration, etc. Clients sometimes request estimates for a variety of solutions to a design project. This is common practice and gives the client a choice of directions.

It is important to explain what these fees *do* include (i.e. design, mechanical, production, type specification, preliminary proofreading, etc.) and more important, what they *do not* include (i.e., out-of-pocket expenses, author's alterations, overtime charges, photographic art direction, long distance travel, etc.). These non-fee expenses, including mark-ups, should be stated and estimates of charges should be included if possible.

When supplying production prices such as printing, be sure to state that these estimates are based on rough verbal specifications and are budget estimates only. More exact quotations can be furnished at such time as a comp or mechanicals are viewed by the printer.

Part 3: Payments: Most design projects are typically quoted and billed by phase, with an initiating fee representing 10-30 per cent of the total estimated fees and reimbursable expenses and an outline of the payment schedule should be provided.

Part 4: Rights, usage and credit: Discuss usage, ownership of rights and artwork, credit lines, approvals and interest charged for late payments and any other terms deemed necessary. For clarification on these items, refer to the standard contracts in this book. Signature lines for both client and artist and date that the agreement is signed should follow. A signed original and copy should be retained by both parties.

Part 5: Collateral material: Include material that will help sell your abilities to the client. These may include background material or biographies, awards, a list of other clients and examples of work completed for them.

The following pages contain the standard Graphic Artist Guild contract forms. It should be noted that while these forms are as comprehensive as possible, some terms may not be suited to a given assignment; but they can used as starting points for your own customized contracts. However, legal language is written to be precise, and simplification of contract terms into "plain English," or deletion of contract terms altogether may leave the artist exposed to misinterpretation and misunderstanding of important aspects of an agreement.

All-Purpose Purchase Order

TO	COMMISSIONED BY
	DATE
	PURCHASE ORDER NUMBER

ASSIGNMENT DESCRIPTION
(remove all italics before using this form)
(indicate any preliminary presentations required by the buyer)
DELIVERY DATE   FEE

BUYER SHALL REIMBURSE ARTIST FOR THE FOLLOWING EXPENSES

RIGHTS TRANSFERRED. BUYER PURCHASES THE FOLLOWING EXCLUSIVE RIGHTS FOR USAGE	
TITLE OR PRODUCT	*(name)*
CATEGORY OR USE	*(advertising, corporate, promotional, editorial, etc.)*
MEDIUM OF USE	*(consumer or trade magazine, annual report, TV, book, etc.)*
EDITION (IF BOOK)	*(hardcover, mass market paperback, quality paperback, etc.)*
GEOGRAPHIC AREA	*(if applicable)*
TIME PERIOD	*(if applicable)*

ARTIST RESERVES ANY USAGE RIGHTS NOT EXPRESSLY TRANSFERRED. ANY USAGE BEYOND THAT GRANTED TO BUYER HEREIN SHALL REQUIRE THE PAYMENT OF A MUTUALLY AGREED UPON ADDITIONAL FEE. SUBJECT TO ALL TERMS ON REVERSE SIDE OF FORM.

Terms:

1. Time for Payment. All invoices shall be paid within thirty (30) days of receipt.

2. Changes. Buyer shall make additional payments for changes requested in original assignment. However, no additional payment shall be made for changes required to conform to the original assignment description. The Buyer shall offer the Artist first opportunity to make any changes.

3. Expenses. Buyer shall reimburse Artist for all expenses arising from this assignment, including the payment of any sales taxes due on this assignment. Buyer's approval shall be obtained for any increases in fees or expenses that exceed the original estimate by 10% or more.

4. Cancellation. In the event of cancellation of this assignment, ownership of all copyrights and the original artwork shall be retained by the Artist, and a cancellation fee for work completed, based on the contract price and expenses already incurred, shall be paid by the Buyer.

5. Ownership of Artwork. The Artist retains ownership of all original artwork, whether preliminary or final, and the Buyer shall return such artwork within thirty (30) days of use.

6. Credit Lines. The Buyer shall give Artist and any other creators a credit line with any editorial usage. If similar credit lines are to be

given with other types of usage, it must be so indicated here:

☐ If this box is checked, the credit line shall be in the form :

© _____ 199____ .

7. Releases. Buyer shall indemnify Artist against all claims and expenses, including reasonable attorney's fees, due to uses for which no release was requested in writing or for uses which exceed authority granted by a release.

8. Modifications. Modification of the Agreement must be written, except that the invoice may include, and Buyer shall pay, fees or expenses that were orally authorized in order to progress promptly with the work.

9. Arbitration. Any disputes in excess of $_____$ (maximum limit for small claims court) arising out of this Agreement shall be submitted to binding arbitration before the Joint Ethics Committee or a mutually agreed upon arbitrator pursuant to the rules of the American Arbitration Association. The Arbitrator's award shall be final, and judgment may be entered in any court having jurisdiction thereof. The Buyer shall pay all arbitration and court costs, reasonable attorney's fees, and legal interest on any award of judgment in favor of the Artist.

10. Acceptance of terms. The signature of both parties shall evidence acceptance of these terms.

CONSENTED AND AGREEZD TO
_____

DATE
_____

ARTIST'S SIGNATURE
_____

COMPANY NAME
_____

AUTHORIZED SIGNATURE
_____

NAME AND TITLE

Artist-Agent Agreement

Agreement, this _____ day of
_____, 19 ___, between

_____

(hereinafter referred to as the "Artist"), residing at:

_____

_____

and _____

(hereinafter referred to as the "Agent"), residing at:

_____

_____

Whereas, the Artist is an established artist of proven talents; and
Whereas, the Artist wishes to have an agent represent him or her in marketing certain rights enumerated herein; and
Whereas, the Agent is capable of marketing the artwork produced by the Artist; and
Whereas, the Agent wishes to represent the Artist;
Now, therefore, in consideration of the foregoing premises and the mutual convenants hereinafter set forth and other valuable consideration, the parties hereto agree as follows:

1. Agency. The Artist appoints the Agent to act as his or her exclusive representative: (A) in the following geographical area:

_____

_____

(B) for the markets listed here (specify publishing, advertising, etc.):

_____

_____

The Agent agrees to use his or her best efforts in submitting the Artist's work for the purpose of securing assignment for the Artist. The Agent shall negotiate the terms of any assignment that is offered, but the Artist shall have the right to reject any assignment if he or she finds the terms thereof unacceptable.

2. Promotion. The Artist shall provide the Agent with such samples of work as are from time to time necessary for the purpose of securing assignments. These samples shall remain the property of the Artist and be returned within thirty (30) days of termination of this Agreement. The Agent shall take reasonable efforts to protect the work from loss or damage, but shall be liable for such loss or damage only if caused by the Agent's negligence. Promotional expenses, including but not limited to promotional mailings and paid advertising, shall be paid _____ % by the Agent and _____ % by the Artist. The Agent shall bear the expenses of shipping, insurance and similar marketing expenses.

3. Term. This Agreement shall take effect on the _____ day of _____, 19 ___, and remain in full force and effect for a term of one year, unless terminated as provided in Paragraph 9.

4. Commissions. The Agent shall be entitled to the following commissions: (A) On assignments secured by the Agent during the term of this Agreement, twenty-five (25%) per cent of the billing. (B) On house accounts, ten (10%) per cent of the billing. For purposes of this Agreement, *house accounts* are defined as accounts obtained by the Artist at any time or obtained by another agent representing the Artist prior to the commencement of this Agreement and are listed in Schedule A attached to this Agreement. It is understood by both parties that no commission shall be paid on assignments rejected by the Artist or for which the Artist fails to receive payment, regardless of the reason payment is not made. Further, no commissions shall be payable in either (A) or (B) above for any part of the billing that is due to expenses incurred by the Artist in performing the assignment, whether or not such expenses are reimbursed by the client. In the event that a flat fee is paid by the client, it shall be reduced by the amount of expenses incurred by the Artist in performing the assignment, and

the Agent's commission shall be payable only on the fee as reduced for expenses.

5. Billing. The ☐Artist ☐Agent shall be responsible for all billings.

6. Payments. The Party responsible for billing shall make all payment due within ten (10) days of receipt of any fees covered by this Agreement. Late payments shall be accompanied by interest calculated at the rate of _____ % per month thereafter.

7. Accountings. The party responsible for billing shall send copies of invoices to the other party when rendered. If requested, that party shall also provide the other party with semiannual accountings showing all assignments for the period, the clients' names, the fees paid, expenses incurred by the Artist, the dates of payment, the amounts on which the Agent's commissions are to be calculated, and the sums due less those amounts already paid.

8. Inspection of the books and records. The party responsible for the billing shall keep the books and records with respect to commissions due at his or her place of business and permit the other party to inspect these books and records during normal business hours on the giving of reasonable notice.

9. Termination. This Agreement may be terminated by either party by giving thirty (30) days' written notice to the other party. If the Artist receives assignments after the termination date from clients originally obtained by the Agent during the term of this Agreement, the commission specified in Paragraph 4(A) shall be payable to the Agent under the following circumstances. If the Agent has represented the Artist for six months or less, the Agent shall receive a commission on such assignments received by the Artist within ninety (90) days of the date of termination. This period shall increase by thirty (30) days for each additional six months that the Agent has represented the Artist, but in no event shall such period exceed one hundred eighty (180) days.

10. Assignment. This Agreement shall not be assigned by either of the parties hereto. It shall be binding on and inure to the benefit of the successors, administrators, executors, or heirs of the Agent and Artist.

11. Arbitration. Any disputes in excess of $ _____ (maximum limit for small claims court) arising out of this Agreement shall be submitted to binding arbitration before the Joint Ethics Committee or a mutually agreed upon arbitrator pursuant to the rules of the American Arbitration Association. The Arbitrator's award shall be final and judgment may be entered in any court having jurisdiction thereof. The Agent shall pay all arbitration and court costs, reasonable attorney's fees, and legal interest on any award of judgment in favor of the Artist.

12. Notices. All notices shall be given to the parties at their respective addresses set forth above.

13. Independent contractor status. Both parties agree that the Agent is acting as an independent contractor. This Agreement is not an employment agreement, nor does it constitute a joint venture or partnership between the Artist and Agent.

14. Amendments and merger. All amendments to this Agreement must be written. This Agreement incorporates the entire understanding of the parties.

15. Governing law. This Agreement shall be governed by the laws of the State of :

_____

In witness whereof, the parties have signed this Agreement as of the date set forth above.

SCHEDULE A: HOUSE ACCOUNTS	
DATE	*(remove all italics before using this form)*
1.	*(name and address of client)*
2.	
3.	
4.	
5.	
6.	
7.	
8.	
9.	
10.	
11.	
12.	

_____
ARTIST

_____
AGENT

Computer Generated Art Job Order Form

FRONT: ARTIST'S LETTERHEAD

AUTHORIZED BUYER	DATE

CLIENT

FOR USE IN	ISSUE	DATE

DEFINITION/TYPE OF ASSIGNMENT

(remove all italics before using this form)

This job order form is a sample of a possible contract for computer generated art. Since the field is so new, artists should view this as a model and amend it to fit their situations and the needs of their client, based on a negotiated agreement.

ADDITIONAL USES   *(promotional, packaging, etc.)*

NUMBER OF SCREENS OR IMAGES
STILL FRAME   *(single frame, multiple frame)*

*SECTOR LENGTH PER SCREEN: MAXIMUM PREFERRED: MINIMUM:

JOB DESCRIPTION (NATURE OF MARKET):

COPY TO READ (BE SURE COPY IS CORRECTLY SPELLED AND TITLED. ARTIST IS NOT RESPONSIBLE FOR ANY COPY OTHER THAN EXACTLY WHAT APPEARS BELOW).

PRODUCTION SCHEDULE:

FIRST SHOWING

REVIEW

FINAL ACCEPTANCE

DISK(S) CAN BE USED ONLY FOR THE FOLLOWING PURPOSES STATED BELOW. ALL OTHER USE(S) AND MODIFICATION(S) IS PROHIBITED. THIS DISK MAY NOT BE COPIED WITHOUT THE ARTIST'S PERMISSION AND MUST BE RETURNED AFTER USE.

RIGHTS TRANSFERRED   *(one time use, etc.)*

TYPE OF USE   *(game program, advertising, etc.)*

MEDIUM OF USE   *(floppy, documentation, packaging, promotion, etc.)*

DISTRIBUTION/
GEOGRAPHICAL AREA   *(method of distribution, electronically downloaded, floppy disk, store distribution)*

TIME/NUMBER OF PRINTINGS   *(for use on specific machine, or compiled into other operation languages)*

SYSTEM APPLICATIONS

PURCHASE PRICE

PAYMENT SCHEDULE

Terms:

1. Time for payment. All invoices are payable within thirty (30) days of receipt. A 1-1/2% monthly service charge is payable on all overdue balances. The grant of any license or right of copyright is conditioned on receipt of full payment.

2. Estimates. If this form is used for an estimate or assignment confirmation, the fees and expenses shown are minimum estimates only. Final fees and expenses shall be shown when invoice is rendered. Client's approval shall be obtained for any increases in fees or expenses that exceed the original estimate by 10% or more.

3. Changes. Client shall be responsible for making additional payments for changes requested by Client in original assignment. However, no additional payment shall be made for changes required to conform to the original assignment description. The Client shall offer the Illustrator the first opportunity to make any changes.

4. Expenses. Client shall reimburse Illustrator for all expenses arising from this assignment, including the payment of any sales taxes due on this assignment and shall advance $ _____ to the Illustrator for payment of said expenses.

5. Cancellation. In the event of cancellation of this assignment, ownership of all copyrights and the original artwork shall be retained by the Illustrator, and a cancellation fee for work completed, based on the contract price and expenses already incurred, shall be paid by the Client.

6. Ownership of Artwork. The Illustrator retains ownership of all original artwork, whether preliminary or final, and the Client shall return such artwork within thirty (30) days of use.

7. Credit Lines. The Illustrator shall be given credit in: (a) floppy disk, (b) documentation, (c) packaging, (d) illustrator's mark on art.

8. Alterations. Any electronic alteration of original art (color shift, mirroring, flopping, combination cut and paste, deletion) creating additional art is prohibited without the express permission of the artist. Any such unauthorized alterations shall constitute additional use and will be billed accordingly.

9. Other operating systems conversions. Illustrator shall be given first option at compiling the work for operating systems beyond the original use.

10. Unauthorized use and program licenses. Client will indemnify Illustrator against all claims and expenses arising from uses for which Client does not have rights to or authority to use. The Client will be responsible for payment of any special licensing or royalty fees resulting from the use of graphics programs that require such payments.

11. Illustrators guarantee for program use. Illustrator guarantees to notify Client of any licensing and/ or permissions required for art generating/driving programs to be used.

12. Arbitration. Any disputes in excess of $ _____ (maximum limit for small claims court) arising out of this Agreement shall be submitted to binding arbitration before the Joint Ethics Committee or a mutually agreed upon arbitrator pursuant to the rules of the American Arbitration Association. The Arbitrator's award shall be final, and judgment may be entered in any court having jurisdiction thereof. The Client shall pay all arbitration and court costs, reasonable attorney's fees, and legal interest on any award of judgment in favor of the Artist.

13. The Client must copy-protect all final art which is the subject of this agreement against duplication or alteration.

14. The Client waives the right to challenge the validity of the Illustrator's ownership of the art subject to this agreement because of any change or evolution of the law.

15. Acceptance of terms. The signature of both parties shall evidence acceptance of these terms.

CONSENTED AND AGREED TO

DATE

ILLUSTRATOR'S SIGNATURE

COMPANY NAME

AUTHORIZED SIGNATURE

NAME AND TITLE

Graphic Designer's Estimate / Confirmation Form

FRONT: DESIGNER'S LETTERHEAD

ESTIMATE	ENGAGEMENT CONFIRMATION	INVOICE
TO		DATE
		COMMISSIONED BY
		ASSIGNMENT NUMBER
		INVOICE NUMBER
		CLIENT'S PURCHASE ORDER NUMBER

ASSIGNMENT DESCRIPTION	DELIVERY DATE
	(PREDICATED ON RECEIPT OF ALL MATERIALS TO BE SUPPLIED BY CLIENT)
	MATERIALS SUPPLIED BY
	FEE

ITEMIZED EXPENSES. CLIENT SHALL REIMBURSE DESIGNER FOR ALL EXPENSES. IF THIS IS AN ESTIMATE OR ASSIGNMENT CONFIRMATION, ANY EXPENSE AMOUNTS ARE ESTIMATES ONLY. IF THIS IS AN INVOICE, EXPENSE AMOUNTS ARE FINAL.

ILLUSTRATION	
PHOTOGRAPHY	
MATERIALS AND SUPPLIES	
MECHANICALS	
MESSENGERS	
PHOTOGRAPHIC REPRODUCTION	
PRINTING	
TOLL TELEPHONES	
TRANSPORTATION AND TRAVEL	
MODELS AND PROPS	
SHIPPING AND INSURANCE	
TYPE	
STATS	
OTHER	EXPENSES SUBTOTAL
	TOTAL
	SALES TAX
	TOTAL DUE

ANY USAGE RIGHTS NOT EXCLUSIVELY TRANSFERRED ARE RESERVED TO DESIGNER. USAGE BEYOND THAT GRANTED TO CLIENT HEREIN SHALL REQUIRE PAYMENT OF A MUTUALLY AGREED UPON ADDITIONAL FEE SUBJECT TO ALL TERMS ON REVERSE.

RIGHTS TRANSFERRED. DESIGNER TRANSFERS TO THE CLIENT THE FOLLOWING EXCLUSIVE RIGHTS OF USAGE. *(remove all italics before using this form)*	
TITLE OR PRODUCT	*(name)*
CATEGORY OF USE	*(advertising, corporate, promotional, editorial, etc.)*
MEDIUM OF USE	*(consumer or trade magazine, annual report, TV, book, etc.)*
EDITION (IF BOOK)	*(hardcover, mass market paperback, quality paperback, etc.)*
GEOGRAPHIC AREA	*(if applicable)*
TIME PERIOD	*(if applicable)*
ANY USAGE RIGHTS NOT EXCLUSIVELY TRANSFERRED ARE RESERVED TO DESIGNER. USAGE BEYOND THAT GRANTED TO CLIENT HEREIN SHALL REQUIRE PAYMENT OF A MUTUALLY AGREED UPON ADDITIONAL FEE SUBJECT TO ALL TERMS ON REVERSE.	

Terms:

1. Time for payment. All invoices are payable within thirty (30) days of receipt. A 1-1/2% monthly service charge is payable on all overdue balances. The grant of any license or right of copyright is conditioned on receipt of full payment.

2. Estimates. If this form is used for an estimate or assignment confirmation, the fees and expenses shown are minimum estimates only. Final fees and expenses shall be shown when invoice is rendered. Client's approval shall be obtained for any increases in fees or expenses that exceed the original estimate by 10% or more.

3. Changes. Client shall be responsible for making additional payments for changes requested by Client in original assignment. However, no additional payment shall be made for changes required to conform to the original assignment description. The Client shall offer the Designer the first opportunity to make any changes.

4. Expenses. Client shall reimburse Designer for all expenses arising from this assignment, including the payment of any sales taxes due on this assignment, and shall advance $ _____ to the Designer for payment of said expenses.

5. Cancellation. In the event of cancellation of this assignment, ownership of all copyrights and the original artwork shall be retained by the Designer, and a cancellation fee for work completed, based on the contract price and expenses already incurred, shall be paid by the Client.

6. Ownership of Artwork. The Designer retains ownership of all original artwork, whether preliminary or final, and the Client shall return such artwork within thirty (30) days of use.

7. Credit Lines. The Designer and any other creators shall receive a credit line with any editorial usage. If similar credit lines are to be given with other types of usage, it must be so indicated here:

_____

_____

8. Releases. Client shall indemnify Designer against all claims and expenses, including reasonable attorney's fees, due to uses for which no release was requested in writing or for uses which exceed authority granted by a release.

9. Modifications. Modification of the Agreement must be written, except that the invoice may include, and Client shall pay, fees or expenses that were orally authorized in order to progress promptly with the work.

10. Arbitration. Any disputes in excess of $ _____ (maximum limit for small claims court) arising out of this Agreement shall be submitted to binding arbitration before the Joint Ethics Committee or a mutually agreed upon arbitrator pursuant to the rules of the American Arbitration Association. The Arbitrator's award shall be final, and judgment may be entered in any court having jurisdiction thereof. The Client shall pay all arbitration and court costs, reasonable attorney's fees, and legal interest on any award of judgment in favor of the Designer.

11. The above terms incorporate Article 2 of the Uniform Commercial Code.

12. Code of Fair Practice. The Client and Designer agree to comply with the provisions of the Code of Fair Practice, a copy of which may be obtained from the Joint Ethics Committee, P.O. Box 179, Grand Central Station, N.Y., NY, 10017.

13. Acceptance of terms. The signature of both parties shall evidence acceptance of these terms.

_____
CONSENTED AND AGREED TO

_____
DATE

_____
DESIGNER'S SIGNATURE

_____
COMPANY NAME

_____
AUTHORIZED SIGNATURE

_____
NAME AND TITLE

Illustrator's Confirmation of Engagement

FRONT: ILLUSTRATOR'S LETTERHEAD

TO	DATE
	AUTHORIZED ART BUYER
	ILLUSTRATOR'S JOB NUMBER
	CLIENT'S JOB NUMBER

ASSIGNMENT DESCRIPTION

DELIVERY SCHEDULE

FEE (PAYMENT SCHEDULE)

ADDITIONAL ESTIMATED EXPENSES

CANCELLATION FEE (PERCENTAGE OF FEE)

BEFORE SKETCHES

AFTER SKETCHES

AFTER FINISH

RIGHTS TRANSFERRED (ALL OTHER RIGHTS RESERVED BY THE ILLUSTRATOR)	
FOR USE IN MAGAZINES AND NEWSPAPERS, FIRST NORTH AMERICAN REPRODUCTION RIGHTS UNLESS SPECIFIED OTHERWISE HERE	
(remove all italics before using this form)	
FOR ALL OTHER USES, THE CLIENT ACQUIRES ONLY THE FOLLOWING RIGHTS	
TITLE OR PRODUCT	*(name)*
CATEGORY OF USE	*(advertising, corporate, promotional, editorial, etc.)*
MEDIUM OF USE	*(consumer or trade magazine, annual report, TV, book, etc.)*
GEOGRAPHIC AREA	*(if applicable)*
TIME PERIOD	*(if applicable)*
NUMBER OF USES	*(if applicable)*
OTHER	*(if applicable)*
ORIGINAL ARTWORK, INCLUDING SKETCHES AND ANY OTHER PRELIMINARY MATERIAL, REMAINS THE PROPERTY OF THE ILLUSTRATOR UNLESS PURCHASED BY A PAYMENT OF A SEPARATE FEE.	

Terms:

1. Time for payment. Payment is due within thirty (30) days of receipt of invoice. A 1-1/2% monthly service charge will be billed for late payment. Any advances or partial payments shall be indicated under Payment Schedule on front.

2. Default in payment. The Client shall assume responsibility for all collection of legal fees necessitated by default in payment.

3. Grant of rights. The grant of reproduction rights is conditioned on receipt of payment.

4. Expenses. The Client shall reimburse the Illustrator for all expenses arising from the assignment.

5. Sales tax. The Client shall be responsible for the payment of sales tax, if any such tax is due.

6. Cancellation. In the event of cancellation or breach by the Client, the Illustrator shall retain ownership of all rights of copyright and the original artwork, including sketches and any other preliminary materials. The Client shall pay the artist according to the following schedule: 50% of original fee if cancelled after preliminary sketches are completed, 100% if cancelled after completion of finished art.

7. Revisions. Revisions not due to the fault of the Illustrator shall be billed separately.

8. Credit lines. On any contribution for magazine or book use, the Illustrator shall receive name credit in print. If name credit is to be given with other types of use, it must be specified here:

_____

☐ If this box is checked by the Illustrator, the Illustrator shall receive copyright notice adjacent to the work in the form:

© _____ 199 ___ .

9. Return of artwork. Client assumes responsibility for the return of the artwork in undamaged condition within thirty (30) days of first reproduction.

10. Unauthorized use. Client will indemnify illustrator against all claims and expenses, including reasonable attorney's fees, arising from uses for which no release was requested in writing or uses exceeding the authority granted by a release.

11. Arbitration. Any disputes in excess of $ _____ (maximum limit for small claims court) arising out of this Agreement shall be submitted to binding arbitration before the Joint Ethics Committee or a mutually agreed upon arbitrator pursuant to the rules of the American Arbitration Association. The Arbitrator's award shall be final, and judgment may be entered in any court having jurisdiction thereof. The Client shall pay all arbitration and court costs, reasonable attorney's fees, and legal interest on any award of judgment in favor of the Illustrator.

12. Acceptance of terms. The signature of both parties shall evidence acceptance of these terms.

_____
CONSENTED AND AGREED TO

_____
DATE

_____
ILLUSTRATOR'S SIGNATURE

_____
COMPANY NAME

_____
AUTHORIZED SIGNATURE

_____
NAME AND TITLE

Illustrator's Invoice

TO	DATE
	AUTHORIZED ART BUYER
	ILLUSTRATOR'S JOB NUMBER
	CLIENT'S JOB NUMBER

ASSIGNMENT DESCRIPTION
FEE

ITEMIZED EXPENSES (OTHER BILLABLE ITEMS)
CLIENT'S ALTERATIONS
SALE OF ORIGINAL ART
MISCELLANEOUS
TOTAL
SALES TAX
PAYMENTS ON ACCOUNT
BALANCE DUE

ORIGINAL ARTWORK, INCLUDING SKETCHES AND ANY OTHER PRELIMINARY MATERIALS, REMAIN THE PROPERTY OF THE ILLUSTRATOR UNLESS PURCHASED BY PAYMENT OF A SEPARATE FEE SUBJECT TO TERMS APPEARING ON REVERSE SIDE.

RIGHTS TRANSFERRED (ALL OTHER RIGHTS RESERVED BY THE ILLUSTRATOR)

FOR USE IN MAGAZINES AND NEWSPAPERS, FIRST NORTH AMERICAN REPRODUCTION RIGHTS UNLESS SPECIFIED OTHERWISE HERE

(remove all italics before using this form)

FOR ALL OTHER USES, THE CLIENT ACQUIRES ONLY THE FOLLOWING RIGHTS

TITLE OR PRODUCT	*(name)*
CATEGORY OF USE	*(advertising, corporate, promotional, editorial, etc.)*
MEDIUM OF USE	*(consumer or trade magazine, annual report, TV, book, etc.)*
GEOGRAPHIC AREA	*(if applicable)*
TIME PERIOD	*(if applicable)*
NUMBER OF USES	*(if applicable)*
OTHER	*(if applicable)*

ORIGINAL ARTWORK, INCLUDING SKETCHES AND ANY OTHER PRELIMINARY MATERIAL, REMAINS THE PROPERTY OF THE ILLUSTRATOR UNLESS PURCHASED BY PAYMENT OF A SEPARATE FEE.

Terms:

1. Time for payment. Payment is due within thirty (30) days of receipt of invoice. A 1-1/2% monthly service charge will be billed for late payment.

2. Default in payment. The Client shall assume responsibility for all collection of legal fees necessitated by default in payment.

3. Grant of rights. The grant of reproduction rights is conditioned on receipt of payment.

4. Credit lines. On any contribution for magazine or book use, the Illustrator shall receive name credit in print. If name credit is to be given with other types of use, it must be specified here:

_____

☐ If this box is checked by the Illustrator, the Illustrator shall receive copyright notice adjacent to the work in the form:
© _____ 199___ .

5. Additional limitations. If Illustrator and Client have agreed to additional limitations as to either the duration or geographical extent of the permitted use, specify here:

_____

6. Return of artwork. Client assumes responsibility for the return of the artwork in undamaged condition within thirty (30) days of first reproduction.

7. Unauthorized use. Client will indemnify Illustrator against all claims and expenses, including reasonable attorney's fees, arising from uses for which no release was requested in writing or for uses which exceed the authority granted by a release.

8. Arbitration. Any disputes in excess of $ _____ (maximum limit for small claims court) arising out of this Agreement shall be submitted to binding arbitration before the Joint Ethics Committee or a mutually agreed upon arbitrator pursuant to the rules of the American Arbitration Association. The Arbitrator's award shall be final, and judgment may be entered in any court having jurisdiction thereof. The Client shall pay all arbitration and court costs, reasonable attorney's fees, and legal interest on any award of judgment in favor of the Illustrator.

9. Acceptance of terms. The signature of both parties shall evidence acceptance of these terms.

CONSENTED AND AGREED TO

DATE

ILLUSTRATOR'S SIGNATURE

COMPANY NAME

AUTHORIZED SIGNATURE

NAME AND TITLE

Model Short Form Licensing Agreement

FRONT: LICENSOR'S LETTERHEAD

1. _____
(the "Licensor") hereby grants to

_____
(the "Licensee") a nonexclusive license to use the image (the "Image") created and owned by Licensor on

_____
("Licensed Products") and to distribute and sell these Licensed Products in:

(territory)
_____
for a term of _____ years commencing _____ , 19 ___ , in accordance with the terms and conditions of this Agreement.

2. Licensor shall retain all copyrights in and to the Image. The Licensee shall identify the Licensor as the artist on the Licensed Products and shall reproduce thereon the following copyright notice:
" © Licensor's name 19_____ ."

3. Licensee agrees to pay Licensor a nonrefundable royalty of (___ %) percent of the net sales of the Licensed Products. "Net Sales" as used herein shall mean sales to customers less prepaid freight and credits for lawful and customary volume rebates, actual returns, and allowances. Royalties shall be deemed to accrue when the Licensed Products are sold, shipped, or invoiced, whichever first occurs.

4. Licensee shall pay Licensor a nonrefundable advance in the amount of $ _____ upon signing of this Agreement. Licensee further agrees to pay Licensor a guaranteed nonrefundable minimum royalty of $ _____ every month.

5. Royalty payments shall be paid on the first day of each month commencing _____ , 19 ___ , and Licensee shall furnish Licensor with monthly statements of account showing the kinds and quantities of all Licensed Products sold, the prices received therefor, and all deductions for freight, volume rebates, returns and allowances. The first royalty statement shall be sent on _____ , 19 ___ .

6. Licensor shall have the right to terminate this Agreement upon thirty (30) days notice if Licensee fails to make any payment required of it and does not cure this default within said thirty (30) days, whereupon all rights granted herein shall revert immediately to the Licensor.

7. Licensee agrees to keep complete and accurate books and records relating to the sale of the Licensed Products. Licensor shall have the right to inspect Licensee's books and records concerning sales of the Licensed Products upon prior written notice.

8. Licensee shall give Licensor free of charge samples of each of the Licensed Products for Licensor's personal use. Licensor shall have the right to purchase additional samples of the Licensed Products at the Licensee's manufacturing cost. "Manufacturing cost" shall be $ _____ per Licensed Product.

9. Licensor shall have the right to approve the quality of the reproduction of the Image on the Licensed Products and on any approved advertising or promotional materials and Licensor shall not unreasonably withhold approval.

10. Licensee shall use its best efforts to promote, distribute, and sell the Licensed Products and said Products shall be of the highest commercial quality.

11. All rights not specifically transferred by this Agreement are reserved to the Licensor.

12. The Licensee shall hold the Licensor harmless from and against any loss, expense, or damage occasioned by any claim, demand, suit, or recovery against the Licensor arising out of the use of the Image.

13. Nothing herein shall be construed to constitute the parties hereto joint ventures, nor shall any similar relationship be deemed to exist between them. This Agreement shall not be assigned in whole or in part without the prior written consent of the Licensor.

14. This Agreement shall be construed in accordance with the laws of _____ ; Licensee consents to jurisdiction of the courts of

_____ .

15. All notices, demands, payments, royalty payments and statements shall be sent to the Licensor at the following address:
_____ ; and to the Licensee at: _____ .

16. Any disputes arising out of this Agreement shall be submitted to binding arbitration before the Joint Ethics Committee or a mutually agreed upon arbitrator pursuant to the rules of the American Arbitration Association in the city of
_____ . The Arbitrator's award shall be final, and judgment may be entered in any court having jurisdiction thereof. The Licensee shall pay all arbitration and court costs, reasonable attorney's fees, and legal interest on any award of judgment in favor of the Licensor.

17. This Agreement constitutes the entire agreement between the parties hereto and shall not be modified, amended, or changed in any way except by written agreement signed by both parties hereto. This Agreement shall be binding upon and shall inure to the benefit of the parties, their successors, and assigns.

IN WITNESS WHEREOF, the parties have executed this Licensing Agreement on the _____ day of _____ , 19 ___ .

_____
LICENSOR

_____
LICENSEE

_____
BY:

_____
(POSITION)

© Caryn Leland 1990

Magazine Purchase Order for Commissioned Illustration

This letter is to serve as our contract for you to create certain illustrations for us under the terms described herein.

1. Job description. We, the Magazine, retain you, the Illustrator, to create _____ Illustration(s) described as follows (indicate if sketches are required):

_____

_____

_____

to be delivered to the Magazine by _____ , 199 ___ , for publication in our magazine titled _____ .

2. Grant of rights. Illustrator hereby agrees to transfer to the Magazine first North American magazine rights in the illustration(s). All rights not expressly transferred to the Magazine hereunder are reserved to the Illustrator.

3. Price. The Magazine agrees to pay Illustrator the following purchase price: $ _____ in full consideration for Illustrator's grant of rights to Magazine.

4. Changes. The Illustrator shall be given the first option to make any changes in the work that the Magazine may deem necessary. However, no additional compensation shall be paid unless such changes are necessitated by error on the Magazine's part, in which case a new contract between us shall be entered into on mutually agreeable terms to cover changes to be done by the Illustrator.

5. Cancellation. If, prior to the Illustrator's completion of finishes, the Magazine cancels the assignment either because the illustrations are unsatisfactory to the Magazine or for any other reason, the Magazine agrees to pay the Illustrator a cancellation fee of 50% of the purchase price. If, after the Illustrator's completion of finishes, the Magazine cancels the assignment, the Magazine agrees to pay 50% of the purchase price if cancellation is due to the illustrations not being reasonably satisfactory and 100% of the purchase price if cancellation is due to any other cause. In the event of cancellation, the Illustrator shall retain ownership of all artwork and rights of copyright, but Illustrator agrees to show the Magazine the artwork if the Magazine so requests so that the Magazine may make its own evaluation as to degree of completion of the artwork.

6. Copyright notice and authorship credit. Copyright notice shall appear in the Illustrator's name with the contribution. The Illustrator shall have the right to receive authorship credit for the illustration and to have such credit removed if the Illustrator so desires due to changes made by the Magazine that are unsatisfactory to the Illustrator.

7. Payments. Payment shall be made within thirty (30) days of the billing date.

8. Ownership of artwork. The Illustrator shall retain ownership of all original artwork and the Magazine shall return such artwork within thirty (30) days of publication. To constitute this a binding agreement between us, please sign both copies of this letter beneath the words "Consented and agreed to" and return one copy to the Magazine for its files.

_____
CONSENTED AND AGREED TO

_____
DATE

_____
ARTIST'S SIGNATURE

_____
MAGAZINE

_____
AUTHORIZED SIGNATURE

_____
NAME AND TITLE

Introduction: Surface Designer/ Agent Agreement

The Surface Designer-Agreement seeks to clarify Designer-Agent Relationships by providing a written understanding to which both parties can refer. Its terms can be modified to meet the special needs of either Designer or Agent. The Agreement has been drafted with a minimum of legal jargon, but this in no way changes its legal validity.

The Agreement balances the needs of both Designer and Agent. The agency in Paragraph 1 is limited to a particular market. In the market the Agent has exclusive rights to act as an agent, but the Designer remains free to sell in that market also (except to accounts secured by the Agent). Because both Agent and Designer will be selling in the same market, the Designer may want to provide the Agent with a list of clients previously obtained by the Designer and keep this list up to date.

If the Agent desires greater exclusivity, such as covering more markets, the Designer may want to require that the Agent exercise best efforts (although it is difficult to prove best efforts have not been exercised) and perhaps promise a minimum level of sales. If the level is not met, the Agreement would terminate.

Paragraph 2 seeks to protect the Designer against loss or damage to his or her artwork, in part by requiring the Agent to execute with the client contracts that protect the designs.

Paragraph 3 sets forth the duration of the Agreement. A short term is usually wise, since a Designer and Agent who are working well together can simply extend the term by mutual agreement in order to continue their relationship. Also, as time goes on, the Designer may be in a better position to negotiate with the Agent. The term of the Agreement has less importance, however, when either party can terminate the agency relationship on thirty (30) days notice as Paragraph 10 provides.

The minimum base prices in Paragraph 4 ensure the Designer of a minimum remuneration. Flexibility in pricing requires that the Designer and Agent consult one another in those cases in which a particular sale justifies a price higher than the base price. The Designer can suggest that the Agent follow the Graphic Artists Guild's *Pricing and Ethical Guidelines* to establish the minimum base price.

The Agent's rate of commission in Paragraph 5 is left blank so the parties can establish an acceptable rate. If the Designer is not paid for doing an assignment, the Agent will have no right to receive a commission. Nor are commissions payable on the amount of expenses incurred by the Designer for work done on assignment. Discounts given by the Agent on volume sales of the work of many designers shall be paid out of the Agent's commission.

Paragraph 6 covers the Agent's obligations when commissioned work is obtained for the Designer. Of particular importance are the terms of the order form secured by the Agent from the client. The Agent should use the order form developed by the Graphic Artists Guild or a form incorporating similar terms.

Holding of designs by clients can present a problem which Paragraph 7 seeks to resolve by establishing a minimum holding time of five working days. Again, the Agent should use the holding form developed by the Graphic Artists Guild or a form with similar terms.

In Paragraph 8 the Agent assumes responsibility for billing and pursuing payments which are not made promptly. The reason for keeping any single billing under the maximum allowed for suit in small claims court is to make it easier to collect if a lawsuit is necessary. The Agent should use the invoice form of the Graphic Artists Guild or a form with similar provisions.

Paragraph 9 allows the Designer to inspect the Agent's books to ensure that proper payments are being made.

Termination is permitted on giving thirty (30) days' written notice to the other party. Paragraph 10 distinguishes between sales made or assignment obtained prior to termination (on which the Agent must be paid a commission, even if the work is executed and payment received after the termination date) and those after termination (on which no commission is payable). Within thirty (30) days of notice of termination, all designs must be returned to the Designer.

Paragraph 11 provides that the Agreement cannot be assigned by either party since the relationship between Designer and Agent is a personal one.

In Paragraph 12, arbitration is provided for disputes in excess of the maximum limit for suits in small claims court. For amounts within the small claims court limit, it is probably easier to simply sue rather than seek arbitration.

The manner of giving notice to the parties is described in Paragraph 13.

Paragraph 14 affirms that both Designer and Agent are independent contractors, which avoids certain tax and liability issues that might arise from the other legal relationships mentioned.

This Agreement is the entire understanding of the parties and can only be amended in writing. In stating this, Paragraph 15 points out a general rule that a written contract should always be amended in writing that is signed by both parties.

Paragraph 16 leaves room for the parties to add in any optional provisions that they consider necessary. Some of the optional provisions that might be agreed appear below.

Finally, Paragraph 17 sets forth the state whose law will govern the Agreement. This is usually the law of the state in which both parties reside or, if one party is out of state, in which the bulk of the business will be transacted.

Optional provisions

Additional provisions could be used to govern certain aspects of the Designer-Agent relationship. Such provisions might include:

The scope of the agency set forth in Paragraph 1 is limited to the following geographic area:

_____

Despite any provisions of Paragraph 1 to the contrary, this agency shall be nonexclusive and the Designer shall have the right to use other Agents without any obligation to pay commissions under this Agreement.

The Agent agrees to represent no more than _____ designers.

The Agent agrees not to represent conflicting hands, such hands being designers who work in a similar style to that of the Designer.

The Agent agrees to have no designers as salaried employees.

The Agent agrees not to sell designs from his or her own collection of designs while representing the Designer.

The Agent agrees to employ_____ full time and_____ part time sales people.

The Agent agrees that the Designer's name shall appear on all artwork by the Designer that is included in the Agent's portfolio.

The Agent agrees to seek royalties for the Designer in the following situations:

_____

The Agent agrees to hold all funds due to the Designer as trust funds in an account separate from funds of the Agent prior to making payment to the Designer pursuant to Paragraph 8 hereof

The Agent agrees to enter into a written contract with each client that shall include the following provisions:

Credit line for designer: The designer shall have the right to receive authorship credit for his or her design and to have such credit removed in the event changes made by the client are unsatisfactory to the designer. Such authorship credit shall appear as follows on the selvage of the fabric:

_____

☐ If this box is checked, such authorship credit shall also accompany any advertising for the fabric:

_____

Copyright notice for designer: Copyright notice shall appear in the Designer's name on the selvage of the fabric, the form of notice being as follows:

© _____ 199_____ .

The placement and affixation of the notice shall comply with the regulations issued by the Register of Copyrights. The grant of right in this design is expressly conditioned on copyright notice appearing in the Designer's name.

☐ If this box is checked, such copyright notice shall also accompany any advertising for the fabric.

Surface Designer/Agent Agreement

Agreement, this _____ day of _____, 19 ____, between (hereinafter referred to as the "Designer"), residing at:

_____

_____

and _____

(hereinafter referred to as the "Agent"), residing at:

_____

_____

Whereas, the Designer is a professional surface designer; and

Whereas, the Designer wishes to have an Agent represent him or her in marketing certain rights enumerated herein; and

Whereas, the Agent is capable of marketing the artwork produced by the Designer; and

Whereas, the Agent wishes to represent the Designer;

Now, therefore, in consideration of the foregoing premises and the mutual convenants hereinafter set forth and other valuable consideration, the parties hereto agree as follows:

1. Agency. The Designer appoints the Agent to act as his or her representative for:
☐ Sale of surface designs in apparel market,
☐ Sale of surface designs in home furnishing market,
☐ Securing of service work in apparel market. Service work is defined to include repeats and colorings on designs originated by the Designer or other designers,
☐ Securing of service work in home furnishing market
☐ Other

_____

_____

The Agent agrees to use his or her best efforts in submitting the Designer's artwork for the purpose of making sales or securing assignments for the Designer. For the purposes of this Agreement, the term *artwork* shall be defined to include designs, repeats, colorings and any other product of the Designer's effort. The Agent shall negotiate the terms of any assignment that is offered, but the Designer shall have the right to reject any assignment if he or she finds the terms unacceptable. Nothing contained herein shall prevent the Designer from making sales or securing work for his or her own account without liability for commissions except for accounts which have been secured for the Designer by the Agent. This limitation extends only for the period of time that the Agent represents the Designer. Further, the Designer agrees, when selling his or her artwork or taking orders, not to accept a price which is below the price structure of his or her Agent. After a period of _____ months, the Designer may remove his or her unsold artwork from the Agent's portfolio to do with as the Designer wishes.

2. Artwork and risk of loss, theft or damage. All artwork submitted to the Agent for sale or for the purpose of securing work shall remain the property of the Designer. The Agent shall issue a receipt to the Designer for all artwork which the Designer submits to the Agent. If artwork is lost, stolen or damaged while in the Agent's possession due to the Agent's failure to exercise reasonable care, the Agent will be held liable for the value of the artwork. Proof of any loss, theft or damage must be furnished by the Agent to the Designer upon request. When selling artwork, taking an order or allowing a client to hold artwork for consideration, the Agent agrees to use invoice, order or holding forms which provide that the client is responsible for loss, theft or damage to artwork while being held by the client, and to require the client's signature on such forms. The Agent agrees to enforce these provisions, including taking legal action as necessary. If the Agent undertakes legal action, any recovery shall first be used to reimburse the amount of attorney's fees and other expenses incurred and the balance of the recovery shall be divided between Agent and Designer in the respective percentages set forth in Paragraph 5. If the Agent chooses not to require the client to be responsible as described herein, then the Agent agrees to assume these responsibilities. If the Agent receives insurance proceeds due to loss, theft or damage of artwork while in the Agent's or client's possession, the Designer shall receive no less than that portion of the proceeds that have been paid for the Designer's artwork.

3. Term. This Agreement shall take effect on the _____ day of _____, 19 ___, and remain in full force and effect for a term of one year, unless terminated as provided in Paragraph 10.

4. Prices. At this time the minimum base prices charged to clients by the Agent are as follows:

Sketch (apparel market):

Repeat (apparel market):

Colorings (apparel market):

Sketch (home furnishing market):

Repeat (home furnishing market):

Colorings (home furnishing market):

Other:

The Agent agrees that these prices are minimum prices only and shall be increased whenever possible as the work becomes larger or more complicated than is usual. Higher prices shall also be charged for rush jobs, whenever possible. The Agent also agrees to try to raise the base price to keep pace with the rate of inflation. The Agent shall obtain the Designer's written consent prior to entering into any contract for payment by royalty. No discounts shall be offered to clients by the Agent without first consulting the Designer. When leaving a design with the Agent for possible sale, the Designer shall agree with the Agent as to the price to be charged if the design should bring more than the Agent's base price.

5. Agent's commissions. The rate of commission for all artwork shall be _____. It is mutually agreed by both parties that no commissions shall be paid on assignments rejected by the Designer or for which the Designer does not receive payment, regardless of the reasons payment is not made.

On commissioned originals and service work, expenses incurred in the execution of a job, such as photostats, shipping, etc. shall be billed to the client in addition to the fee. No Agent's commission shall be paid on these amounts. In the event that a flat fee is paid by the client, it shall be reduced by the amount of expenses incurred by the Designer in performing the assignment, and the Agent's commission shall be payable only on the fee as reduced for expenses. It is mutually agreed that if the Agent offers a client a discount on a large group of designs including work of other designers, then that discount will come out of the Agent's commission since the Agent is the party who benefits from this volume.

6. Commissioned work. Commissioned work refers to all artwork done on a nonspeculative basis. The Agent shall provide the Designer with a copy of the completed order form which the client has signed. The order form shall set forth the responsibilities of the client in ordering and purchasing artwork. To this the Agent shall add the date by which the artwork must be completed and any additional instructions which the Agent feels are necessary to complete the job to the client's satisfaction. The Agent will sign these instructions. Any changes in the original instructions must be in writing, signed by the Agent, and contain a revised completion date. It is mutually agreed that all commissioned work generated by the Designer's work shall be offered first to the Designer. The Designer has the right to refuse such work.

The Agent agrees to use the order confirmation form of the Graphic Artists Guild, or a form that protects the interests of the Designer in the same manner as that form. The order form shall provide that the Designer will be paid for all changes of original instructions arising out of no fault of the Designer. The order form shall also provide that if a job is

cancelled through no fault of the Designer, a labor fee shall be paid by the client based on the amount of work already done and the artwork will remain the property of the Designer. In a case in which the job being cancelled is based on artwork which belongs to the client such as a repeat or coloring, a labor fee will be charged as outlined above and the artwork will be destroyed. If the artwork is already completed in a satisfactory manner at the time the job is cancelled, the client must pay the full fee.

7. Holding policy. In the event that a client wishes to hold the Designer's work for consideration, the Agent shall establish a maximum holding time with the client. This holding time shall not exceed five (5) working days. Any other arrangements must first be discussed with the Designer. The Agent agrees to use the holding form of the Graphic Artists Guild, or a form that protects the interests of the Designer in the same manner as that form. All holding forms shall be available for the Designer to see at any time.

8. Billings and payments. The Agent shall be responsible for all billings. The Agent agrees to use the invoice form of the Graphic Artists Guild, or a form that protects the interests of the Designer in the same manner as that form. The Agent agrees to provide the Designer with a copy of all bills to clients pertaining to the work of the Designer. The Designer will provide the Agent with a bill for his or her work for the particular job. The Designer's bill shall be paid by the Agent within one (1) week after the delivery of artwork or, if the Agent finds it necessary, within ten (10) working days after receipt of payment from the client. The terms of all bills issued by the Agent shall require payment within thirty (30) calendar days or less. If the client does not pay within that time, the Agent must immediately pursue payment and, upon request, inform the Designer that this has been done. The Agent agrees to take all necessary steps to collect payment, including taking legal action if necessary. If either the Agent or Designer under-

takes legal action, any recovery shall first be used to reimburse the amount of attorney's fees and other expenses incurred and the balance of the recovery shall be divided between the Agent and Designer in the respective percentages set forth in Paragraph 5. The Agent agrees, whenever possible, to bill in such a way that no single bill exceeds the maximum that can be sued in small claims court. Under no circumstances shall the Agent withhold payment to the Designer after the Agent has been paid. Late payments by the Agent to the Designer shall be accompanied by interest calculated at the rate of 1-1/2% monthly.

9. Inspection of the books and records. The Designer shall have the right to inspect the Agent's books and records with respect to proceeds due the Designer. The Agent shall keep the books and records at the Agent's place of business and the Designer may make such inspection during normal business hours on the giving of reasonable notice.

10. Termination. This Agreement may be terminated by either party by giving thirty (30) days written notice by registered mail to the other party. All artwork executed by the Designer not sold by the Agent must be returned to the Designer within these thirty (30) days. In the event of termination, the Agent shall receive commissions for all sales made or assignments obtained by the Agent prior to the termination date, regardless of when payment is received. No commissions shall be payable for sales made or assignments obtained by the Designer after the termination date.

11. Assignment. This Agreement shall not be assigned by either of the parties hereto. It shall be binding on and inure to the benefit of the successors, administrators, executors, or heirs of the Agent and Designer.

12. Arbitration. Any disputes in excess of $ _____ (maximum limit for small claims court) arising out of this Agreement shall be submitted to binding arbitration before the Joint Ethics Committee or a mutually agreed upon arbitrator pursuant to the rules of the American Arbitration Association. The Arbitrator's award shall be final and judgment may be entered in any court having jurisdiction thereof. The Agent shall pay all arbitration and court costs, reasonable attorney's fees, and legal interest on any award of judgment in favor of the Designer.

13. Notices. All notices shall be given to the parties at their respective addresses set forth above.

14. Independent Contractor Status. Both parties agree that the Agent is acting as an independent contractor. This Agreement is not an employment agreement, nor does it constitute a joint venture or partnership between Designer and Agent.

15. Amendments and merger. All amendments to this Agreement must be written. This Agreement incorporates the entire understanding of the parties.

16. Other provisions

_____

_____

_____

_____

_____

_____

17. Governing law. This Agreement shall be governed by the laws of the State of _____ .

18. Acceptance of terms. The signature of both parties shall evidence acceptance of these terms. *In witness whereof,* the parties have signed this Agreement as of the date set forth above.

_____
DESIGNER

_____
AGENT

Surface Designer's Holding Form

TO	DATE

NUMBER OF DESIGNS HELD		
DESIGN I.D. NUMBER		SKETCH PRICE
DESIGN I.D. NUMBER		SKETCH PRICE
DESIGN I.D. NUMBER		SKETCH PRICE
DESIGN I.D. NUMBER		SKETCH PRICE
DESIGN I.D. NUMBER		SKETCH PRICE
DESIGN I.D. NUMBER		SKETCH PRICE
DESIGN I.D. NUMBER		SKETCH PRICE

Terms:

The submitted designs are original and protected under the copyright laws of the United States, Title 17 United States Code. These designs are submitted to you in confidence and on the following terms:

1. Ownership and copyrights. You agree not to copy, photograph, or modify directly or indirectly any of the materials held by you, nor permit any third party to do any of the foregoing. All artwork photographs, and photostats developed from these designs, including the copyrights therein, remain my property and must be returned to me unless the designs are purchased by you.

2. Responsibility for artwork. You agree to assume responsibility for loss, theft, or any damage to the designs while they are being held by you. It is agreed that the fair market value for each design is the price specified above.

3. Holding of artwork. You agree to hold these designs for a period not to exceed _____ working days from the above date. Any holding of artwork beyond that period shall constitute a binding sale at the price specified above. You further agree not to allow any third party to hold designs unless specifically approved by me.

4. Arbitration. Any disputes in excess of $ _____ (maximum limit for small claims court) arising out of this Agreement shall be submitted to binding arbitration before the Joint Ethics Committee or a mutually agreed upon arbitrator pursuant to the rules of the American Arbitration Association. The Arbitrator's award shall be final, and judgment may be entered in any court having jurisdiction thereof. The party holding the designs shall pay all arbitration and court costs, reasonable attorney's fees, and legal interest on any award of judgment in favor of the Surface Designer.

5. The above terms incorporate Article 2 of the Uniform Commercial Code.

6. Acceptance of terms. The signature of both parties shall evidence acceptance of these terms.

CONSENTED AND AGREED TO

DATE

DESIGNER'S SIGNATURE

COMPANY NAME

AUTHORIZED SIGNATURE

NAME AND TITLE

Surface Designer's Confirmation Form

FRONT: DESIGNER'S LETTERHEAD

TO	DATE
	PATTERN NUMBER
	DUE DATE

ESTIMATED PRICES
SKETCH
REPEAT
COLORINGS
CORNERS
TRACINGS
OTHER

DESCRIPTION OF ARTWORK		
REPEAT SIZE		
COLORS		
TYPE OF PRINTING		
1/2 DROP	☐ YES	☐ NO

SPECIAL COMMENTS

Terms:

1. Time for payment. Because the major portion of the above work represents labor, all invoices are payable fifteen (15) days net. A 1-1/2% monthly service charge is payable on all unpaid balances after this period. The grant of textile usage rights is conditioned on receipt of payment.

2. Estimated prices. Prices shown above are minimum estimates only. Final prices shall be shown in invoice.

3. Payment for changes. Client shall be responsible for making additional payments for changes requested by Client in original assignment.

4. Expenses. Client shall be responsible for payment of all extra expenses rising from assignment, including but not limited to photostats, mailings, messengers, shipping charges, and shipping insurance.

5. Sales tax. Client shall assume responsibility for all sales taxes due on this assignment.

6. Cancellation fees. Work cancelled by the client while in progress shall be compensated for on the basis of work completed at the time of cancellation and assumes that the Designer retains the project whatever its stage of completion. Upon cancellation, all rights, publication and other, revert to the Designer. Where Designer creates corners which are not developed into purchased sketches, a labor fee will be charged, and ownership of all copyrights and artwork is retained by the Designer.

7. Insuring artwork. The client agrees when shipping artwork to provide insurance covering the fair market value of the artwork.

8. Arbitration. Any disputes in excess of $ _____ (maximum limit for small claims court) arising out of this Agreement shall be submitted to binding arbitration before the Joint Ethics Committee or a mutually agreed upon arbitrator pursuant to the rules of the American Arbitration Association. The Arbitrator's award shall be final, and judgment may be entered in any court having jurisdiction thereof. The Client shall pay all arbitration and court costs, reasonable attorney's fees, and legal interest on any award of judgment in favor of the Surface Designer.

9. The above terms incorporate Article 2 of the Uniform Commercial Code.

10. Acceptance of terms. The signature of both parties shall evidence acceptance of these terms.

_____

CONSENTED AND AGREED TO

_____

DATE

_____

DESIGNER'S SIGNATURE

_____

COMPANY NAME

_____

AUTHORIZED SIGNATURE

_____

NAME AND TITLE

Surface Designer's Invoice

TO	DATE
	INVOICE NUMBER
	PURCHASE ORDER NUMBER
	STYLIST
	DESIGNER

PATTERN NUMBER	DESCRIPTION	PRICE
		SUBTOTAL

ITEMIZED EXPENSES
SUBTOTAL
TOTAL
SALES TAX
TOTAL DUE

Terms:

1. Receipt of artwork. Client acknowledges receipt of the artwork specified above.

2. Time for payment. Because the major portion of the above work represents labor, all invoices are payable fifteen (15) days net. The grant of textile usage rights is conditioned on receipt of payment. A 1-1/2% monthly service charge is payable on unpaid balance after expiration of period for payment.

3. Adjustments to invoice. Client agrees to request any adjustments of accounts, terms, or other invoice data within ten (10) days of receipt of the invoice.

4. These terms incorporate Article 2 of the Uniform Commercial Code.

5. Arbitration. Any disputes in excess of $_____$ (maximum limit for small claims court) arising out of this Agreement shall be submitted to binding arbitration before the Joint Ethics Committee or a mutually agreed upon arbitrator pursuant to the rules of the American Arbitration Association. The Arbitrator's award shall be final, and judgment may be entered in any court having jurisdiction thereof. The Client shall pay all arbitration and court costs, reasonable attorney's fees, and legal interest on any award of judgment in favor of the Designer.

6. Acceptance of terms. The signature of both parties shall evidence acceptance of these terms.

_____
CONSENTED AND AGREED TO

_____
DATE

_____
DESIGNER'S SIGNATURE

_____
COMPANY NAME

_____
AUTHORIZED SIGNATURE

_____
NAME AND TITLE

On the Guild

The Graphic Artists Guild was founded by a group of specialized illustrators employed by Detroit ad agencies serving the automotive industry. Perhaps these artists saw that unionized assembly-line workers were getting paid more to bolt together Motown iron than they were getting to create the polished images essential to selling it. Their militant efforts, culminating in the Guild's one and only strike (against Campbell Ewald in 1971) were not notably successful, but they did organize a branch in New York which grew and prospered while the Detroit parent declined. It was the New York chapter that became the nucleus of the present Graphic Artists Guild.

While few in the present-day Guild would advocate a strike, the Guild retains its "union" status and continues to pursue its constitutional goals: "to advance and extend the economic and social interests of (our) members" and to "Promote and maintain high professional standards of ethics and practice and to secure the conformance of all buyers, users, sellers and employers to established standards." The Guild's constitution explicitly endorses the articles of the *Code of Fair Practice* formulated by the Joint Ethics Committee as the expression of such professional standards of business relations. You'll find a copy of the Code in the chapter on *Ethical Standards*.

In its pursuit of these objectives, the Guild has become the largest and most effective artists' advocacy organization in the history of the United States. Since the majority of Guild members are employed on a freelance basis, a form of employment that's old hat for artists but which seems to be a wave of the future for other kinds of workers, the Guild is in a sense at the vanguard of the labor movement. As we develop ways to represent "self-employed" freelance workers effectively, the Guild is becoming a valuable model for other organizations concerned with the loss of traditional manufacturing jobs and the growth of high-tech "cottage industries" in the service sector.

Foremost among the Guild's activities is our ongoing effort to educate members and non-members alike about the *business* of being a graphic artist. Both nationally and at the chapter level, we run regular programs on negotiation and pricing strategies, tax issues, self-promotion, time management, and all the other essential business skills that are not, by and large, taught in the art schools. The Guild provides a means for experienced artists to share their understanding of the advertising, publishing and corporate markets with young artists, and a way for artists at every level of attainment to share concerns and information. Many artists join the Guild for the information and "networking" it offers, and find themselves drawn into other activities as well.

Some Guild Chapters directly assist their members in the marketing of their work. In New York, the Guild's "Professional Practices Committee" helps resolve misunderstandings between artists and clients. In Boston, annual "See Parties" place the work of many illustrators before a steady stream of buyers who come to survey the talent available. The Indianapolis and Vermont chapters run graphics-industry trade shows which bring all kinds of illustrators and designers, as well as color separators, typographers, printers, and other members of the graphic arts community together at one time. The response of artists and buyers to these shows has been very enthusiastic.

But it's not enough to help artist-members to cope with the market as it is. When the market stacks the deck unfairly against artists, the Guild is determined to do something about it. The widespread use of "work-for-hire" contracts by publishers and other buyers is a case in point. There's an innocuous-sounding provision in the copyright law, originally intended to vest copyright ownership in employers when artists are conventionally employed. Salary, benefits and vacations are perhaps a fair trade for copyright ownership, but somehow this work-for-hire provision has engulfed many artists who receive none of the benefits of traditional employment.

Although a recent Supreme Court decision narrowed the applicability of "work for hire," abuses continue. Such contracts are often presented on a take-it-or-leave-it basis, sometimes even in the outrageous form of an after-the-fact paragraph on the back of a check, which must be signed to cash the check. A detailed discussion on "work for hire" can be found in the chapter on *Professional Issues*.

While we make every effort to help clients understand why the surrendering of authorship is offensive to artists, the Guild realizes that the real remedies are legislative. Clearly, the "work-for-hire" provision should be made applicable only to artists who receive a regular paycheck and other employee benefits as compensation.

The Guild's track record suggests that we will accomplish this goal in the end. Legislative struggles require patience and determination, but these qualities abound in the Guild. We're not new to the process; we've successfully promoted artists' rights legislation in four states, and we've made our voice heard in Washington as well.

Recently, the Guild led a coalition of seventy-five artists' groups, who together succeeded in overturning, against very long odds indeed, a tax provision that created an unreasonable burden on artists. This "uniform tax capitalization" law, which was intended to put an end to the sham tax shelters of movies never made and books never written, was established with legislation so broadly and imprecisely written that it appeared to forbid artists and other creators to deduct the expenses of creating artwork *until it is sold* and then only in proportion to the percentage of the work's total value received. The bookkeeping burden alone was crippling, and the absurdity of treating creative artwork as items of inventory was offensive. If uniform tax capitalization had been allowed to stand, it would have severely injured the creative life of this country. But artists, in the sincere belief that they were struggling in the nation's best interest as well as their own, stuck together and won.

The U. S. Constitution acknowledges that creativity itself is encouraged when creators profit from their own inventions.

That's why we believe that when we fight to end the abusive practices grouped under "work-for-hire," we're also fighting in the nation's best interest. And that's why we're confident that we'll eventually prevail.

Active membership in the Graphic Artists Guild is the best way to ensure the advancement of creator's interests and equitable professional conditions for all. Today, most graphic artists join the Guild to act together to protect their professional integrity and their art by sharing information, discussing problems in the industry and working to improve the profession. Guild members work together on contract issues and artists' rights legislation-communicating with each other to take advantage of the experiences of the group.

Guild members have established a strong track record on successful lobbying on behalf of artists on state and federal levels, developing trailblazing publications on professional practices and pricing strategies, establishing educational seminars, and group health, life and disability insurance plans.

The Graphic Artists Guild is a national organization whose headquarters are located in New York City. Local chapters of the Guild exist in Florida, Georgia, Indiana, Massachusetts, Upstate and Downstate New York, and Vermont.

National benefits and services

The national organization offers a wide range of benefits and services to members, whether they are attached to a specific chapter or are members at-large. These programs and services were developed as a direct result of members' expressed needs.

National newsletter

The National *Guild News* is published and distributed quarterly to all Guild members. It features important and timely information on industry trends, professional concerns, legislative developments and rights issues. The paper is directed by an editor-in-chief who also serves on the national board of directors.

Individual members, board members and chapters are encouraged to use the newsletter to share information about local activities and professional concerns; to foster dialogue about issues of mutual concern; to bring up ideas for the Guild's national policy agenda. This can be done through letters to the editor, contributing columns and planning announcements.

Legal referral network

Because independent contractors often face legal questions particular to their type of business, the Guild has a referral system listing lawyers around the country who are familiar with artists' issues and who are willing to work with our members for reduced fees. Lawyers who are members of the referral network have been screened by the Guild's legal counsel to insure the appropriateness of their experience. This *member only* service is available throughout the country.

Areas for which members might consult lawyers include: contract review, bill collection, copyright and patent advice, incorporation and partnership, tax questions, and real estate, among others.

Chapters and individual members can recommend lawyers with whom they work for inclusion in the service by writing or calling the national office.

Insurance

The Guild offers group insurance to its members for health, life and disability coverage. Also available are valuable papers insurance that protects original artwork and a legal insurance plan which will handle most routine business problems for an annual retainer. All members, with the exception of students, are eligible to apply for these plans.

Professional education programs

This project arranges seminars and workshops on subjects such as negotiation, marketing, self-promotion, and financial planning for groups of artists around the country. Members can request these programs through their local chapter or by contacting National directly.

Another component of this project is curriculum development for art schools, in which teachers who are Guild members share information about teaching professional practices on the undergraduate level.

The Guild also sponsors courses and workshops in cooperation with art schools, undergraduate art departments and related organizations.

Professional practices monitoring

The national organization monitors problems that occur throughout the industry and tracks member complaints on issues concerning standards, practices and pricing. For those members whose grievances cannot be solved at the chapter level, the national office will consider grievances with clients on issues such as late-payment, contract disputes, collections, return of original artwork, etc. Either through legal referral or action by the national board of directors, members can receive support for their rights when a case has been accepted.

Public policy and legislation

Artists are recognized as special contributors to our society and economy. As such, they are accorded special status within the U.S. Constitution and through the 1976 Copyright Act. The Guild has a legislation and public policy committee that monitors federal and state policy developments and works to protect artists' rights in local, state and federal arenas. Activities of the committee and legislative developments are reported regularly in the National *Guild News*.

The Guild-authored Copyright Justice Act, which seeks to reform the work-for-hire provision of the Copyright Law, is pending in the U.S. Congress. The national organization is also the leader of a creators' coalition that includes writers, photographers, performing artists and visual artists who have joined in the effort for work-for-hire reform.

Other lobbying projects include Moral Rights, which protects an artist's original work from alteration, defacement or damage, even after reproduction rights are sold; Fair Practices, which clears up the ambiguity of ownership of the original work; Tax Equity, to ensure that artists can claim full market-value deductions for works donated to charitable institutions; and creators' rights in light of the developments in new technologies.

Bills on Moral Rights and Fair Practices have been passed in New York, Massachusetts, Maryland, Oregon and California.

National board of directors

The national board of directors, which has oversight responsibility for the organization, is comprised of elected artist-

members. Each local chapter has representatives on the national board and the full
board meets twice a year to establish goals
and priorities, share information on program
development and approve the organization's
budget. During the rest of the year, the
board meetings are held bi-monthly in New
York City to consider ongoing issues and
programs.

Chapters

Each chapter of the Guild runs its
own programs oriented to the needs of its
region and members, under the direction of
elected artist-members. The local chapters
are the "lifeblood" of the Guild, where
members' direct input influences services
and programs. As the chapters identify
needs and concerns, local programs are
developed; if an issue becomes a concern for
more than one chapter, or more than one
group of members, it is then referred to the
national board for assessment and action.

Local services and benefits

Newsletters

Each chapter publishes its own
newsletter covering issues of regional
interest, announcing meetings and programs, and reporting on members' activities.
Most chapter newsletters are published on a
quarterly basis.

Artist-to-artist hotline

Chapters across the country have
established artist-to-artist hotlines that are
staffed by member volunteers. Members
with questions about professional issues,
such as pricing, contracts or negotiating, can
call seasoned professionals in the Guild for
help. Information received through the
hotlines is often used in assessing markets
and targeting problems in the field.

Discounts on supplies

Many chapters have developed
discount programs with suppliers in their
areas, where members can receive from 5 to
20 per cent off art supplies and services.

Grievance committees

Grievance procedures for members
who are experiencing contractual or
professional disputes with clients exist in
most chapters. These committees help
resolve disputes through informal contact
with the client. If these disputes are not
resolved through committee assistance, it
many make recommendations for further
action that the artist may take. These
committees may also provide support letters
for court cases.

Meetings and networks

Regular member meetings are
features of all Guild chapters. At these
meetings, programs on issues such as self-
promotion, pricing, negotiating or resource-
swaps are highlighted. Members are able to
confer directly with peers on business
issues, keep updated on the latest developments in their field and socialize.

Professional education programs

Local chapters may run in-depth
seminars and workshops on subjects such as
pricing, marketing and negotiation. Members are active in helping to develop the
curricula for these programs, which are
coordinated under the direction of the
chapter boards and staff.

Chapters sometimes arrange
cooperative programs with local art schools
or art departments in colleges and universities, which attract wide audiences.

The Graphic Artists Guild Foundation

The Graphic Artists Guild Foundation was formed in 1983 to "foster,
promote, and advance greater
knowledge, appreciation and understanding
of the graphic arts...by the presentation and
creation of the graphic arts, activities
designed to promote, aid and advance the
study of existing work, and to promote the
creation, presentation and dissemination of
new works; to sponsor workshops, training
sessions, symposia, lectures and other
educational endeavors."

Further, the Foundation's constitution states among its goals, "to help monitor and establish rules governing industry practices and to contribute to modifying these when necessary."

The Foundation receives grants and donations to conduct studies whose information will benefit the industry, the public and the arts in general. It has concluded a two-year study, partially sponsored by the National Endowment for the Arts, of art contests and competitions. The study assessed the nature of contests and competitions and developed a set of ethical guidelines and standards for these events and is published in the chapter on *Professional Issues*.

Directory of Illustration

Published by Serbin Communications Inc. and sponsored by the Graphic Artist Guild, this advertising directory for illustrators offers discounted rates for Guild members and has a free distribution of at least 18,000 art directors and buyers nationwide. The publication date for Volume 8 is fall, 1991. For more information or to reserve pages in the directory, please contact Glen Serbin, President, Serbin Communications, 511 Olive Street, Santa Barbara, CA 93101, (800) 876-6425.

On joining the Guild

When you join the Guild, you're making a very definite statement of your conviction that graphic artists deserve the same respect our society affords other professionals.

Joining the Guild affirms the value of artists working together to improve standards of pay and working conditions in our industry. Joining is an endorsement of the highest standards of ethical conduct in the marketplace.

Joining the Guild is joining the effort to advance the rights and interests of artist through legislative reform. Examples: our ongoing fight to end the widespread abuse of the copyright law's "work-for-hire" language; our successful battle against unfair taxation of artists.

Joining the Guild may provide you with a vehicle for contract bargaining — with your employer if you are a staff artist, or even with your client if you are one of a group of freelance artists regularly working for a given client.

Joining the Guild puts you in contact with other artists who share your concerns. It's a way to share ideas, information, and business skills with your colleagues.

Joining the Guild has immediate practical benefits:

Members receive the latest edition of the *Graphic Artists Guild Handbook, Pricing & Ethical Guidelines*. This best-seller contains a wealth of information about pricing and trade practices in every corner of the graphic arts. Many consider it an industry "bible."

Group health insurance as well as disability and retirement plans are available to members at favorable rates.

Members receive a subscription to national and local chapter newsletters.

Your local chapter may provide direct marketing assistance through job referral services, trade shows, and other activities.

Members receive substantial discounts on supplies from many dealers, and on page rates in many illustration and design directories.

Chapters also run "hotlines" to give members access to advice and referrals to Guild-approved lawyers and accountants should you need them.

Chapters produce educational programs and social events for members.

The Graphic Artists Guild is the only organization of its kind in the United States. If you want to work together with other artists to effect positive change in the status of artists in the marketplace and in society, you belong in the Guild!

Graphic Artists Guild Membership Application

Please photocopy this page, fill out all portions of this form and mail it with your dues payment and initiation fee to:
Graphic Artists Guild, 11 West 20th Street, 8th Floor, New York, NY 10011-3704

NAME		
ADDRESS		
CITY	STATE	ZIP
BUSINESS TELEPHONE	HOME TELEPHONE	

The Graphic Artists Guild is a national organization with local chapters. Membership applications are processed at the national office; you'll be enrolled either in a local chapter serving your area or in the "At-Large" chapter if there is no local chapter near you.

Membership Status
Guild Membership comprises two categories: Member and Associate Member. Only working graphic artists are eligible to become full Members. Interested people in related fields who support the goals and purposes of the Guild are welcome to join as Associate Members, as are graphic arts students and retired artists. Associate Members may participate in all Guild activities and programs, but not hold office or vote.

☐ I earn more than half of my income from my own graphic work I am therefore eligible to join the Guild as a Member.

☐ I wish to join the Guild as an Associate Member.

Employment Status
If you are on staff and do freelance work as well, please write "1" for staff and "2" for freelance.

___ Staff

___ Freelance (includes business-owners, partners, and corporation principals)

☐ Retired Graphic Artist

☐ Student

☐ School

___ Year of graduation (Students must include photocopy of current college I.D.)

Discipline
Please write "1" for the area in which you do most of your work, and "2" and "3" for additional specialties.

___ Art Direction
___ Artists' Rep

___ Cartooning
___ Computer Arts
___ Graphic Design
___ Illustration
___ Photography
___ Pre-Production Art
___ Production Art
___ Surface Design
___ Teaching
___ Video/Broadcast design
___ Other: _____

For office use only:
AZW____ PEGS____ CARD____

Dues and Initiation Fee
To offset the administrative expense of processing new memberships, the Guild collects a $25 one-time fee with each membership application.

Guild dues depend upon membership category and income level. Income level refers to your total adjusted gross income from your federal tax return.

(Please check category)
Member Dues

☐ Income under $12,000/yr. $100 per year

☐ Income $12,000-$30,000 $135 per year

☐ Income over $30,000 $175 per year

Associate Member Dues

☐ Students $55 per year

☐ Others $95 per year

Method of Payment

☐ Check/Money Order

☐ Visa   ☐ Master Card

_____
CARD NO.

_____
EXPIRATION DATE

Initiation fee: $25 *

Total enclosed $ _____

You may remit one-half of your dues with this application (plus the initiation fee), we will bill you for the second half, which must be paid within 60 days.

Returned checks are subject to a $10 service charge.

On occasion, the Guild allows use of its mailing list by companies selling products of interest to our members. Please check this box if you do not wish to have your name made available in this manner. ☐

Membership Statement
(Please read and sign the following)

I derive more income from my own work as a graphic artist than I do as the owner or manager of any business which profits from the buying and/or selling of graphic artwork.*

I, the undersigned, agree to abide by the Constitution** of the Graphic Artists Guild and do hereby authorize the Guild to act as my representative with regard to negotiation of agreements approved by the Guild membership to improve pricing and ethical standards of the graphic arts profession. I further understand that my membership in the Graphic Artist Guild is continuous and that I will be billed for membership dues annually on the anniversary of my original application. If I wish to resign from the Graphic Artists Guild, I understand that I must resign in writing, and that I will be responsible for the payment of any dues owed prior to the date of my resignation.

This statement does not apply to associate members.

**Your membership package will contain a copy of the Constitution. To obtain one prior to joining, send $1 with your request to the national office. The document is also on file at national and chapter offices for inspection.*

_____
SIGNATURE *(for membership statement)*   DATE

Other resources

These books and audio cassettes are available from the Graphic Artists Guild National Office, 11 West 20th Street, 8th Floor, New York, New York, 10011, (212) 463-7730 by pre paid check or by Visa/MasterCard charges. New York tax of 8.25 per cent is applicable to orders mailed to addresses in New York State. Shipping and handling charges of $3.50 should be added for the first book or cassette ordered, $1.00 for each additional book or cassette. Guild Members are entitled to a 25 per cent discount off the list price.

Crawford, Tad. *Legal Guide for the Visual Artist.* The professional's handbook. Revised and expanded. New York: Allworth Press, 1990. $18.95.

Crawford, Tad, and Doman Bruck, Eva. *Business and Legal Forms for Graphic Designers.* Thirty three ready-to-use forms; use and negotiation checklists; extra tear-out forms. New York: Allworth Press, 1990. $15.95.

Gordon, Elliott and Barbara. *How to Sell Your Photographs and Illustrations.* A step-by-step business-building plan for freelance photographers and illustrators, including: building a selling portfolio and getting assignments; the secrets of self-promotion; how to price your work (10 key pricing questions you must ask); setting up a profitable business plan. New York: Allworth Press, 1990. $16.95.

Graphic Artists Guild Directory of Illustration. Volume 7 of this book contains some of the world's most talented illustrators. More than 1,000 illustrations showcase a remarkable depth and range of talent. For use by art directors and buyers, graphic design firms and educators. California: Serbin Communications, Inc., 1990. $39.95.

Leland, Caryn R. *Licensing Art & Design.* A professional's guide for understanding and negotiating licenses and royalty agreements. New York: Allworth Press, 1990. $12.95.

Rossol, Monona. *The Artist's Complete Health and Safety Guide.* Everything you need to know about art materials to make your workplace safe and in compliance with United States and Canadian right-to-know laws. New York: Allworth Press, 1990. $16.95.

Wilson, Lee. *Make It Legal.* For graphic designers; advertising copywriters, art directors, and producers; commercial photographers; and illustrators. A guide to copyright, trademark, and libel law; privacy and publicity rights; false advertising law. New York: Allworth Press, 1990. $18.95.

Crawford, Tad. *Protecting Your Rights & Increasing Your Income* (audio cassette). A guide for authors, graphic designers, illustrators, photographers. 60 minutes. New York: Allworth Press, 1990. $12.95.

Glossary

accessories, clothing: Hat, gloves, shoes or slippers, jewelry, socks, belt, suspender, necktie, collar, cuffs, scarf, umbrella, hair decoration, apron, handbag, tote, etc.

accessories, home furnishings: Floral arrangement, basket, lamp, coat hanger, storage box, garment bag, shoe organizer, drying towel, pot holder, shower curtain, tissue cover, toilet lid cover, bolster, pillow, cushion, doorstop, bookends, frame, appliance cover, laundry bag, etc. (Note: Some home accessories can overlap as novelties.)

account executive: A representative of an advertising agency who handles specific accounts and acts as a client liaison to the art director, creative director and others creating advertising for the account.

adult clothing: Clothing in sizes for teengirls, teenboys, misses', miss petite, junior, junior petite, women's, half-sizes and men's.

advance: An amount paid prior to the commencement of work or in the course of work. It may be to cover expenses or it may be partial payment of the total fee. An advance as partial payment is common for a time-consuming project.

advance on royalties or advance payment against royalties: An amount paid prior to actual sales of the commissioned item or work; sometimes paid in installments. Advances are generally not expected to be returned, even if unearned in sales. Both the terms and the size of the advance are negotiable.

afghan: A small blanket, sometimes called a nap blanket, designed for use by one person. It can be formed in a variety of techniques, such as crochet, knitting, weaving, etc.

agreement: See *contract*.

all rights: The purchase of all rights of usage for reproduction of an artwork forever.

animator: An artist who is responsible for articulation of characters' movements.

appliqué or applied work: To apply or stitch one layer of fabric over another so that the applied pieces form a motif. See also *reverse appliqués*.

art director: One whose responsibilities include the selection of talent, purchase of visual work and the supervision of the quality and character of visual work. Usually an employee of the advertising agency, publishing house, magazine or other user of the graphic artist's work, although some organizations hire free-lance art directors to perform these duties.

art staff: A group of artists working for a company such as an advertising agency, publisher, magazine or large design studio and under art director supervision.

artwork: Any finished work of a graphic artist.

assistant animator: Cleans up the animator's drawings according to a model sheet and does in-betweens. In some larger studios the assistants solely do the clean-up work.

author's alterations (AAs) or author's corrections (ACs): Alterations or corrections of type that has been set due to the client's errors, additions or deletions. The typographer's or printer's changes for making AAs are usually passed on to the client. See also *printer's error*.

background: One who paints backgrounds which have already been designed.

bailment: An obligation on the part of the individual(s) with whom art is left to take reasonable care of it. This is a legal requirement and applies to situations such as leaving a portfolio for review.

basketry: The art of forming baskets from wood, reeds, yarns, etc., by weaving, braiding, coiling or other techniques.

bedspread: The final or top cover for a bed of any size, primarily used for decorative purposes. See also *quilt*.

blanket: A layer of bedclothing placed over the top sheet and under the bedspread, used primarily for warmth. See also *quilt*.

bleed: A small extra area on the exterior dimensions of a page to allow for trimming. Also called "trim" area; the printing that runs into this area.

braiding: To plait together strands of yarn or strips of fabric to form a larger ply to be coiled and sewn together flat or dimensionally to make rugs, mats, baskets, etc.

built-up lettering: Letters, numerals or ampersands used to create various forms.

camera-ready art or camera copy: Usually a mechanical or pasteup accompanied by finished art that is prepared for photographing for plate-making.

cancellation fee: When a project is terminated or not used by the client, this fee is paid as compensation for the artist's or studio's effort in developing the illustration or design.

cartoonist: A professional artist who creates art in a humorous and satirical style and/or as political commentary.

castoff: To provide a breakdown or estimate of length. In knitting, to take stitches off a knitting needle. In publishing, to estimate the typeset length or number of pages from manuscript or galley proof. In textiles, sometimes used as a synonym for knock-off; refers to a pattern or design that a company wishes to alter for a new pattern while retaining similarity to the original.

cel: Short for celluloid. A transparent sheet of celluloid on which the finished drawings are inked.

center truck: The center page spread in a magazine or newspaper that is a premium space for the placement of advertisements.

children's clothing: Sizes pertaining to boys and girls from toddlers to teens.

Chromalin proofs: A proprietary term for a color proof process employing a photosensitized clear plastic. Color separation film negatives are exposed to the plastic in such a way that process color will adhere to dots on the plastic. Four sheets (one for each process color) are exposed, treated with the separate process colors, placed in register and then laminated. Such proofs are used for presentations and for checking register, obvious blemishes and size. The color may be very accurate but is subject to variation due to exposure and the application of the process color. Also *transfer key*. See also *Color Key* and *progressive proofs*.

chrome: See *transparency*.

Cibachrome: A proprietary term for a full-color positive photographic print made from a transparency.

client accommodation: To work at fees below the normal rate in order to accommodate budgetary restrictions and to preserve a long-term working relationship.

Color Key: A proprietary term of the 3M Company; sometimes referred to as "3Ms." A method for obtaining separate film positives showing progressive color breakdown of thee color separation negatives. Such proofs are useful for presentation and for checking register, obvious blemishes and size; they are not a true indication of final printed color. *Chromalin proofs* are preferred for more accurate (though still not exact) color representation. *Progressive proofs* using process inks on press are the most accurate method for checking color. See also *Chromalin proofs* and *progressive proofs*.

color proofs: The first full-color printed pieces pulled off the press for approval before the press is considered ready to roll for the entire press run. Sometimes called *simple colored proofs*, these proofs are useful for making corrections in color on press, particularly for those problems resulting from improper registration and the effects of overprinting. *Progressive proofs* are the preferred method for accurately checking color.

commission *(n)* **commission** *(v)***:** Percentage of a fee paid by an artist to the artist's agent or gallery for service provided or business transacted. The act of giving an artist an assignment to create a work of art.

comprehensive *or* **comp:** A visualization of the idea for an illustration or a design usually created for the client and artist to use as a guide for the finished art. *Tight comp* or *loose comp* refers to the degree of detail, rendering and general accuracy used in the comprehensive.

confirmation form: A contract form that is used by an artist when no purchase order has been given or when the purchase order is incomplete with respect to important terms of the contract, such as amount of fee, rights transferred, etc.

contract: An agreement, whether oral or written, whereby two parties bind themselves to perform certain obligations. Synonyms: *agreement* or *letter of agreement* (if the contract takes the form of a letter).

converter: A company that transfers designs onto printed or woven fabric.

copy: The text of an advertisement; editorial concern of a magazine or a newspaper or the text of a book.

copyright: The right to copy or authorize the copying of creative work. Any freelance artist creating artwork automatically owns the right of that work unless provisions have been made prior to the commencement of the project to transfer the copyright to the buyer.

corners: A type of layout for specific textile designs in which a single layout of a complete corner is used for the repeated design on all four corners. Commonly used in home furnishings (e.g., the design for the corners of a tablecloth, napkin or scarf).

C print *or* **inter-neg:** A full-color positive print from a negative transparency.

creative director: Usually an employee or officer of an advertising agency whose responsibilities may include over-all supervision of all aspects of the character and quality of the agency's work for its client. The creative director's background may be art, copy or client contact.

crochet: A method of making a lace or a textile structure from any yarn, fabric strip or stringy material with a hook, using the chain stitch or variations on the chain to form the textile.

croquis: Rough sketches made by an artist, particularly by fashion illustrators.

design brief: An analysis of a project prepared either by the publisher or the designer. When the designer assumes this responsibility it should be reflected in the design fee. The design brief may include: (1) a copy of the manuscript, with a selection of representative copy for sample pages and a summary of all typographical problems, copy areas, code marks, etc.; (2) an outline of the publisher's manufacturing program for the book: compositor and composition method, printer and paper stock, binder and method of binding; and (3) a description of the proposed physical characteristics of the book, such as trim size, page length, list price, quantity of first printing and whether the book will print in one color or more than one. The publisher should also indicate whether any particular visual style is expected.

director: One who oversees the complete picture from conception to finish. Has complete control over all phases: character design (which is usually supplied by an agency), layout, sound, etc.

dummy: A book, brochure or catalog idea in a roughly drawn form usually made up to contain the proper number of pages and used as a reference for positioning, pagination and in position.

dye transfer: Similar in appearance to a color photograph but different in the important respect that it is produced from a transparency by printing continuous tones of color dyes.

embroidery: A general term referring to decorating the surface of any fabric with freeformed stitches that are based on plain sewing. For example: embroidery with wool or a wool-like yarn on fabric is called *crewel embroidery.* Stitches and fabric vary according to the will of the designer. Also *counted embroidery:* The formation of regimented stitches on even-weave fabrics on needlepoint canvas known by various names that denote their style of stitches (e.g., hardanger, black work, drawn thread work). *Cross stitch embroidery:* Can be either freeformed embroidery over Xs printed on the fabric or counted embroidery worked on an even-weave fabric or canvas.

employee, freelance: Terms of freelance employment include: Work hours, determined by assignment, using one's own workspace and materials; freelancers generally provide their own benefits. The freelancer often collects state sales tax from clients and pays his or her own income taxes.

engineered design: A pattern specifically designed to fit certain size factors and to be repeated in a particular fashion (e.g., panel print to fit a Tressi blouse or dress design).

finished art: Usually an illustration, photograph or mechanical that is prepared and ready for the engraver or printer.

first North American serial rights: The right to be the first magazine to publish art for use in one specific issue to be distributed in North America.

first rights: The right to be the first user of art for one-time use; frequently used to describe the right to publish art in a magazine serial or drawn from a book in which the art will appear.

floor covering: Any textile structure or painting technique that is used to cover a floor partially or completely for either decorative or functional purposes.

format: An arrangement of type and illustration that is used for many layouts; an arrangement used in a series.

Fortune double-500 company: *Fortune* magazine's annual listing based on sales revenues of the 1,000 largest corporations in the United States.

general apprentice: One who does a little of everything except camera work.

graphic artist: A visual artist working in a commercial area.

graphic designer: A professional graphic artist who works with the elements of typography, illustration, photography and printing to create commercial communications tools such as brochures, advertising, signage, posters, slide shows, book jackets and other forms of printed or graphic communications. A visual problem solver.

graphic film artist: One who is skilled in creating special effects on film by use of computerized stands, matting and/or adding computerized movement to artwork (e.g., television logos with glows, set movement).

graphics: Visual communications.

group head: Some advertising agencies divide their clients into groups under a group head who supervises the work of art directors on the various accounts.

guild: An association of like-minded professionals seeking to protect and better their status and/or skills. When employees are members in equal proportion to freelancers, such a guild qualifies with the United States government as a union. In this capacity, a guild may represent employees who are its members in collective bargaining.

gutter: The area in a magazine, newspaper or book where the left (verso) and right (recto) pages meet. Important elements are often not placed in this area because of the fold.

half-body garments: A garment that is worn either from the waist up or from the waist down, such as a vest, sweater, poncho, pants, skirt, etc.

hand letterer: A professional artist who creates letterforms for use in logotypes, alphabets and specific titles or captions.

hard furniture: Any furniture that requires the designer to use a hard substance such as wood, metal, etc. for structural support or decorative purposes. It may also incorporate padding and a textile surface.

illustrator: A professional graphic artist who communicates a pictorial idea by creating a visual image using paint, pencil, pen, collage or any other graphic technique except photography for a specific purpose.

image: A pictorial idea.

in betweener: One who does the drawings depicting motion in-between the drawings that have been cleaned up by the assistant, thereby animating them.

infant clothing: Refers to newborn and baby sizes up to toddler sizes.

inker: One who inks onto cels the lines of finished drawings.

invoice: A statement given to a client showing the amount due on an assignment. Usually submitted after work has been completed unless advance payments are to be made. When advance payments are made, the invoice should reflect these and show the balance due.

jacquard sketches: A sketch usually done on graph paper to be used on jacquard woven fabrics such as tablecloths, upholstery and towels.

junior checker: (paint and ink only): One who inspects cels for the proper and thorough application of the correct paint colors.

key line artist: A sometimes pejorative term for a mechanical or pasteup artist.

kickback: A sum of money or a large figure paid to an artist by a supplier for the artist's part in passing on work such as printing. Or kickbacks are demanded by art buyers from artists in exchange for awarding commissions. Kickbacks are illegal. Often the supplier's kickback costs are hidden in its invoices submitted to the client for work completed.

knitting: The method of forming a lace or a textile structure from any yarn, fabric strip or stringy material with two or more eyeless needles, pegged tools or sticks, etc. using various looped stitches to form the structure.

knock-off *(n)* **knock off** *(v)* **:** A term most often used in the textile design industry to identify a design that at the request of the client or stylist has been copied by a different artist than the one who created it. Broadly used to mean the copying of an artist's style or artwork when no creative input and/or significant changes are made by the artist in creating the knock-off. Knock-offs are unethical and often illegal.

lace: A general term for any openwork or sheer fabric with holes formed by any technique including knitting, crochet, bobbin lace, netting, hairpin lace, tatting, eyelet, needle lace, etc.

latch hook: A method of knotting short or long lengths of yarn over crosswise threads of a rug canvas with a latch hook tool. The technique is generally used for rugmaking, pillows and wall hangings.

layette: A coordinated ensemble for the newborn consisting of a receiving blanket, cap, jacket and booties.

layout: The design, usually in sketch form, of the elements of an advertisement, magazine or book page or any other graphic work (e.g., brochures, catalogs, etc.) intended for reproduction. Used as a guide and usually executed by an art director or illustration graphic designer.

layout: An artist who lays out and arranges backgrounds**.**

letter of agreement: See *contract.*

line sheet See *sales catalog.*

live area: The area on the camera copy of a page or a publication beyond which essential elements should not be positioned.

logo: A mark or symbol created for an individual, company or product that translates the impression of the body it is representing into a graphic image.

logotype: Any alphabetical configuration that is designed to identify by name a producer, company, publication or individual.

lucey: One of several optical devices used to enlarge or reduce images.

macramé: A method of ornamental knotting for cords and yarns, generally used to form cringes,

hammocks, wall hangings, plant holders, etc.

markup *(n)* **mark up** *(v)* **:** A service charge added to expense account items to reimburse the artist for the time to process the billing of such items to the client and the cost of advancing the money to pay such expenses; the process of adding such a charge.

arkers: Felt-tipped pens used in a technique for illustrating comprehensives or for sketching a rough in black-and-white or color. Proprietary synonyms: *Magic Markers, Stabilo.*

mechanical: Ruled and pasted flats or boards composed by a prodution artist for the printer to use in the printing and engraving process.

moonlighting: A freelance commission taken on by a salaried person to be completed in the person's spare time.

needlepoint *or* **canvas work:** The formation of regimented stitches over the meshes or threads of a special open-weave fabric called canvas.

novelties: A general term for gift or boutique-type items or for clever decorative or functional items such as an eyeglass, comb or mirror case; Christmas decorations (stockings, tree skirt ornaments, etc.); calendar; clock; cosmetic bag; jewelry bag; typewriter cover; golf bag and club covers; exercise or beach mat, etc. Also, wax transfer patterns for embroidery or appliqué motifs. (*Note:* some novelties can overlap as home accessories.)

opaque projector: A projector that uses reflected light to project the image of a non-transparent object onto a canvas, board or screen; the image is then used by an artist to copy or show work.

overhead: Nonbillable expenses such as rent, phone, insurance, secretarial and accounting services and salaries.

page makeup: Assembling in sequence the typographic and/or illustrative elements of a brochure, catalog, book or similar item.

pasteup *(n)* **:** Usually reproduction copy of galley type fastened in position with wax or glue by a production artist for the use of the engraver in the platemaking process. Also, *paste-up (adj.)* and *paste up (v).*

patchwork: Piecing, sewing or joining together pieces of fabric to form motifs or a complete fabric structure. Generally, the pieces are cut in planned shapes. When shapes are unplanned or take on a helter-skelter appearance it is called *crazy patchwork* or *crazy quilt.*

per diem: A day rate given to a professional by a client to complete an assignment.

portfolio *or* **artist's book:** Reproductions and/or originals that represent the body of an artist's work.

preplanner/checker: One who checks that the animation is in sync and flows correctly (before camera).

presentation boards: Color illustrations of a

grouping of styles from the design collection that a manufacturer wishes to feature. Mounted on display boards with fabric swatches, they are used for presentation during market week sales.

printer's error (PE): A mistake made in the film negatives, platemaking or printing that is not due to the client's error, addition or deletion. These alterations are normally absorbed by the printer or typographer. See also *author's alterations.*

price list: See *sales catalog/line sheets.*

production artist: A professional artist who works with a designer in taking a layout through to mechanicals, pasteups and often on through the printing process.

production coordinator: One who is responsible for making sure that everything is in order before it goes under the camera.

professional: One who strives for excellence in business and follows fair practices in every professional endeavor.

profit: The difference remaining (i.e., net income) after overhead, expenses and taxes are subtracted from income received (gross income).

progressive proofs *or* **progs:** Proofs of color separation negatives that have been exposed to offset plates and printed using process inks. Presented in the sequence of printing, i.e., (1) yellow plate alone, (2) red alone, (3) yellow and red, (4) blue alone, (5) yellow, red and blue, (6) black alone and (7) yellow, red, blue and black. The preferred way for checking the color of the separation negatives using the same inks, paper, ink densities and color sequence as intended for the production run. See also *color proofs.*

proposal *or* **estimate:** A graphic designer's detailed analysis of the cost and components of a project. Used to firm up an agreement before commencing work on a project for a client.

punch needle: Refers to both a fine, delicate embroidery technique (fine yarns or threads and fine fabrics and needles) and to a heavy rug technique (using heavy yarns and coarse fabrics and needles) where loops of varying lengths are formed on the surface of the fabric by pushing a handled-needle through the fabric from the wrong side. Fine versions are generally used for decorations in clothing or home accessories; coarse versions for chair cushions, mats, rugs and wall hangings.

purchase order: A form given by a client to an artist describing the details of an assignment and, when signed by an authorized person, authorizing work to commence.

quilt: A bedcovering that functions as both a blanket and/or a bedspread that consists of two fabric layers, one placed above and the other below a filling layer. The filling can be a non-woven layer of cotton or polyester batting or a woven layer of cotton or polyester batting or a woven fabric such as flannel. Small hand running stitches, machine stitches or yarn tufts formed through all layers over the item produce the quilted structure and design. Also, the quilted structure can be used as a technique to produce clothing and other decorative or functional items.

readers: Copies with type prepared for the author or client to proofread and mark corrections on. They are nonreproduction quality and their value is only in checking corrections.

ready-made: Refers to clothing or fabric that was purchased in a store or available to the designer at the stage when it could have been purchased at retail.

reel: A film or number of films spliced together.

reference file: File compiled by an illustrator or designer made up of clippings from newspapers, magazines and other printed pieces that is referred to for ideas and inspiration as well as technical information.

repeat: The textile design process by which consecutive press impressions may be made to put together imperceptibly so that the textile will appear as one consecutive image and the process run may be continued indefinitely.

representative *or* **rep:** A professional agent who promotes specific talent in illustration, photography or surface design and negotiates contracts for fees and commissions. Usually receives a percentage of the negotiated fee as payment for the services provided to the talent.

reprint rights: The right to print something that has been published elsewhere.

reproduction copy *or* **repro:** Proofs printed in the best possible quality for use as camera copy for reproduction. Also *reproduction proof.*

resident buying service: These buying services purchase fashion illustrations depicting available styles and reproduce them on retail ad mats which are sent to subscribing retail outlets.

residuals: Payments received in addition to the original fee, usually for extended usage of a work. See also *royalty.*

retoucher: A professional artist who alters a photograph to improve or change it for reproduction. Usually works on transparencies or color and black-and-white prints.

reverse appliqué *or* **cut through appliqué:** When two or more layers of fabric are handled together, with the upper layer(s) cut away and stitched separately in order to reveal the under layer(s) and thus form a motif.

roughs: Loosely drawn ideas, often done in pencil on tracing paper, by an illustrator or designer. Usually several roughs are sketched out before a comprehensive is developed from them.

royalty: Payments to the artist that are based on a percentage of the revenue generated through the quantity of items sold (e.g., books, cards, calendars). See also *advance on royalties.*

sales catalog/line sheet: Used by apparel manufacturer's sales staff as a hand-out to buyers; a black-and-white illustrated list of all the styles in a collection or line, showing available size, color, pattern and prices.

sales tax: Each state government establishes the rate of taxation on items sold. It varies between 4 and 8 percent of the amount billed the client, which the freelance graphic artist is often required to be licensed to charge, collect and remit to the state on a quarterly basis.

second rights: The right to use art that has appeared elsewhere. Frequently applied to use by magazines of art that has appeared previously in a book or another magazine.

shoot (v): In advertising, a day's filming or a day's shooting of still photography.

showroom illustrations: Color illustratoins of key styles from an apparel manufacturer's design collection or line, used to heighten showroom atmosphere and promote showroom sales.

simultaneous rights: The right to publish art at the same time as another publication. Normally used when the two publications have markets that do not overlap.

sizing: The process of marking an original with a percentage or a multiplier for reduction or enlargement on camera.

sketch: Design for textiles not done in repeat. See also *roughs*.

soft furniture: Any furniture that uses only a soft filling such as batting, foam pillows, etc. to form the inner structure.

soft sculpture: A decorative dimensional item formed from fabrics or in one of the many textile structures which is stuffed with a soft filling.

speculation: Accepting assignments without any guarantee of payment after work has been completed. Payment upon publication is also speculation.

spine: The area between the front and back book bindings on which the author, title and publisher are indicated.

spot: A small drawing or illustration used as an adjunct to other elements in an advertisement, editorial or book page.

spot: A television commercial.

stenciling: A method of painting on a surface using a template and a stiff bristle brush with a blunt end.

storyboards: A series of sketches drawn by artists in small scale to a television screen and indicating camera angles, type of shot (e.g., close-up, extreme close-up), backgrounds, etc. Essentially a plan for shooting a commercial for television; often accompanied by announcer's script and actor's lines.

storyboards: Sketches of action for animation. Synonyms: *story* or *story sketches*.

studio: The place where an artist works. Also an organization offering a complete graphic service. In surface design, an agency representing designs by more than one surface designer.

style: A particular artist's unique form of expression; also referred to as "a look." In surface design referred to as "hand."

subsidiary rights: In publishing, those rights not granted to the publisher but which the publisher has the right to sell to third parties, in which case the proceeds are shared with the artist.

surface designer: A professional arist who creates art usually to be used in repeat on surfaces such as fabric, wallpaper, wovens or ceramics.

tablewear: Functional items that are used at the dining room or kitchen table, such as placemat, napkin, napkin ring, runner, tea cozy, hot pad, tablecloth, coaster, etc.

talent: A group of artists represented by an agent or gallery.

technique: Refers to the particular medium used by a graphic artist.

textbook: In book publishing, applies to any book that is to be sold through schools and used for educational purposes.

thumbnail *or* **thumbnail sketch:** A very small, often sketchy visualization of an illustration or design. Usually several thumbnails are created together to show different approaches to the visual problem being solved.

trade book: In book publishing, applies to any book that is to be sold in bookstores to the general public.

transparency *or* **chrome:** A full-color translucent photographic film positive. Color slides are also referred to as transparencies.

union: A group of people in the same profession working to monitor and upgrade the business standards in their industry.

weaving: A method of interlacing yarns or any stringy material in both a lengthwise and crosswise manner simultaneously. A traditional loom is generally used to control the interlacing technique, but other devices may also be used.

whole-body garments: Any one-piece garment worn from the neck and stopping anywhere below mid-thigh, such as dresses, coats, capes, etc.

workbook: In book publishing, applies to any book accompanying a textbook, usually at the elementary school level, for students to complete exercises in by following written and pictorial instructions.

work-for-hire: For copyright purposes, "work-for-hire" or similar expressions such as "done-for-hire" or "for-hire" signify that the commissioning party is the owner of the copyright for the artwork as if the commissioning party is, in fact, the artist.

Index

N O T E S

NOTES